High-Stakes Schooling

High-Stakes Schooling

What We Can Learn from Japan's Experiences with Testing, Accountability, and Education Reform

CHRISTOPHER BJORK

The University of Chicago Press
Chicago and London

Christopher Bjork is professor and the Dexter M. Ferry Chair of Education at Vassar College. He is the author of *Indonesian Education* and editor or coeditor of many other books, including *Education and Training in Japan*, *Educational Decentralization*, *Taking Teaching Seriously*, and *Japanese Education in an Era of Globalization*.

The University of Chicago Press, Chicago 60637
The University of Chicago Press, Ltd., London

Printed in the United States of America

25 24 23 22 21 20 19 18 17 16   1 2 3 4 5

ISBN-13: 978-0-226-30938-5 (cloth)
ISBN-13: 978-0-226-30941-5 (paper)
ISBN-13: 978-0-226-30955-2 (e-book)
DOI: 10.7208/chicago/9780226309552.001.0001

Library of Congress Cataloging-in-Publication Data

Bjork, Christopher, author.
High-stakes schooling : what we can learn from Japan's experiences with testing, accountability, and education reform / Christopher Bjork.
pages ; cm
Includes bibliographical references and index.
ISBN 978-0-226-30938-5 (cloth : alk. paper) — ISBN 978-0-226-30941-5 (pbk. : alk. paper) — ISBN 978-0-226-30955-2 (ebook) 1. Educational change—Japan. 2. Curriculum change—Japan. 3. Educational tests and measurements—Japan. 4. Educational change—United States. I. Title.
LA1311.83.B66 2016
370.952—dc23

2015019957

♾ This paper meets the requirements of ANSI/NISO Z39.48–1992 (Permanence of Paper).

CONTENTS

List of Tables / vii

ONE / Searching for Solutions / 1

TWO / Framing the Education Crisis / 18

THREE / Examining the Impact of Reform Policies / 34

FOUR / The Teaching Force / 63

FIVE / Nurturing Enthusiasm in Elementary School Students / 81

SIX / Responses to Change in the Middle Schools / 102

SEVEN / Curricular Reform, Academic Achievement, and Educational Opportunity / 119

EIGHT / Shifting Student-Teacher Relationships / 141

NINE / Broadening the Discussion / 163

TEN / US Teachers Reflect on Japanese Elementary School Instruction / 184

ELEVEN / Looking Forward / 198

Epilogue / 213 *Acknowledgments / 219* *Notes / 221*
References / 227 *Index / 243*

TABLES

1.1. Trends in Instructional Time: Elementary School (6-Year Totals) / 6
1.2. Trends in Instructional Time: Middle School (3-Year Totals) / 7
2.1. Comparison of NCLB and Relaxed-Education Goals / 25
2.2. International Comparison of Student Happiness / 27
3.1. Characteristics of Schools Studied / 41
5.1. Student Ranking of Their Favorite Subjects / 92
5.2. Teacher Opinion of Integrated Studies / 98
5.3. Comparison of Current and Previous Curriculum / 98
6.1. Instructional Approaches in Academic Lessons / 113
6.2. Instructional Approaches in IS/Elective Lessons / 113
7.1. Influence of Mother's Level of Education / 122
7.2. Parent Survey Results / 135
7.3. Parent Priorities / 137
9.1. PISA Results: Top 10 Performers over Time / 166
9.2. TIMSS Results: Top 10 Performers over Time / 167
11.1. Japan's TIMSS Performance over Time (1995–2011) / 209
E.1. Changes in the Elementary School Curriculum / 214
E.2. Changes in the Middle School Curriculum / 215

ONE

Searching for Solutions

Education systems around the globe continually struggle to strike an appropriate balance between academically rigorous curricula and engaging instruction. In the United States, concerns about the nation's mediocre performance on international achievement tests—combined with expanding gaps between high- and low-achieving students—have generated enthusiasm for raising learning standards in the schools. Initiatives such as the No Child Left Behind Act (NCLB) and Race to the Top (RTT) place testing at the center of school reform in an attempt to pressure school districts to demand more of their students. Proponents of this approach assert that if school decision making is more directly informed by statistical measures of student achievement, teachers "will have a clear framework for creating a challenging and dynamic curriculum" (Bambrick-Santoyo 2010, 8). Data-driven instruction is presented as a more effective alternative to approaches that give teachers the autonomy to determine what and how they teach (Dyck 2006; Mandinach and Jackson 2012; Popham 2010). Although many school districts are still in the process of determining data-collection and -analysis procedures, reform currents push the school accountability movement forward. Districts that choose not to follow this trend risk losing credibility and funding.

In other locations, education planners are grappling with similar issues. Examinations have traditionally occupied a central position in the education systems of many Asian nations. But across the region, education planners have begun to reconsider the role that testing plays in schools. From South Korea to Singapore, observers lament that pupils may perform well on standardized tests but often lack the skills and attitudes necessary to become productive members of society. Responding to criticism that schools have become intense pressure cookers, education officials are encouraging teachers to pay more attention to the development of the "whole child." Reforms implemented throughout the region emphasize the need to cultivate children's creativity, critical thinking skills, and love for learning (Bjork 2006).

In Japan, testing has exerted a particularly powerful influence on education-related decision making. Interestingly, one of the first people to promote increased emphasis on examinations in Japanese schools was David Murray, an American who served as senior advisor to Minister of Education Mori Arinori during the Meiji reformation. Murray encouraged the Japanese to use examinations to determine advancement between grades, and as a mechanism for increasing student motivation (Amano 1990). By the 1920s, high-stakes tests were commonplace and the term "examination hell" (*juken jigoku*) had entered the Japanese lexicon. The emphasis on testing has been pointed to by some as an effective mechanism for securing students' commitment to studying—and by others as a primary reason that large numbers of children become stressed out and lose their interest in learning (Bjork and Tsuneyoshi 2005; Tsuneyoshi 2004b).

In the 1970s, the Japanese government began to consider strategies that might be used to overhaul its schools. A group of government officials and policy advisers, concerned that the rigidity of the education system was harming its students, asserted that practices that had served the nation well during its reconstruction after World War II required modification. Reports published by the Ministry of Education, Culture, Sports, Science and Technology (MEXT) in succeeding years emphasized the need to making schools more flexible and inspiring settings for learning. In 2002, after years of discussing and debating the merits of various reform approaches, the ministry enacted a series of reforms collectively known as "relaxed education" (*yutori kyoiku*). In attempt to relieve academic intensity in the schools, the school week was shortened to five days, the volume of concepts teachers were required to cover was reduced significantly, and the national Course of Study (*gakushu shido yoryo*) was revised to give students more opportunities to study topics that interested them. In addition, teachers were advised to incorporate more hands-on activities, problem solving exercises, and student-centered learning into their courses (Tsuneyoshi 2004a).

Introduction of these policies raised the possibility that a system known for its resistance to change would undergo major restructuring. According to ministry guidelines, curricula, pedagogy, and student-teacher relationships would all be modified to make learning less intense and more meaningful. Cave emphasizes the significance of *yutori kyoiku*, calling the movement "the most radical since the introduction of a national curriculum in the late 1950s" (Cave 2001, 179). The Ad Hoc Education Council labeled relaxed education the Third Major Education Reform initiative in Japanese history (the first two being the Meiji restoration and the post–World War II reconstruction). Not surprisingly, the reforms provoked intense debates about the direction of the nation's schools. Rarely does one pick up a newspaper or turn on the television in Japan without glimpsing a report examining the effects of recent changes in the schools. Reform advocates decry problematic aspects of the traditional schooling with as much fervor as critics of relaxed education trumpet the deleterious effects of test-driven instruction. Yet outside of East Asia, knowledge about this reform movement is limited. Impressions of the Japanese education system continue to draw primarily from reports published during the economic boom era.

Why Look East?

The fact that a system that only a decade earlier had been regarded as one of the most successful in the world was undertaking such a significant overhaul is intriguing. By the mid-1980s, Japan had "achieved one of the highest levels of quality for schooling, as illustrated by such measures as enrollment ratios, retention or graduation rates, daily attendance rates, and academic performance" (Fujita 2010, 21) in the world. Japanese students consistently scored near the top of global rankings that compared the performance of pupils on achievement tests such as TIMSS and PISA. Searching for clues for understanding "the so-called Japanese education miracle" (Arnove 1999, 6), Western countries looked to Japan for inspiration. In many instances, the Japanese education system was held up as a model deserving emulation. Why would a system that was enjoying such success undertake such an ambitious reform project? Could a system anchored by an examination system that produced cohesion and dependability—but also great stress—be reshaped to nurture children's individuality, creativity, and intellectual curiosity? And how would education stakeholders respond to the changes advocated by the Ministry of Education, Culture, Sports, Science and Technology (MEXT)? Would they support the ministry's vision for the future?

The answers to the above questions should interest individuals who follow the Japanese education system, as well as those with a more general interest in the effects of standardized testing on curriculum and instruction. Pushing children to reach their academic potential while maintaining their interest in learning is a daunting task. This is especially true in environments in which students are compared, ranked, and sorted. Even changes that seem minor on the surface can have a powerful effect on school cultures. When new mechanisms for determining academic success or failure are adopted, members of a learning community are expected to adjust their behavior to fit reform directives. Given the complexity of this process, it is not surprising that few fundamental reforms have had lasting impacts on school practice (Cuban 1990; Tyack and Cuban 1995).

Policies such as NCLB and RTT have cast their shadows over all K–12 schools in the United States. They have aroused strong opinions among parents, teachers, and administrators. More important, they are shaping the experiences of children who are compelled to attend school. Yet discussion of these policies tends to be driven by ideology rather than evidence. Ironically, at the same time that the US Department of Education is trumpeting the benefits of "evidence-based policies and practice" (NCLB 2001; Slavin 2002; USDOE 2007), it is implementing an ambitious reform agenda that lacks solid empirical foundation. Both NCLB and RTT are guided by the premise that high-stakes testing will galvanize teachers and schools across the country to elevate academic standards. According to advocates of these measures, a primary reason that US students do not excel on international achievement tests is that neither they nor their teachers have been held accountable for their performance. Instituting a challenging set of examinations and attaching rewards and sanctions to the results, it is argued, will provide the impetus for system-wide improvement. But the United States has had limited experience with the accountability systems that anchor the two initiatives. Even today, unreliable data make it difficult to "discern whether school reforms are, in reality, raising student achievement" (Fuller et al. 2006, 21).

Given the muddled reform environment in the United States, it makes sense to look abroad to deepen our understanding of the effects of high-stakes testing. Studying the outcomes of educational reforms introduced in other countries can provide valuable insights into the potential ramifications of policy decisions made at home. The field of comparative education is uniquely organized to yield such perspectives. As Harold Noah, a pioneer in the field, once posited, "Knowledge of what is being proposed and tried in cognate situations abroad is indispensable for reasoned judgment about what we need to do at home" (Noah 1984, 552). This is true even when the school systems and societies being analyzed differ from our own; their unique attributes can push us to think about education from distinct vantage points. Over the past half century, the governments that facilitated and maintained the most impressive progress in education all constructed reform plans after carefully studying strategies that have proven successful in other settings (Tucker 2011). American government officials, on the other hand, have rarely looked abroad for inspiration. Such insularity makes no sense, given the multitude of challenges that currently confront our schools. It is in our best interests "to compare broad goals, policies, practices, and institutional structures, as well as relative standing on common measures, in order to understand what another country is trying to achieve, how it has gone about achieving it, what it would have done differently, what mistakes it made, and it addressed them, which factors most account for its achievement, and so on" (Tucker 2011, 173).

This is an opportune moment to follow the advice of Noah and Tucker—to study Japan's experiment with relaxed education and apply the lessons learned to education decision making in other locations. Education pundits inside Japan may decry conditions in schools, but their students continue to excel on international achievement tests. As Tucker and Brown report,

> The performance of Japan's students relative to those in the other OECD countries in mathematics and science is legendary, and their comparative performance on the PISA reading survey, though not in the top very ranks, is nonetheless impressive. There is nothing new about this consistently superior performance. Japan has placed at or near the top of the international rankings on all such surveys since they began. (Tucker and Brown 2011, 79)

The Japanese school system remains an important reference point for educators and policymakers in the United States. That is especially true now that American schools are grappling with issues tied to high-stakes testing. Individuals who find Japan's efforts to reduce academic intensity admirable—as well as critics of those changes—can benefit from careful study of the effects of the *yutori kyoiku* movement. The mechanisms used to build and refine the Japanese education system "should surely be considered by any country that wants to match its achievements" (OECD 2010, 154).

Components of Japan's Relaxed-Education Policies

"Relaxed education" refers to both a philosophical approach to learning and a concrete set of initiatives designed to support that vision. Definitions of the concepts are often ambiguous, as flexible as the form of education they promote. While MEXT documents frequently refer to *yutori kyoiku,* it is not always clear which specific programs or initiatives fall under that umbrella. In my study, I consider the following developments as the central components of the relaxed-education movement:

Shortened school week. Beginning in 1992, MEXT reduced the number of minutes Japanese students spend in school each year. The sheer volume of time children were required to attend school, some believed, was symbolic of the excessive demands placed on students and teachers. The decisions to cut the school week represented such a significant modification to traditional practice that it was introduced in stages. In 1992—which could be identified as the beginning of the relaxed-education era—one Saturday per month was designed as a vacation day. Three years later, an additional Saturday each month was removed from the school calendar. Finally, in 2002, all public schools in the country were required to follow the comprehensive five-day school week (*kansen shu itsukasei*).

Modifications to the Course of Study. A series of revisions to the national Course of Study represented another significant step in the ministry's reform plans. Similar to the strategy used to reduce the school week, the curriculum was cut in small increments over a span of two and a half decades, announced in revisions to the Course of Study implemented in 1978, 1992, and 2002 (See tables 1.1 and 1.2).[1] Although it is difficult to quantify the extent of these reductions, MEXT usually used a figure of 30% in reports on curricular changes. Ministry officials believed these changes were necessary after both media reports and government surveys attested that students' interest in studying was declining (MEXT 2002b). Reducing the number of hours teachers were required to devote to core academic instruction was regarded as one way to rekindle students' interest in academics. Trimming the contents of the Course of Study, MEXT asserted, would allow children to explore concepts in greater depth and to feel more engaged in the classroom.

Table 1.1. Trends in intended instructional time: Elementary school (6-year totals)

	1978	1992	2002
Japanese	1,532	1,601	1,377
Social studies	558	420	345
Mathematics	1,011	1,011	869
Science	558	420	350
Music	418	418	358
Fine arts	418	418	358
Home economics	627	627	540
Physical education	627	627	540
Ethics	209	209	209
Special activities	209	209	209
Integrated Studies	—	—	430
Total	**5,785**	**5,785**	**5,367**

Table 1.2. Trends in intended instructional time: Middle school (3-year totals)

	1978	1992	2002
Japanese	455	455	350
Social studies	385	350–385	295
Mathematics	385	385	315
Science	350	315–350	290
Music	175	140–175	115
Fine arts	175	140–175	115
Physical education	315	315–350	270
Technology/home economics	245	210–245	175
Foreign language	—	—	315
Moral education	105	105	105
Special activities	210	105–210	105
Electives	—	—	155–280
Integrated Studies	—	—	210–335
Total	**3,150**	**3,150**	**2,940**

Note: Standard class times are 45 minutes for elementary schools and 50 minutes for middle schools. Prior to 1998, foreign language was considered an elective subject.
Source: MEXT 2005

Introduction of the Integrated Studies subject. The creation of a new subject called Integrated Studies (*sogoteki na gakushu*), which became part of the national curriculum in 2002,[2] represented the symbolic embodiment of the relaxed approach to education advocated by MEXT (Bjork 2009). Schools could select topics for integrated study that fit the unique characteristics of their surrounding communities and the interests of their students. Ministry officials hoped that introduction of Integrated Studies (IS) curricula would catalyze substantial changes in instructional methodology, as well as students' views about learning. IS was regarded as a vehicle that would encourage the investigation of provocative issues that children face in their daily lives. According to MEXT guidelines, students would explore those topics in an integrated fashion, drawing from a variety of relevant disciplines, as one naturally does in looking for answers to real-life questions. Taking part in such investigations would make learning more stimulating and personally relevant for students. Although IS became a distinct course, no additional instructors were hired to teach this subject. Instead, teachers from all disciplines were expected to take part in IS planning and implementation.

Expansion of elective offerings. Another strategy adopted to augment student motivation to learn was the expansion of elective courses offered at the secondary level. This shift created more frequent opportunities for pupils to "study in accordance with their interests, career inclinations, and level of proficiency. . . . Thus, students can study subject in more depth—as deeply as their level of motivation takes them" (MEXT 2000). As was true of the framework for IS, the Course of Study specified the total number of hours that should be devoted to elective studies, but schools were given the authority to organize those courses to fit their own goals. For example, at the upper secondary level, the minimum total number of credits for instruction in the core academic subjects was reduced from thirty-eight to thirty-one hours per week, to make more room in the schedule for elective coursework. Schools could offer electives that expanded on concepts introduced in the existing curriculum, or they could create new courses designed to appeal to students, such as environmental studies or photography (MacDonald 2006).

Innovative pedagogy. MEXT viewed the contents of the curriculum as well as the instructional methods used to present concepts as essential elements of relaxed education. Just as the policies were framed as an antidote to outdated practices, innovative instructional practices were presented as preferable to traditional modes of teaching. Responding to concerns that Japanese schools placed "too much emphasis on conformity (MEXT 2002b, 7), the Ministry exhorted teachers to design lessons that promoted a "zest for living" (*ikiru chikara*).[3] New abilities demanded new pedagogical approaches, most of which would fall under the term "student-centered" as it is understood in the West. Moving away from the lecture and test model was considered an essential step toward relieving pressure on students. Teachers were encouraged to experiment with instructional strategies that were better aligned with the "new abilities" MEXT was promoting. Rather than simply memorize facts, students would be challenged to discuss, evaluate, and analyze information. One report, for example, states that "experiential learning such as experiences with nature, experiences in everyday life, observations, experiments, field trips and research, and problem-solving approaches to learning should be actively applied" (MEXT 2002b, 23) in the classroom.

Supportive teacher guidance/class management. In the past, teachers in Japan were given great latitude to respond to student misbehavior as they saw fit. At the secondary level, the combination of "intimacy coupled with severity" (Rohlen 1983, 201) was considered an effective way to encourage adolescents but also keep them in line. In some cases, however, teachers responded to pupil misconduct with excessive force (Miller 2010). Beginning in the 1990s, MEXT encouraged teachers to refrain from all forms of physical punishment. Instead, instructors were advised to mentor their students using more compassionate techniques. Shifting to more relaxed class management and guidance methods would reduce the prevalence of the social maladies that were attracting extensive media coverage. (See chapter 8 for more information about this topic.)

More than a decade has passed since *yutori kyoiku* was introduced. Education stakeholders have witnessed firsthand the repercussions of MEXT's attempts to alleviate pressure in the schools. Many of those people are equipped to compare conditions in the schools before and after the Course of Study was revised in 2002. Veteran educators have taught when the curriculum was more voluminous and examinations more pervasive; they have also implemented the new curriculum designed to give children more "room to grow." Administrators have witnessed the effects of *yutori kyoiku* on the schools they oversee. They understand the demands associated with such an ambitious reform, and the specific conditions that may support or impede its implementation. Parents, too, have observed the effects of relaxed education on their children. They can shed light on the degree to which relaxed education has augmented their children's creativity, independence, and love for learning. In combination, these perspectives can provide valuable insights into the process of altering attitudes about testing, accountability, and academic achievement.

In Japan as well as the United States, the populations of students served by the schools are more diverse and complex in recent years (Gordon et al. 2009; Tsuneyoshi, Okano, and Boocock 2011). The work of educators employed in the two systems has become more challenging as a result. As I detail in the next chapter, in both countries, proclamations of educational crisis have prompted policy makers to endorse policies that have forced education stakeholders at all levels of the system to reexamine their core beliefs about the purpose of schooling. Yet the two nations have employed fundamentally different strategies to address perceived deficiencies in students and schools. In the United States, the solutions attracting the most attention have emphasized the need to set more ambitious standards for students, teachers, and schools, and provide sanctions to those that do not meet those standards. In Japan, those types of solutions have been decried as the very root of the problems currently plaguing the schools.

Underlying the relaxed-education initiatives were widespread concerns about the state of Japanese youth, who were portrayed as stressed out, lacking motivation, undisciplined, uncaring, and deficient in basic academic skills—in sum, socially, and intellectually unprepared to face the challenges of modern society. Interestingly, many of the negative traits applied to the younger generation implicitly juxtaposed contemporary children against previous generations of children, as if the solution to all education-related problems was to convince young citizens to fit a mold of the ideal student embraced in the past. Yet the policies embraced by MEXT were distinctly forward looking, representing a break from traditional educational practices. The relaxed-education reforms were anchored by the notion that the traditional model of schooling in Japan was no longer meeting the needs of students or society.

Arguments in favor of *yutori kyoiku* emphasized the importance of reshaping the schools to fit the realities of contemporary society, the dispositions of their students, and the demands of the business world. Central to this conception of reform was a belief that schools should be more supportive and engaging settings for children. Both the curriculum and the methods used to deliver it needed to be revised so as to enhance students' interest in studying. Requiring pupils to memorize a large body of facts was no longer considered an effective approach. Instead, MEXT encouraged teachers to design learning activities that required children to participate actively in the discovery and application of knowledge. Through such experiences, students would acquire skills that could be nimbly applied to the unpredictable challenges they face in their lives.

What has been the impact of relaxed-education reforms? Have they met the goals outlined in MEXT reports? It has been difficult to answer these questions, despite a plethora of information pertaining to *yutori kyoiku*. According to MEXT forecasts, relaxed education would make learning more relevant and appealing to students, and would create more balance in their lives. However, MEXT predictions have not been matched with solid supporting evidence. The effects of policy changes on actual schools and classrooms have been overshadowed by fiery debates about the state of the schools, driven by ideology rather than evidence. As Tsuneyoshi (2004b) observes, those debates "seemed to have the attraction of a talk show, where prominent critics took their stance and the audience could cheer for their favorites" (371). Most discussions of relaxed education have provided incomplete—and sometimes inaccurate—information about the effects of the reforms. This study was designed to provide a more nuanced analysis of *yutori kyoiku*.

Focus of the Study

In the chapters that follow, I analyze the effects of the relaxed-education reforms on teaching and learning in Japanese schools. My primary objective for this project was to delve below the rhetorical level and study the concrete effects of *yutori kyoiku*. The research methodology I used was designed to fit that goal. Rather than evaluate the merits of claims made by the commentators most often cited in news reports, I documented the activities that took place in classrooms, hallways, playing fields, and faculty rooms. Determined to understand the impact of relaxed education on student learning, I immersed myself in the cultures of a sample of elementary and middle schools. Over a six-year period, I traveled around the country interviewing students, parents, teachers, administrators, academics, and ministry officials about their experiences with *yutori kyoiku*.

Drawing from the information provided by these informants, I examine the challenges, rewards, frustrations, and tensions generated by relaxed education. This ground-level view of reform provides valuable insights into a system that is frequently mischaracterized, sensationalized, and misunderstood. I pay particular attention to the following aspects of the reform process:

Teachers' Efforts to Realize the Goals of Yutori Kyoiku

The success or failure of MEXT reform plans depended in large part on the actions of teachers. In an attempt to encourage instructors to assume ownership over the new curriculum, the ministry deliberately kept the directives it communicated to instructors to a minimum. Reports on relaxed education are often premised on the supposition that school employees faithfully followed policy guidelines disseminated by MEXT. Yet the education officials I spoke with admitted that they knew very little about how teachers were actually responding to those plans. A number of questions remained unanswered: Did teachers embrace the proposed changes? Did they support the ministry's goals related to reducing academic intensity? If so, did they have the skills and necessary to facilitate the shift from test-driven to student-centered instruction? In what ways did the organizational culture of their schools support or impede teachers as they attempted to follow reform directives?

The Effects of Reform on Student Learning and Attitudes Toward School

Previously published research tends to emphasize the central role that education has played in the lives of Japanese youngsters (Fukuzawa and LeTendre 2001; Shimahara and Sakai 1995; White 1987). Commitment to education created cohesion among the populace that proved invaluable during the postwar years, but also placed demands on children that could be overwhelming. According to education critics, those pressures were interfering with children's social and intellectual development. One of the objectives of relaxed education was to make school more engaging and meaningful to students. Has introduction of *yutori kyoiku* enhanced children's commitment to learning? Have revisions to the curriculum or the more child-centered instructional approaches advocated by MEXT made schools more "user friendly" in the eyes of students? Has relaxed education, as its name would suggest, alleviated the stress children experience? Up to this point, little attention has been devoted to student perspectives on relaxed education.

The Depth of Parental Commitment to Relaxed Education

While the primary targets of this reform movement were teachers, parents and community leaders were also expected to help tailor the curriculum to fit students' interests. Arguments in favor of the five-day school week maintained that parents would use the extra day of leisure to support the goals of relaxed education. It was unclear, however, how adults would respond to these opportunities to participate more actively in their children's education. Their views about MEXT's plans for change have not been examined thoroughly. Did parents support the decision to reduce the contents of the national curriculum in attempt to make their children's lives more relaxed? Did they agree that teachers should spend less time preparing students for exams and more time developing "twenty-first-century abilities"? And were they equipped to facilitate the type of academic enrichment activities described in MEXT reports? Exploring these questions can serve as a litmus test of how Japanese citizens feel about educational reform—their primary concerns, goals for their children, and commitment to transforming schools.

Responses in the Schools

My analysis reveals that Japanese teachers are much more willing to act autonomously than has been acknowledged in the past. Research on schooling in Japan tends to emphasize MEXT's pervasive and cogent influence over the nation's schools (Kida 1986; Schoppa 1991a). With authority to shape education policy, determine the national curriculum, and manage personnel, the ministry appears to wield almost unchecked power over the schools. In the schools I visited, teachers displayed an awareness of MEXT expectations for classroom practice—but did not organize their actions to fit those prescriptions. Even individuals who agreed with the objectives of new policies struggled to alter their behavior to fit MEXT's plans for *yutori kyoiku*. When new policies did not consistently produce the outcomes forecast by MEXT, teachers tended to revert to tried-and-true practices.

The evidence I collected casts doubt on the assertion that adoption of the relaxed-education policies triggered a system-wide state of crisis. Attempts to modify the system produced limited changes in the learning experiences provided to children. Although all the schools I studied produced reports indicating that they were adhering to reform guidelines, teachers resisted pressure to alter established practices. Instructors may have conformed to ministry guidelines at a surface level, but their instructional practices and core beliefs endured. Elementary school teachers did design learning activities that supported the objectives of relaxed education, but that was true prior to the adoption of the 2002 Course of Study. Middle school instructors' skepticism about those same goals resulted in widespread resistance to change that was obscured by superficial compliance with policy guidelines. Due to this tendency, the learning environments in which children spend a majority of their waking hours have not been modified in any significant way.

I discovered that parents as well as teachers tended to agree with the goals of relaxed education, but struggled to fully commit to the proposed changes due to their concerns about how children educated in a more flexible system would perform on high school and university entrance examinations. Conscious that students' educational futures were determined primarily by their performance on entrance exams, instructors focused lessons on material that was likely to appear on those assessments, using pedagogies that made it possible for them to cover large bodies of facts efficiently. Even individuals who had initially expressed support for relaxed education reverted to pedagogical practices that *yutori kyoiku* was designed to eliminate. The sense of accountability to prepare students for examinations was so strong that teachers could not de-emphasize those instruments. Only elementary school instructors, whose students would not be required to take entrance examinations for several years, consistently implemented learning activities that met the goals for relaxed education outlined in MEXT documents.

Responses to the relaxed-education reforms offer some important lessons for countries such as the United States that have expanded the role of testing in schools in attempt to boost accountability. The Japanese case highlights the broad and powerful reach that high-stakes tests have on decision making in schools. The ramifications of those tests should not be underestimated. Individuals at all levels of the system adjust their behavior in recognition of the rewards and sanctions linked with those exams. Keenly aware of the mechanisms used to evaluate students (and school employees), teachers often feel compelled to focus on learning activities explicitly designed to prepare pupils for exams—even when those activities conflict with their core values about education. Schools reorganize instructional programs to fit the demands of tests. We have already seen evidence of this tendency in the United States, where schools have begun to eliminate music, art, physical education, and science, if those subjects are not included on the exams. And once schools make that shift, it becomes remarkably difficult to undo the changes that have been instituted.

Testing also has a direct impact on student behavior. Proponents of high-stakes examinations assert that test-based accountability systems represent an effective means of securing student commitment to their studies (Paige 2006). Policies such as NCLB and RTT are premised on the idea that instituting more rigorous accountability systems will stimulate all students to reach their academic potential. My research suggests otherwise. In Japan, tests did reinforce some students' attachment to school. However, while test-related pressure did motivate high-achieving middle school students in my sample to work diligently, less academically capable pupils quickly lost interest in school. Low test scores sent the clear message to those individuals that they had little chance of earning acceptance to a competitive high school. This realization, coupled with uninspiring instruction, often extinguished their enthusiasm for studying. Japan concomitantly offers glimpses of the promise that public education affords and the significant costs of relying on examinations to motivate adolescents to study.

The findings of this study should interest individuals located in other settings currently grappling with questions related to the influence of testing on instructional practices and children's attachment to school. With a few notable exceptions, high-stakes testing is currently regarded by education policy makers in Western settings as something of an elixir. The United States and the United Kingdom, in particular, have enthusiastically adopted initiatives that rely on examinations to leverage school improvement without carefully studying the structure and effects of systems that have long histories of relying on examinations to bolster commitment to education. Responses to Japan's relaxed-education reforms highlight some troubling by-products of examination-driven education. The students, teachers, and parents I interviewed all described how the focus on examinations undercut children's interest in learning—but they also recognized that the system had become impervious to change. If we think that tests exert an excessive influence in Japanese schools, we would be wise to learn from the country's experiences. Otherwise, we may also be faced with a generation of students who are stressed out, disinterested in learning, and lacking the skills necessary to contribute to a knowledge-based economy. Continuing to pursue an education-reform agenda that prizes accountability, data-driven instruction, and standardized testing could exacerbate the very problems education policy makers in the United States are currently attempting to disrupt.

Outline of the Book

High-Stakes Schooling investigates the issues and questions raised above. Drawing from interviews with education stakeholders, observations of lessons conducted in elementary and middle schools located across Japan, and evidence collected during a yearlong ethnographic study of six schools, I examine the translation and implementation of relaxed-education policies. Each chapter looks the effects of *yutori kyoiku* from a different perspective, and connects Japan's experiences with education reform to issues currently confronting schools in the United States.

Chapter 2, "Framing the Education Crisis," situates the themes of this book in broader social and political contexts. It compares the forces that have been driving calls for educational reform in Japan and the United States over the past twenty-five years. My analysis indicates that while politicians in both locations have relied on a rhetoric of crisis to support their education-reform agendas, the evidence used to justify those claims—as well as the proposed solutions—differed markedly. At the same time that the US Department of Education was promoting expanded testing and accountability in schools, MEXT was decrying those very factors as responsible for the "crisis" the Japanese education system was experiencing.

Chapter 3, "Examining the Impact of Reform Policies," introduces the setting of the study: Nishiyama, a medium-size city located in northern Japan. After presenting a broad overview of the area, I describe the six schools that are the focus of the study. Next, I summarize the research methods that guided the study. Chapter 4, "The Teaching Force," explores the roles that instructors played in implementing the government's plans for *yutori kyoiku*. The first section investigates the rhetorical arguments that were used to support the devolution of authority to school-based educators. The next section analyzes teachers' views about the ministry's plans for change. Particular attention is paid to tensions between new responsibilities delegated to school employees and traditional values about the responsibilities of educators.

Adoption of relaxed-education reforms created challenges for all educators, but teachers internalized the repercussions of the reform differently, depending to a great extent on their location within the system. Chapter 5, "Nurturing Enthusiasm in Elementary School Students," looks closely at those differences and examines their impact on the learning opportunities provided to children. Evidence presented in this chapter establishes that elementary school teachers cultivated the academic abilities and mental dispositions identified by both conservative and progressive critics as those required for success in contemporary society. The analysis provided indicates that elementary teachers managed to meet the goals for *yutori kyoiku* precisely because they were not subject to the examination pressures pervasive in secondary schools.

In the middle schools, however, teachers often had trouble adjusting their behavior to fit reform guidelines. As I detail in Chapter 6, "Responses to Change in the Middle Schools," middle school employees continued to shape decisions to fit practices that had proven, over long periods of time, "consistent with the stable web of beliefs and assumptions that are part of the culture" (Stigler and Hiebert 1999, 87). Those beliefs and assumptions were tied to the exigencies of entrance examinations rather than to ideals about children's love for learning. Interview and observation data signal that teachers were pressed to move in one direction—but the foundation on which they operated remained stationary. The evidence presented in Chapter 7, "Curricular Reform, Academic Achievement, and Educational Opportunity," analyzes the impact of that pattern on student learning. I observe that changes to the curriculum introduced with the goal of making learning more appealing to all students actually had the opposite effect in the middle schools: achievement-oriented pupils capitalized on the opportunities offered to them while their less motivated peers fell further behind.

Parallel to the curricular revisions that grounded the relaxed-education reforms, the student-guidance system also underwent significant modifications. The flexibility incorporated into the curriculum was accompanied by a loosening of discipline procedures that has received negligible attention in the research literature. As Chapter 8, "Shifting Student-Teacher Relationships" illustrates, these shifts had important implications for student-teacher interactions in the middle schools. The combination of increasingly rebellious students and more accommodating guidance approaches complicated the work of educators. Deterred from employing tactics that had proven effective in the past, middle school teachers struggled to apply *yutori* approaches to student guidance in settings where their authority was challenged frequently.

Chapter 9, "Broadening the Discussion," expands the scope of the discussion to include evidence from other nations that have introduced ambitious educational reforms recently. The commonalities between initiatives enacted in Japan, China, Korea, Singapore, Indonesia, and Malaysia are striking. In all of these places, ministries of education are promoting policies that, like *yutori kyoiku,* aim to dilute the influence of examinations. Another common theme is the desire to make learning more relevant and motivating to students. Next, I identify key factors that help to explain the success of the education systems currently regarded as success stories.

As I was conducting fieldwork for this book, I also took part in a cross-national study of teaching practices in Japan, China, Singapore, and the United States. In Chapter 10, "US Teachers Reflect on Japanese Elementary School Instruction," I report on the findings of that study, paying particular attention to American teachers' opinions about a sample of lessons that were videotaped in Japan. Their responses to those videos reveal that the goals of educators in the United States and Japan overlap in many areas. Heightened pressures associated with high-stakes tests, however, are making it difficult for American teachers to use methods designed to enhance children's creativity, critical thinking skills, and problem-solving abilities. Chapter 11, "Looking Forward," summarizes the evidence presented in previous chapters and extends the findings to broader questions about educational reform, testing, and accountability. In all the schools I studied, considerations rooted in the local community exerted a more direct and powerful influence over educators as they responded to policy directives than did concerns about MEXT expectations.

TWO

Framing the Education Crisis

Declarations of education crisis are pervasive to such a degree that the absence of such rhetoric would be more surprising than its presence. It is difficult to recall a time when an education system did not provoke debates about the effectiveness of its schools or the academic performance of its students. Absent crisis, politicians lack the ammunition to advance their own ideas about how public institutions should operate. How can someone make the case for fundamental reform if the schools are successfully carrying out their missions? Crisis rhetoric, on the other hand, "serves to arouse an emotional, rather than analytic, response in people, making the public fearful of the 'crisis' and thus more receptive to drastic intervention" (Takayama 2007, 427). Reform proponents in Japan and the United States have recently capitalized on such fears to promote extensive changes in schools. In the United States, the No Child Left Behind (NCLB) Act was passed in 2001 and signed into law in January 2002. Japan's relaxed-education (*yutori kyoiku*) reforms were introduced nation-wide in April 2002.

Both reform efforts were identified as groundbreaking in terms of their scope and implications. Responding to escalating calls of systemic problems, politicians in the two countries pushed forward ambitious plans to overhaul the schools. However, the "crises" that led to educational reform were framed quite differently. The rationales employed to support entreaties for change were linked to contrasting views about the root of the challenges that faced schools and the role that government should play in addressing those issues. NCLB relied on high-stakes testing to augment students' motivation to study, outlining detailed rewards and sanctions for schools based on their ability to prepare pupils for those tests. One system decried the evils of testing and sought to alleviate academic intensity; the other attempted to heighten the pressures experienced by a generation of complacent students and teachers. Given the increasingly transnational flow of educational policies (Steiner-Khamsi 2012) these contrasting education reform trajectories are intriguing.

In this chapter, I look closely at the framing of educational crisis in Japan and the United States. A comparison of these two reform pathways points to strikingly different visions of the challenges that currently confront public schools. My analysis of those divergent reform trajectories points to critical differences in views about the fundamental purposes of education and teachers' responsibilities to their students. In addition, this comparison provides unique perspectives on the shifting role of government in both national contexts. The insights generated have the potential to lead to more effective decision making in Japan, the United States, and elsewhere.

Arguments for Change in the United States

A series of reports and policies disseminated over the last fifty years have decried the sorry state of the schools in the United States. Since the launch of Sputnik in 1957, commentators of all political stripes and colors have warned that unless American schools are overhauled, our society will lose ground to students and businesses in other countries. Those cries of alarm are sounded regardless of the state of the economy at the time. Perhaps the document that stated the appeal for reform most cogently—and generated the strongest response from the public—was *A Nation at Risk: The Imperative for Educational Reform*, which was published by the National Commission on Excellence and Education in 1983. Authors of the report declared that "the educational foundations of our society are presently being eroded by a rising tide of mediocrity that threatens our very future as a Nation and a people" (NCEE 1983, 9). Evidence cited to support this statement included declining scores on international achievement tests, the SAT, and College Board achievement tests. For example, according to the report, "Average achievement of high school students on most standardized tests is now lower than 26 years ago when Sputnik was launched" (ibid., 11). Furthermore, too many schools were emphasizing "such rudiments as reading and computation at the expense of other essential skills, such as comprehension, analysis, solving problems, and drawing conclusions" (12). To remedy these conditions, the United States needed to become a "Learning Society" that valued education occurring in both formal and informal settings. Proposed strategies for accomplishing this goal included setting more extensive high school graduation requirements, adopting more rigorous and measurable standards, lengthening the school day and year, and enhancing the quality of teaching.

In the years that followed, despite the uproar generated by *A Nation at Risk*, American schools did not show significant progress in the areas deemed in need of attention by NCEE. High school graduation rates did not rise noticeably, the length of the school year was not extended in many districts, and the challenging curricular requirements referred to in the report were rarely implemented as outlined. Nevertheless, state and government leaders continued to advocate heightened accountability through content standards and testing over the next two decades (Derthick and Dunn 2009). For instance, the Improving America's Schools Act (IASA), adopted in 1994 under President Clinton, directed all states to establish content and performance standards, assess student learning at all three levels of the system, and develop systems for identifying underperforming students. Clinton also endorsed the Goals 2000: Educate America Act, which moved forward the outcomes-based approach to educational reform that had been gaining momentum since the publication of *A Nation at Risk*. An important shift in the education-reform legislation was an increased emphasis on the role that testing would play in leveraging change.

Efforts to make schools more accountable reached a new level in January 2002, when President George W. Bush, with the support of politicians from both parties, signed the No Child Left Behind Act into law. The goals of NCLB echoed those that guided policies introduced by Bush and Secretary of Education Rod Paige during their tenure in Texas: "The purpose of this title is to ensure that all children have a fair, equal, and significant opportunity to obtain a high-quality education" (NCLB, Sec. 1001). In communicating the need for reform to the public, officials in the Bush administration emphasized altruistic aspects of the new policies. President Bush repeatedly declared his resolve to end "the soft bigotry of low expectations" that undermined the educational opportunities delivered to many American children. Requiring school districts to set specific achievement goals for low-income, minority, and LEP (limited English proficient) students would force educators to respond to systemic inequalities that demanded more focused efforts. According to Secretary Paige, this requirement was motivated by "a determination to educate all of our kids" (Kongshem 2002, 16). This would be accomplished by "improving and strengthening accountability, teaching, and learning by using State assessment systems designed to ensure that students are meeting challenging State academic achievement and content standards and increasing achievement overall, but especially for the disadvantaged" (ibid.). A central pillar of Bush's "compassionate conservatism," NCLB was structured to encourage schools to pay closer attention to the academic progress made by all of their students. According to the timetable written into NCLB, 100% of all students in the country would become proficient in reading and mathematics by the year 2014. Observers of all political leanings applauded this unprecedented attention to the academic performance of students who faced significant challenges in their lives.

Although states were granted the authority to decide which tests would be used to measure student progress, NCLB was quite prescriptive in terms of the frequency of testing, data-analysis procedures, and the consequences of failing to meet target scores.[1] The act required states to develop "adequate yearly progress" (AYP) objectives for the following subgroups of students: economically disadvantaged children, students with disabilities, pupils from major racial/ethnic minority groups, and LEP students. To generate the data necessary to determine if these objectives were met, the language arts and mathematics assessments adopted by states would be administered annually in grades three through eight, with at least 95% of eligible students completing the tests. In addition, schools were directed to disseminate the results of those tests to the public. Students who attended schools that did not meet their AYP goals for two successive years would be provided with tutoring services and given the option of transferring to more successful schools. Institutions that failed to demonstrate satisfactory progress were labeled "in need of improvement" and were subject to consequences that ranged from "supplemental services" (such as tutoring) to restructuring.

Another notable aspect of the act was its emphasis on accountability. Secretary Paige maintained that the previous absence of clearly defined accountability measures was the primary reason that American students were underperforming:

> Our public education system, however, flourished in that environment because there was little external accountability, little information available about school quality, and little pressure to compete for students. . . . In other words, the child's education was delivered as educators determined, and although some parents did voice their opposition to this process, most had little option but to accept it. (Paige 2007, 471)

Instituting more rigorous accountability structures would yield data that teachers could use to make informed decisions about the instructional services they provided, and would create stronger incentives for educators to invest in their work. The language in Paige's statement—and in NCLB legislation—implied that a lack of incentives was at the root of the nation's educational problems. NCLB was designed to generate pressures that would alter that. "This new definition of accountability," Paige asserted, "will do more to shape the future of our education system than any law passed by Congress" (ibid., 472). No longer would schools be free to evaluate their own progress. The new reporting requirements required them to set ambitious goals for student achievement and develop concrete strategies for meeting them. Teachers and schools could respond productively to those pressures, or suffer the consequences.

This approach to reform was significant for a number of reasons. First, the recommendations included in the policy focused on creating systems to make the delivery of educational services more efficient, uniform, and measurable. Although the ultimate beneficiaries of the reform were children, NCLB placed greater emphasis on assessment mechanisms than on the specific ways that students stood to benefit from the reform. The stress placed on streamlining institutions and procedures so as to make them more efficient recalled the language of a business report. Paige himself drew parallels between corporate practice and the goals of NCLB:

> Some years ago, management literature was dominated by a concept called Total Quality Management. That means fixing the production process so that defects are corrected before the product gets to the end of the pipeline. That's kind of analogous to what we're doing here. We're switching to a zero-defect attitude and saying that each step along the teaching pipeline has to correct its own defects—so that when a person goes through the system and exits on the other end, they are assured mastery of concepts expected by the high standards in that particular state. So when we say 'no child left behind,' that's another way of saying "zero deficits." (Kongshem 2002, 2–3)

Schools, like corporations, would be evaluated using statistical evidence of the progress they made (or did not make) toward concrete goals. To keep that process manageable, the evidence used to make those determinations was limited to include scores on standardized mathematics and language arts tests. Subjects such as social studies, art, music, and physical education were not included in the evaluations; nor were factors such as students' moral development, interest in learning, or ability to work with others. The procedures for assessing success or failure were designed so that they could be implemented on a massive scale, and would produce results that could be easily quantified and communicated to the public.

NCLB also represented a significant shift in thinking regarding the professional responsibilities of educators. In the United States, the teaching profession has historically attracted individuals eager to "make a difference" in the lives of children. In exchange for their labor, teachers have been granted extensive autonomy in designing and implementing curricula (Ayers 1995; Sarason 1993). As Lortie (1975) has observed, "It is of great importance to teachers to feel that they have 'reached' their students—their core rewards are tied to that perception. Other sources of satisfaction . . . pale in comparison" (106). NCLB called into question the wisdom of depending on teachers to work diligently out of an intrinsic desire to help children. Altruism alone is not enough to overcome the challenges that schools currently face: "Committed educators are providing the required educational opportunities . . . However, without the legislation, there would be no guarantee, no assurance that this would be done. Good teachers are everywhere, but they must perform within a system" (Paige 2006, 466). NCLB created such a system—one that provided incentives to teachers who succeeded in raising their students' test scores, as well as consequences for those who did not. The core belief underlying this approach was that the threat of negative sanctions would persuade students and teachers to work harder, and their performance would improve as a result (Nichols, Glass, and Berliner 2005).

Together, these changes induced a significant shift in federal government's role in public education. Previously, state governments were responsible for coordinating both policymaking and funding associated with education. The powers entrusted to Department of Education (DOE) were limited.[2] The Constitution, for example, does not include any references to the federal government's role in providing education. The DOE was not created until 1979, and only two years later Ronald Reagan attempted to abolish it.[3] The DOE website currently states that "education is primarily a State and local responsibility in the United States" (USDOE 2012). Despite its limited role, the DOE "works hard to get a big bang for its taxpayer-provided bucks by targeting its funds where they can do the most good" (ibid.). NCLB was the instrument relied on to generate that explosion.

NCLB was structured to induce states to accept the DOE's recommendations related to testing, assessment, and accountability in exchange for a relatively small amount of financial support. States continued to pay approximately 88% of the costs of primary and secondary education (ibid.), yet the federal government assumed a much larger role in shaping policies at all levels of the system than that number suggests. One reason was that although the total amount of funds associated with NCLB constituted only a small percentage of overall funding, it was substantial enough to influence subnational decision making; the loss of Title I funding would be crippling to many states. Another key factor was the "compensatory legitimation" that governments acquire when they adopt policies attracting broad support nationally or internationally. Weiler (1984) posits that "an important consideration for those who design policies is not only what outcomes these policies will achieve (greater equity, more efficient schools, more employment of graduates, etc.) but also how these policies will affect the search for added legitimacy" (40).[4] Not only would states that opted not to follow NCLB mandates be subject to sanctions from the government—they would also risk appearing out of step with current educational reform trends. Cognizant of this situation, federal authorities managed to leverage a comparatively small amount of money to dramatically expand their influence. In this way, NCLB marked "yet another historic step toward a greater federal role in our traditionally decentralized education system" (Paige 2006, 466). This trend continued with the Race to the Top Program introduced under President Obama, which made minor modifications to NCLB but continued to reward states that required school districts to rely on high-stakes tests to hold school districts accountable for student achievement.

NCLB passed with bipartisan support. It was shaped to fit the agendas of business leaders rather than any particular party. The principles guiding the reform had been used to run corporations, not educational institutions, and tended to appeal to conservative as well as liberal leaders. Policymakers with various affiliations agreed that adopting accountability systems was an effective approach to incentivizing school improvement (Manna 2006; Nitta 2008). Though NCLB was modeled after the policies enacted in Texas by Bush and Paige, it also resembled Goals 2000, President Clinton's signature education initiative. Opposition to the act was minimal: the Senate passed NCLB by a vote of 91–8; in the House, the vote was 384–45. A handful of education interest groups, such as the National Education Association and the American Association of School Administrators, criticized the bill. Influential members from the business sector, however, drowned out those voices.[5] A variety of economic and political forces had converged to create a broad consensus for heightened accountability. Some questions were raised about the implementation timetable and the resources that schools would receive; yet NCLB was enacted with great fanfare and little opposition.

Japan's Goals for Reform

As table 2.1 indicates, the construction of the "crisis" in Japanese education—as well as the proposed solutions to perceived problems in the schools—differed markedly from those put forth by the US government. At the time that relaxed-education policies were being promulgated, children's academic performance was not MEXT's primary concern. According to one ministry report, "From comprehensive analysis of results from international and national research projects done so far, it can be said that, on the whole, the learning status of Japanese children is generally good" (MEXT 2003, 21). Education officials were more concerned about the social and emotional state of the nation's youth. Calls for fundamental reform were usually supported with evidence of "educational pathologies"

Table 2.1. Comparison of NCLB and relaxed-education goals

Overview of requirements for states under NCLB	Goals of relaxed-education reforms in Japan
States must create a state assessment system to monitor student progress toward meeting these state-defined standards.	Foster open and warmhearted Japanese through participation in community service and various programs.
States must require schools and districts to publish report cards identifying academic achievement of its students in aggregate and disaggregated by ethnicity and other sub groups (e.g., for racial minorities, students for whom English is a second language (ESL), and special education students).	Improve the learning environment to one which is enjoyable and free of worries.
States must create a system of labels that communicate to the community how local schools and districts are performing.	Promote the creation of schools trusted by parents and communities.
States must create a plan (i.e., adequate yearly progress or AYP) that would ensure 100% of its students will reach academic proficiency by the year 2014/15.	Train teachers as "education professionals."
States must come up with a system of accountability that includes rewards and sanctions to schools, educators, and students that are tied to whether they meet state's goals outlined in the AYP plan.	Promote the establishment of universities of an international standard.
	Establish a new educational vision for the new century and improve the foundations of education.

Sources: Nichols, Glass, and Berliner 2005; MEXT 2002

(*kyoiku byori*) rather than statistics that measured students' performance on tests. Reports published by MEXT as well as the mass media drew attention to the prevalence of social maladies such as bullying (*ijime*), violence in school (*konai boryoku*), and truancy. Analysis of these problems tended to point to excessive emphasis on testing and rote learning as responsible for such problems. One report, for example, maintained that "with nerves worn thin from excessive examination competition, it becomes difficult to cultivate a rich sense of humanity without sufficient opportunities to experience everyday life experiences, social experiences, and experiences of nature" (MEXT 1997, 9). *Yutori kyoiku* policy was crafted in response to concerns about testing and academic pressure that had been building for decades. Students may have been scoring well on standardized measures of achievement, but according to a vocal group of educators, the intensity of the school system was extinguishing children's interest in learning.

During this period, MEXT also endorsed a set of structural reforms that emphasized the benefits of decentralization, diversification, and deregulation of education. In contrast with plans to relieve academic pressure promulgated by progressive educators, the structural reforms were endorsed by business leaders who held influential positions in the Ministry of Trade and Industry (MITI), business think tanks, and the Japanese Business Federation (*Keidanren*). Concerned that the schools were not producing a labor force with the skills and creativity necessary to revitalize the economy, these powerful actors endorsed revisions to the education system that followed the logic of neoliberalism and New Public Management (Nitta 2008, 118). Among the ideas they promoted were charter schools, school choice, and a decentralization of education budgets. Although these changes were noteworthy, I will not focus on them in this book for two reasons: (1) the structural reforms have already been carefully studied in another book (*The Politics of Structural Education Reform*, by Keith Nitta); and (2) in 2003, when I was developing the research questions that formed the basis of this study, changes introduced in conjunction with relaxed education were having the most powerful effect on the educators I interviewed. Though school-based actors were aware of the structural reforms, those policies were not directly influencing their daily work.

Relaxed-education initiatives focused on students' dispositions toward school, other pupils, and the communities in which they lived. MEXT reports published in conjunction with *yutori kyoiku* emphasized the affective dimensions of schooling. The charts and graphs included in those reports devoted scant attention to students' scholastic achievement. More prevalent were results from surveys that gauged students' feelings about a vari-

Table 2.2. International comparison of student happiness

Measures of student satisfaction	Japan	United States	China
I feel useless sometimes.	19.1	12.8	9.2
I am mostly satisfied with myself.	9.4	53.5	24.3
I am as worthy as other people.	8.8	51.8	49.3
I feel confident to complete my work once it is planned.	9.8	54.2	32.8
I do not have much to be proud of.	14.9	9.1	10.2

Source: Mext 2002

ety of school-related topics. Those survey data highlighted some troubling changes in school-aged youth. Compared with their peers from previous generations, contemporary youth reported spending less time studying, finding school less interesting, and experiencing greater levels of stress (MEXT 2001). Furthermore, Japanese children appeared to have lower self-esteem than their counterparts in other countries (see table 2.2).

MEXT policy recommendations were shaped to fit these realities. *Creating Dreams for Japan's Tomorrow*, a report published by MEXT in 2002, identified seven reform priorities:

1. Improve the students' basic scholastic proficiency in easy-to-understand classes
2. Foster open and warm-hearted Japanese [citizens] through participation in community and various programs
3. Improve the learning environment to one which is enjoyable and free of worries
4. Promote the creation of schools trusted by parents and communities
5. Train teachers as "education professionals"
6. Promote the establishment of universities of an international standard
7. Establish a new educational vision for the new century and improve the foundations of education

(MEXT 2002, 7)

The substance and tone of these statements contrast sharply with the language found in NCLB policy documents. The perceived crisis that MEXT was responding to was social and emotional trauma that resulted from widespread stress on academics.

While concerns about children's mental outlook received the most attention in government reports, MEXT also emphasized the need to prepare students to function more effectively in a globalized, knowledge-driven world. The ministry is often depicted as a highly centralized, almost monolithic organization, but in reality it is a large bureaucracy with internal divisions (Hood 2001, Hood 2003, Nitta 2008; Takayama 2011). In addition, the recommendations delivered by education advisory boards, such as the National Council on Educational Reform (NCER) and the Council for Education Rebuilding (CER), tend to reflect the priorities of the businesspeople who serve on them (Fujita 2010). This diverse group of stakeholders may have agreed that recent social and economic changes have complicated the lives of children, but their ideas about how schools should respond to those changes reflected their distinct orientations. As a result, the recommendations included under the umbrella of relaxed education covered a wide range of issues connected in some way to the seven priorities listed above.

Teachers' Roles in Implementing Reform Policies

MEXT granted a significant amount of autonomy to educators as they implemented the *yutori* curriculum. Though schools were expected to adhere to detailed outlines regarding the total number of hours they allocated to each subject in the Course of Study, they were given the latitude in terms of the topics explored and the instructional methods used. The ministry emphasized the important roles that school-based actors would play in realizing its vision for change. In an attempt to encourage teachers to assume ownership for the new curriculum, MEXT deliberately kept its directives to schools to a minimum: "Each school is to organize its own distinctive curricula in accordance with the relevant laws and ordinances and Courses of Study, taking into consideration the conditions of the local community and the school itself, the stages of mental and physical growth and the characteristics of children" (MEXT 2002, 15). No textbooks for either Integrated Studies or elective subjects were published. Rather than offer detailed prescriptions regarding the content and delivery of these subjects, teachers were given great flexibility to determine the material that would be introduced, the arrangement of instructional content at each grade level, and the methods for assessing student learning. As one Ministry of Education official explained to me, "We wanted the teachers to create the curriculum by themselves, producing their own original ideas without the influence of the ministry" (pers. comm.). This shift was notable, given the ministry's reputation for tightly monitoring activity at all levels of the system. Teachers were offered unprecedented levels of power. Ministry officials assumed that instructors would embrace the autonomy that was offered to them.

Notably absent from relaxed-education policy documents was any mention of how the success or failure of reform initiatives would be measured. MEXT did not specify instruments that would be used to assess the impact of *yutori kyoiku,* or set performance goals for students or teachers. Ministry reports do not refer to inputs or outputs, as is common in education policy legislation. Discussion of the desired effects of relaxed education includes broad statements such as, "[students] with a self-motivated learning attitude . . . get higher scores on tests" (MEXT 2003, 20). This lack of emphasis on achievement test data fits with the overarching goal of reducing academic pressure. Instituting a rigorous system of monitoring the impact of the new policies could be seen as undermining that goal. Furthermore, the desired effects of relaxed education do not naturally lend themselves to quantitative assessment. What instruments could be used to gauge, with any degree of precision, a student's "self-realization," "ability to live independently," or "rich sense of humanity" (MEXT 1997, 5)? On what basis do you determine whether a school has become "an emotional resting place for children" (MEXT 2003, 52)? One prominent feature of relaxed-education policy reform guidelines was an implicit expectation that teachers had the skills and commitment required to realize plans for improving the schools. Teachers were not offered any extrinsic rewards for following those plans, nor were they threatened with any sanctions if they fell short. Schools were expected to evaluate the effects of their efforts and to revise instructional and management methods accordingly, but the "specifics of self-evaluation are left in the hands of schools or school boards of education" (MEXT 2003, 70). No accountability systems were deemed necessary.

MEXT reports may have proclaimed that its reform agenda was the product of collaborative planning between various constituencies, and that both progressive educators and business leaders involved in its formulation embraced *yutori kyoiku.* In actuality, even though MEXT succeeded in gaining enough support to advance relaxed-education reforms, critics questioned—often quite cogently—the wisdom of the policies that were adopted. Even before the new Course of Study was enacted in 2002, commentators forecast the onset of an achievement crisis (*gaku ryoku teika*). A group of prominent math and science professors, for instance, attracted a great deal of attention after declaring that the achievement levels of university students had dropped (Nitta 2008; Tsuneyoshi 2004b). Despite the fact that most of those students had been educated prior to the introduction of *yutori kyoiku,* warnings that the intellectual level of the nation's youth was dropping elevated public anxiety about the effects of MEXT's reform plans. Although such criticism did not impede introduction of relaxed education, as often occurs when governments attempt to devolve authority over curricula (Bjork 2006), the ongoing, often contentious debates about the direction of the education system did raise the stakes for reform. That reality was strikingly apparent to anyone connected with Japanese schools.

Comparing Reform Rationales and Trajectories

As the previous sections detail, near the beginning of the millennium, cries of crisis swirled around Japanese and American schools. In both locations, critics asserted that the education systems were in a downward spiral that demanded immediate and serious responses. The schools needed to be modified so as to prepare graduates to enter the workforce and ensure each nation's global competitiveness. Yet the definitions of the problems at the root of those proclaimed crises, as well as the solutions devised for addressing them, pushed the two systems along different trajectories. Japanese and American policymakers were intent on reshaping schools to fit the demands of the twenty-first century, but their ideas about how to accomplish that goal shared few commonalities.

Driving Japan's relaxed-education initiatives were concerns about excessive emphasis on examinations, and evidence that students were suffering as a result of the intense pressures they experienced in school. In contrast, the education reforms that George W. Bush enacted as governor and as president responded to concerns that US schools had suffered as a result of having become *too* "relaxed." Preoccupation with children's self-esteem and creativity had caused American teachers to lose sight of their fundamental responsibility: to ensure that their pupils developed a solid foundation in the core academic subjects. Students who failed to develop that curricular base would emerge from the school system unprepared to contribute to society, no matter how secure or well adjusted they may have felt. Although American policy planners, like their counterparts in Japan, were motivated to produce citizens with the skills and attitudes required to succeed in the twenty-first century, the reforms they endorsed encouraged a narrowing rather than a broadening of the curriculum.

Education policies promulgated in the United States borrowed from restructuring approaches commonly used to overhaul corporations. A system that had, since its creation, been highly decentralized was reconfigured into a more vertical hierarchy, with expanded powers granted to the USDOE. Under NCLB, accountability was regarded as the critical ingredient in educational reform. The legislation required all public schools to implement a detailed set of requirements for assessing student achievement and school performance. Implementation plans suggested that if teachers and students felt enough pressure to follow change plans, they would modify their behavior to fall in line with reform prescriptions. That represented a significant departure from the localized system of entrusting schools to make decisions about curriculum and instruction that had been in place for decades.

The language used to articulate USDOE change plans echoed the businesslike approach to reform that was being promoted. NCLB outlined reform mandates in concise, legalistic language, leaving little room for misinterpretation. The legislation included numerous references to "academic assessments," "accountability systems," "academic standards," and "alignment." Goals, assessment procedures, and desired outcomes were all described with precision. Teachers were encouraged to embrace "data-driven instruction" and to monitor student progress through rigorous analysis of standardized test scores. Schools were not only required to assess student achievement—they were mandated to do so annually, to disaggregate the data for four subgroups of students (economically disadvantaged students, students from major racial and ethnic groups, students with disabilities, and students with limited English proficiency), and to ensure that at least 95% of each group completed the assessments. Districts were expected to use those data to demonstrate that each subgroup was meeting adequate yearly progress (AYP) goals. Schools that did not meet those goals were subject to a clearly outlined set of sanctions, which became more severe when schools missed their targets a second or third time. Like companies that do not meet revenue targets, schools that failed to raise test scores would be put out of business.

The relaxed-education policies pushed Japan in the opposite direction, structurally and philosophically. In promoting *yutori kyoiku*, MEXT communicated its commitment to devolve authority over the education system to local levels. Schools were provided expanded decision-making powers in the areas of curriculum and instruction. Rather than simply implement plans formulated in Tokyo, teachers were expected to act as policy planners, curriculum designers, and pedagogical experts. MEXT delivered reform guidelines to the schools but entrusted them to devise concrete strategies for realizing those plans. The *School in the New Era* report, for example, noted that relaxed-education initiatives depended "each teacher to engage in daily education activities with expertise, a sense of mission, and passion" (MEXT 2003, 6). According to MEXT, reducing the volume of the national curriculum would liberate teachers from "time constraints and mental pressure" (Tsuneyoshi 2004b, 385) so that they could pay more attention to the unique needs of their students.

Another notable aspect of *yutori kyoiku* reform guidelines was their inexact articulation of policy outcomes. Descriptions of the objectives and implications of relaxed education sound quite vague, especially when compared with NCLB legislation. Rather than identify scores or pass rates that would indicate success or failure, MEXT exhorted schools to "evaluate the learning status of each and every child even more carefully than before" (MEXT 2003, 24). Individual institutions were entrusted to translate that advice into concrete assessment procedures. The autonomy provided to schools implied that high levels of teacher professionalism obviated the need to establish a uniform set of performance-based rewards or sanctions. Teachers would perform optimally if supported rather than monitored.

In stark contrast to NCLB, relaxed education focused on the affective dimensions of learning. MEXT presented traditional pedagogy centered on the acquisition of facts as something to be avoided. Instead, teachers were encouraged to design lessons that fostered creativity, critical thinking, and independence. Phrases such as "the job of self-existence and self-realization," "a mind that is sensitive yet vibrant," and "respecting the individuality of each child" pervaded ministry reports (MEXT 1996; MEXT 1997a; MEXT 2003). Government reports implied that the education system had recently strayed from its core mission. As Japan became more prosperous, the schools gradually shifted their attention from children's social and emotional development to test preparation. Eager to address this issue, MEXT revised the national Course of Study so that children would have more opportunities to explore topics that interested them and related to their lives outside of school.

The idea that teachers will work diligently to improve schools if they are given extensive autonomy is quite appealing. And a curriculum tailored to fit students' unique interests seems preferable to one shaped to fit the contents of standardized tests. Who wouldn't want their children to attend schools that cultivate their creativity, independence, and self-direction? But are these images of education more idealistic than practical? If the objectives and implementation plans for NCLB and relaxed education are compared on paper, Japan's reform blueprints may seem preferable, but are they feasible? Is it prudent to implement a set of ambitious reforms nation-wide without requiring schools to produce specific and quantifiable outcomes? Accountability systems may ruffle the feathers of progressive educators, but are they necessary, given the costs of a major education-reform effort? Introduction of the relaxed-education initiatives provided a unique opportunity to explore these questions. In the chapters that follow, I examine the specific factors that supported and impeded efforts to alleviate academic pressure in Japanese schools. Careful analysis of the challenges, complications, and accomplishments experienced by the members of those learning communities can lead to more-effective policy planning in Japan, the United States, or any country grappling with questions related to high-stakes tests.

THREE

Examining the Impact of Reform Policies

What does it feel like to participate in the daily activities that organize life in a Japanese school these days? Has that experience been altered significantly by curricular changes designed to reduce the intensity of K–12 education? To what extent do examination pressures shape curriculum and instruction in the schools? What incentives are provided to Japanese teachers in attempt to enhance their commitment to their work? How do Japanese "accountability systems" for teachers compare to those currently in favor in the United States? These questions are remarkably difficult to answer, despite the seemingly unending supply of reports about the current education "crisis" that appear in newspapers, books, and on television in Japan. This glut of information about *yutori kyoiku* provokes a wide range of responses, but opinions about the reforms are rarely grounded in a thorough understanding of the impact those policies have had on actual schools or students. As a result, discussions of educational reform tended to provoke strong feelings that were not always based on firsthand knowledge of conditions in schools.

Important questions about how students and teachers are responding to changes in curricula tend to be obscured by heated discussions about the declining morals of contemporary youth or the drop in Japan's relative standing on international achievement tests. Outside of Asia, awareness of *yutori kyoiku* is limited. Images of students clad in meticulously tailored uniforms sitting obediently in rows remain lodged in the memory of many Westerners, despite the anachronous nature of such views. Although most of the people I talk with have heard a great deal about Japan's notorious entrance examination system, few realize that the government introduced a set of reform initiatives designed to alleviate the pressures experiences by students.

Critical analysis of local responses to the relaxed-education initiatives can add valuable insights into the role of the teacher, the influence of cultural on instructional practices, and the challenge of balancing children's academic and social needs. As I have noted, governments around the world are grappling with these issues. Eager to boost their standing on international achievement tests—and to create a more productive citizenry—education planners in the United States and Europe promulgated policies designed to make schools more academically rigorous. In Asia concerns about the negative effects of high-stakes tests prompted ministries of education to promote policies that aim to make school more engaging and less stressful. Common to most of these reform efforts is a dearth of information about the effects of the policies on actual teaching and learning.

The lack of empirical evidence of the effects of educational reform limits our ability to benefit from the experiences of other school improvement initiatives. Although Japanese schools and teachers have extensive firsthand knowledge about the specific conditions that create pressure on students as well as the challenges associated with reducing that pressure, their perspectives have been largely absent from assessments of *yutori kyoiku*. Until recently, the same was true of reports on No Child Left Behind (NCLB) and Race to the Top (RTT). As I will show in the chapters that follow, omitting the school-level view from assessments of a reform effort can produce incomplete or inaccurate inferences. Assessments of *yutori kyoiku* tend to assume that school-based actors are faithfully implementing policy directives; most analyses offer positivistic conclusions that obscure the complexity of the policy translation process (Tsuneyoshi 2004b). This is not surprising, given the powerful influence that rational choice models have historically exerted on governmental decision making (Diamond 2007; Spillane, Reiser, and Reimer 2002). However, framing the analysis of education-reform efforts in this way can yield reductionist descriptions of reform ventures that do not accurately capture the impact of those initiatives (Rhoten 2000). Policy implementation is rarely a linear process; instead, the individuals relied on to implement reform initiatives modify those policies in response to factors such as intraorganizational relations, commitment, capacity, and institutional complexity (Lipsky 1983). As McLaughlin (1987) observes, at each point in this process, "a policy is transformed as individuals interpret and respond to it. What is actually delivered or provided under the aegis of a policy depends finally on the individual at the end of the line, the 'street level bureaucrat'" (174). Neo-institutional theorists also emphasize the decoupled nature of policy environments and classroom activity—and the resulting autonomy provided to individuals involved in the process of policy implementation (Coburn 2004; Rowan 1990). Analyses that examine reform initiatives in an "embedded context" can therefore provide more nuanced and thorough understandings of those change efforts than studies framed by rational choice models of organizational behavior (McLaughlin and Talbert 2001).

This study employs such an approach, documenting the experiences of the education stakeholders most directly affected by adoption of a reform movement. It analyzes their interpretations of education policies and links their actions to the societal, historical, and institutional conditions shaping their behavior. The conclusions I draw are based on data collected over a six-year period (2003–2009). The first stage of my fieldwork was a three-month survey of education stakeholders' opinions and experiences related to *yutori kyoiku*. During that period I interviewed approximately forty teachers and administrators working in eight different prefectures, as well as bureaucrats employed by MEXT. I visited schools located in urban centers experiencing serious challenges associated with recent social changes, plus institutions located in rural areas that rarely attract the attention of foreign observers. That preliminary study helped me identify key issues and challenges that had surfaced in connection with the relaxed-education reforms. While the interviews conducted in 2003 did enhance my understanding of educators' views about relaxed education, their observations were self-reported. I was curious to see how, over time, they reconsidered, modified, and ultimately translated their ideas in the classroom. Having conducted research on policy implementation in other contexts (Bjork 2005), I knew that the process is often messy and unpredictable.

Eager to observe how teachers were applying the MEXT's plans on the ground level, I returned to Japan two years later and spent a full year studying the impact of the relaxed-education policies on a sample of elementary and middle schools located in a prefecture located in northwest Japan. First, I conducted a pilot study in two elementary schools in a rural part of the prefecture, observing classes, interviewing teachers, and fine-tuning data-collection instruments. Over the course of that three-week period, I developed a set of questions that guided my succeeding fieldwork. Next, I conducted an in-depth ethnographic study of implementation of the relaxed-education policies.

At the same time I was studying *yutori kyoiku*, I was invited to take part in a cross-national study of teaching in elementary schools. The team of researchers involved in that project videotaped learning activities that took place in elementary schools in Japan, China, Singapore, and the United States. We showed the videos to teachers and parents in all four countries and interviewed them about what they observed. As I wrote this book, I used data from that project as an additional source. The interviews with American teachers provided a valuable link between reform efforts in Japan and the United States; chapter 10, "US Teachers Reflect on Japanese Elementary School Instruction," explores those connections. The analysis offered in that chapter draws attention to factors that support and impede educators in both locations as they attempt to revise their practices in response to reform mandates and changes in their students.

Broadening the Scope of Research on Japanese Education

Much of the research on Japanese education published over the last twenty years is based on activity in urban schools, which are often unique in terms of the students they serve, the challenges they face, and the methods used to improve their instructional programs. Researchers base themselves in Tokyo and Osaka for logical reasons. The two urban centers contain multiple institutions of higher education and resources—such as libraries—that support their research goals. Metropolises are also populated by families with unique backgrounds and needs. For example, immigrants often flock to the greater Tokyo area, and Osaka is home to a substantial number of people of Ainu ancestry. Research that examines the education experiences of children from marginalized groups or those who have experienced discrimination adds valuable depth to our understanding of schools. In the past, disregard of those perspectives led to inaccurate assumptions about the homogeneity of Japanese society (Gordon 2008; Tsuneyoshi, Okano, and Boocock 2011; Okano and Tsuchiya 1999; Tsuneyoshi 2001). I value the contributions of researchers who draw attention to issues and voices that have previously been overlooked. I am also motivated to produce research that adds balance to scholarship focused on urban settings; to capture the realities of schools located in areas that are rarely profiled on national television or in the newspapers. To understand the consequences of reforms such as the relaxed-education policies, it is essential to study their reverberations in urban areas that set national trends, as well as those located outside centers of power and culture.

With this situation in mind, I established a base in northwest Japan and began searching for research sites. Kita Prefecture (a pseudonym) is located in northwest Japan, approximately three hours from Tokyo by train. The Japan Sea serves as its western border. As one would expect, fishing is a major industry in the coastal cities and towns. A string of mountain ranges parallel the ocean. This unique topography produces abundant snow in most parts of the prefecture: when the moisture-laden air from the ocean strikes nearby mountains, the volume of snow that is produced can be paralyzing. Heavy snowfalls are welcomed by the numerous ski resorts in the prefecture but can cause problems for everyday citizens. During the winter months, it is common for local television stations to air stories about villages in the mountains that become unreachable for several days. Despite the extreme swings in the weather, agriculture remains Kita's major industry. It ranks first in terms of total rice planting area in the country, and second in terms of total production of rice (Global Agricultural Information Network 2011). Farmers in the prefecture also harvest a variety of other crops, including soybeans, grapes, and cucumbers. Other major industries in the prefecture include manufacturing, fishing, and shipping (JETRO 2011).

Although Kita has long been known for its agricultural output, as with many areas of Japan, its aging population has created challenges for the farming industry. In the first decade of the twenty-first century, the prefecture's total population declined by more than 4%. Local governments struggle to attract more young people to move into or remain in the area, and to develop sustainable industries to compensate for the waning interest in farming. Members of the younger generation tend not to find the prospect of maintaining the family farm as appealing as their parents or grandparents once did. In addition, over the last twenty years, the population has decreased as a consequence of declining birthrates and an outflow of people to urban hubs.

The schools have also been affected by these demographic trends, though not as directly as one might expect. In the larger cities in the prefecture, school enrolments have remained fairly steady over the past twenty years. However, in some rural areas, the drop in school-age children has been dramatic. One of the schools I studied, for example, had formerly housed more than 1,000 students, but only 150 children were enrolled when I conducted my fieldwork there. Yet deeply rooted values about the role of the neighborhood school have prevented most schools from closing, even those with only a handful of students at each grade level. In contrast to the common practice in the United States of consolidating schools with low enrollments, in Japan local boards of education generally treat schools as integral components of local communities, and avoid closing them except under dire circumstances. One of the teachers I interviewed had previously worked at an elementary school serving a total of twelve students. Despite this low number, the school remained open and employed a full-time principal and a nurse, and teachers for each grade level.

Initially, I planned to visit schools that differed primarily in terms of academic reputation. I had employed that approach in previous research projects and been satisfied with the results. However, informants (parents, teachers, administrators, and academics) residing in the area seemed puzzled by this way of thinking about school diversity. What distinguished schools, they told me, was not academic effectiveness. Rather than focus on students' test scores or rates of matriculation to competitive high schools, I was advised to select schools based on their geographical location and employment patterns in the communities they served. Following the advice of local informants, I selected a sample of schools located "in the mountains, in the city, and near the sea." Adopting this approach, they suggested, would provide me with a variegated group of schools and communities to study. The topography of the area shifts noticeably as one moves away from the ocean, as do occupational patterns. In the neighborhoods near the shore, families with deep ties to the fishing industry proliferate. Just a few kilometers inland, neighborhoods are filled with small family businesses and shops that have been operating for decades, even centuries. A few kilometers further east, agriculture is the most common source of income.

My goal was to produce a detailed analysis of the education offered in small sample of schools, for I have found research framed in this manner to be particularly revealing. Yet I also sought to conduct a study that would bridge levels of schooling. In Japan, most children attend neighborhood schools through the ninth grade, at which point they apply to high schools spread throughout a prefecture. Previous research on Japanese education has emphasized contrasts between elementary and secondary education (Fukuzawa 1994; LeTendre 2000; Rohlen 1983). This is not surprising, given changes in the personalities and capabilities of children as well as the complex topics that children are expected to master. Literature on Japanese education tends to focus on a single level of the system, or to identify patterns in practices common to schools located in different parts of the country and at different levels of the academic hierarchy. Although a number of perceptive studies of elementary schools and secondary schools have been written, I have yet to read a single study that looks at both levels with precision. As a result, readers are usually required to study different levels of schools in isolation, and to draw connections between studies marked by significant methodological and analytical dissimilarities. Examining the effects of relaxed-education policies at multiple tiers of the system, I decided, would allow me to develop a more thorough understanding of the effects of the specific strategies adopted in support of the relaxed-education movement. Looking closely at how certain changes influenced the lives of students at teachers operating in a variety of contexts would encourage exploration of the reasons *why* those alterations produced particular outcomes, rather than yield facile conclusions about success or failure of the reforms. In addition, I was motivated to learn about the course of students' academic experiences as they progress through the system.

Due to my interest in the trajectory of student experience, I selected two schools in each area (the mountains, the city, and the sea) in or near Nishiyama City, a medium-size city in Kita Prefecture.[1] Studying pairs of schools (one elementary and one middle school) that served the same communities, I decided, would allow me to compare approaches to educating children of different ages, and to examine children's responses to shifting expectations and instructional techniques as they advanced up the academic hierarchy. This approach would also draw attention to the job definitions of elementary and middle school teachers, and how the framing of their professional responsibilities might modulate their responses to the MEXT's reform agenda. As I note above, education pundits and individuals with the resources required to capture the attention of the media have dominated most debates about the relaxed-education policies. The opinions of people with the most extensive and direct experience with the changes that have been introduced—the children and adults who spend the bulk of their time inside the schools—have been overshadowed by those expressed by more-vociferous high-profile commentators.

After consulting with numerous parents, teachers, and university faculty, I selected three pairs of schools to include in my sample.[2] This collection of schools is not offered as a representative sample of institutions in the prefecture, or in Japan. Because the majority of children in Japan attend the school closest to their home through the ninth grade, the characteristics of the schools I studied were not as distinct as would have been the case if I had observed high schools.[3] Nevertheless, at the conclusion of my period of fieldwork, the mix of schools in my sample had provided me with windows into school cultures organized to fit different personalities and orientations, despite their location within a centralized system. Clearly, students received unique educational experiences, depending on which of the schools below they attended. The official curriculum may have been consistent, but learning activities were molded to fit the personalities and proclivities of the members of each learning community. Walking through the halls of each school, one could not avoid differences in the nature of human interactions, students' connections to the institution, or the activi-

Table 3.1. Characteristics of schools studied

School name	Number of students	Number of teachers*	Academic reputation	Location
Oka Elementary	108	6	average	mountains
Oka Middle	68	6	average	mountains
Chuo Elementary	415	14	high	city center
Chuo Middle	493	22	high	city center
Hama Elementary	170	6	average	seaside
Hama Middle	472	21	low	seaside

*This includes only full-time teachers; administrators, nurses, and part-time teachers are not included.

ties that anchored life in each school. The longer I stayed at each site, the more pronounced those contrasts became.

The Schools

Oka Elementary School

Only two years old, Oka Elementary School (OES) looks nothing like your typical Japanese primary school. Located in the mountains approximately forty-five minutes from Nishiyama City, the campus was designed to blend in with the hills and stream that surround it. Ironically, that emphasis on cohesion with the natural environment draws attention to it. As one drives through the small, nondescript town, sight of the elementary school provides an expected pleasure. In contrast to the functional, undistinguished concrete buildings that house most Japan educational institutions, Oka Elementary School looks modern and inviting. The single level visible from the exterior is distinguished by an interplay of shapes and colors. It reminded me more of a museum than a school. Sharply sloping grass walls connect the classrooms to an expansive dirt playground, where children engage in a panoply of activities. The cement walkways that connect outdoor spaces are distinct, etched with tessellating patterns that create a sense of movement, even when no children are present.

As one moves from the exterior to the interior of the building, the dominant surfaces shift from cement to wood and glass. Almost all floor and walls are constructed of bleached wood. Several teachers explain to me that members of the school community constructed the wooden furniture to match the permanent architecture. A large two-story gymnasium that doubles as a theater lies at the center of the building. Classrooms line one side of the gym, with rooms with special functions bordering the other three; these include the library, cooking room, computer laboratory, science laboratory, and a *tatami* room (where students can practice tea ceremony). The floor plan appears to have been designed to promote collaboration. As is true of most Japanese schools, a sliding door connects each classroom with the school's main corridor. But behind this facade of traditional segmentation lies an interlocking set of learning spaces. A large section of one wall in each space is open, allowing one to walk from the first-grade to sixth-grade rooms without interruption. This openness sometimes results in relatively high noise levels and some unusual aural interplay. For example, one morning I observed the sixth graders practicing a dance routine accompanied by a music video, while the fifth graders in the connecting room were conferring with their teacher about upcoming parent-teacher conferences. On numerous occasions, I had trouble hearing a teacher because her words were drowned out by noise from neighboring rooms. But this physical arrangement also supports a sense of community among students and teachers, making it easy for children to work together with those from neighboring rooms. Even the design of the lunchroom reinforces this goal. Students in Japanese schools usually eat lunch in their classrooms. But at Oka, everyone—students, teachers, and administrators—eats together in a dining hall located near the entrance of the school.

Students as well as teachers seem comfortable with this arrangement. People move freely from room to room without hesitation or irritation. It is not unusual to come across children skipping through hallways or singing. Although I rarely witnessed learning activities structured to encompass multiple grade levels, teachers did often ask colleagues in neighboring rooms for assistance or checked to see what was going on in the room next door. The physical layout promotes a continuous flow of activity at OES.

Teachers at Oka capitalize on the children's enthusiasm and energy. Although they are mandated to follow the national curriculum, faculty members regularly expand on curricular guidelines to bring subject matter to life for students. For example, after observing first-grade students making sculptures out of tissue boxes, toilet paper rolls, and other used household objects, I asked their teacher if that activity was included in the textbook. She responded, "No, I thought it would be a good way to reinforce their study of shapes, from the textbook. If I just teach them the ideas in the book, students might forget them quickly. I try to think of ways to connect things in the book to the children's lives." Another notable feature of instructional activity at Oka is the regular incorporation of movement into instructional activities. Students rarely remain in their seats for long periods of time, especially at the lower grade levels. Instead, teachers design lessons that allow children to move about the room, to work with their friends, and to use their bodies to enact subject matter. The second-grade teacher, for instance, has her students hop in place as they recite their multiplication tables. None of the rooms include a list of class rules, as is common in the United States. Instead, teachers post the goals for their homerooms. A poster in the fifth-grade room urges its members to "have a bright attitude," "do things with a smile on your face," and "be fifth graders who keep taking challenges." This is not to say that students at OES always are always attentive and focused. As one would expect, a fair amount of horseplay and chatting does occur. But teachers do not often acknowledge such activity, other than to encourage those involved to focus on their work. Punishments are rarely distributed, and I never observe a teacher command a student to leave a classroom or serve any type of detention.

OES employees feel fortunate to work in such a supportive environment. Several of them emphasize to me what an excellent job the principal has done in establishing a tone of trust and support. They all speak highly of their students and colleagues. In an informal conversation, one teacher tells me that several of the children have grown angels' wings. Teachers working with students in the upper grades do occasionally express concern about the mental disposition of some of their pupils. "The problem isn't their intelligence," the sixth-grade teacher explains to me, "but their ability to concentrate. If they try hard and can't do the work, I wouldn't be upset, but they often daydream, which is why I sometimes push them hard." And the fifth-grade teacher facilitates a series of meetings among the girls in her class after she observes signs of bullying among them. None of these issues create serious obstacles to learning in OES classrooms. In stark contrast to the images broadcast by the media of urban schools plagued by "classroom collapse" (*gakkyu hokkai*), Oka is a tranquil setting for teaching and learning.

While most teachers underscore the positive aspects of Oka Elementary, they also acknowledge that their work can be draining. At a faculty party that takes place just before I complete my fieldwork at the school, instructors discuss the work-related stress they experience. The members of the group explain to me that while they find their work gratifying, the long hours can be exhausting. In recent years, their work has become more difficult, yet the salaries of all teachers in the prefecture were recently cut by 1%, and most of the educators I interview expect additional cuts in the future. Balancing professional and personal demands can be difficult for the teachers, all of whom have children. Faculty and staff generally arrive at school before eight (first period begins at 8:40) and remain on campus until six or seven in the evening. One might expect teachers to express approval of the elimination of classes on Saturdays, but opinions are mixed: some individuals value the additional time they can spend with their families; others state that they now work later in the evenings to complete tasks previously left for Saturdays. After telling one teacher that I am impressed by her enthusiasm, she responds that because she invests so much energy in her work, she is too tired to give her own children the attention they need. When she goes home, she wants to go to sleep as soon as possible. Another instructor reflects that "now we have less time in school. That makes more work for teachers. We have to spend the limited time we have in school focused on students and finish our work on weekends. I wonder how students use the Saturdays now they don't have school. There are probably kids who spend time doing interesting things with their families, but there are also kids who are left by themselves."

Given the strong support for education on display at OES and the near absence of discipline problems, one might expect the school to serve a wealthy, highly educated community. That is not the case. While large numbers of adults can be depended on to show up for special school events—such as the annual marathon running race through the town or the cultural festival (*bunkasai*)—I am struck by the down-home feel at those activities. When I initiate conversations with attendees, their strong local dialects are sometimes difficult for me to decipher. Most work on farms, in small family businesses, or a combination of the two. Some parents make the commute to Nishiyama City each day, but they are likely to hold white-collar jobs that provide steady (though not lucrative) salaries. The school does not keep track of parental income or educational aspirations for their children, but a teacher estimates that 50 to 60 percent of OES students will eventually matriculate to college. The town exhibits few signs of wealth or opulence. The narrow main road is lined with the types of shops one finds in most Japanese towns: ramen shops, farm supply stores, convenience stores, and photo stores. Oka is a small, unexceptional rural town that has made a strong commitment to support its single elementary school.

Oka Middle School

After graduating from OES, students move on to Oka Middle School (OMS), which is located approximately a kilometer up the street, on the opposite side of the road. Despite their physical proximity, however, the two schools share few commonalities. Soon after I begin my fieldwork at the middle school, the institution celebrates its fiftieth anniversary. The building actually looks much older than this. The three rectangular buildings that organize life at OMS have been stained by decades of exposure to severe weather. The green metal roof capping the gymnasium provides the only contrast to the faded gray that washes over all other surfaces. Lines of windows—organized into groups of four—on each of the three floors of the main building add a degree of regularity to front facade that is interrupted in the center by the main entrance. Like many Japanese secondary schools, the facility could be mistaken for a factory. The gymnasium and the playing field located at the front of the campus are the only obvious markers of its educational function. Squat gray pillars spaced evenly across the roof add to the industrial character.

The dreary impression made by OMS is more striking when viewed after visiting the elementary school. When I ask people to explain the differences between the two campuses, they tell me that the town wanted to demonstrate its strong commitment to education, but had only enough money to fund the construction of one new school. Hoping to create a strong educational foundation for children, the town opted to invest in the elementary school facility. Students who begin their careers in the classroom with warm feelings about school, it is believed, will remain enthused as they progress through the school system.

The middle school campus provides ample space to the students and staff members who populate it.[4] The number of students in Oka has gradually, but significantly, declined. Early in the twentieth century, three middle schools in the town operated at full capacity. By the 1950s, however, decreasing enrollments forced the Board of Education to consolidate the three schools into a single institution. At that time, three homeroom classes at each grade level were needed to accommodate the OMS student body. Currently, each grade has only one homeroom class, and the sizes are small by Japanese standards: an average of twenty-three children per grade. During most periods of the day, only three of the thirteen classrooms are in use. The quietness can feel eerie.

The goals that frame daily life at OMS contrast sharply with those at the elementary school down the road. Tellingly, the signs posted in OES classroom that encourage students to meet their potential as students and citizens have been replaced in OMS by lists of rules to be followed. For instance, in one ninth-grade homeroom, a poster instructs students:

> School cleaning (*soji*) starts at 1:35
> Don't waste paper
> Be in the classroom by 8:10 in the morning!

Very few of the lessons I observe at OMS could be described as lively or engaging. Most students docilely accept this reality, rarely displaying an interest in their classes—but not causing problems for the teachers either. The school day unfolds in a series of countervailing waves: uninspiring lectures are followed by nonacademic activities (physical education, music, lunch), during which students come to life and release pent-up energy. During these breaks from academics, children show signs of the vitality that pervades OES classrooms.

As is true at most middle schools in Japan, OMS pupils are required to wear school uniforms: navy-blue skirts and sailor-style blouses for girls and black military-looking suits for boys. On a typical day, however, students spend very little time in these outfits. Pupils usually arrive on campus wearing their formal uniforms but change into their gym tracksuits before their first academic class, and back into formal attire just before heading home at the end of the day.[5] They also display great ingenuity in bending school rules pertaining to acceptable physical appearance. In his study of middle school students in Japan and the United States, LeTendre (2000) observes that "Japanese schools demand tremendous conformity in external presentation. . . . Any regularities in the basic routines—whether an incorrect uniform, use of nail polish, or too much talking at student assembly—were interpreted as signaling potential problems" (55). Attitudes toward student appearance are noticeably more relaxed at OMS (as well as the other middle schools in my sample). It is often difficult to spot a required article of clothing that has not been altered in some obvious way. Many students cut slits that run up to the knees of their gym suits. The trend among boys is to wear their pants as low as possible without showing their underwear (which is forbidden), some appearing to defy gravity. Many of the girls, in contrast, adjust the hems of their skirts so that they fall closer to the waist than to the knee.

Despite outward signs of rebellion—the slit pants, frosted hair, body piercings—these are good kids, as their teachers frequently tell me; they are the *same* kids that attended OES, no longer excited about school or convinced that they will succeed in the academic competition that has begun for them. Teachers describe their pupils with positive terms such as *sunao* (well behaved, docile) and *yasashii* (friendly). Although boys sometimes engage in horseplay during breaks in the academic schedule, they understand that instructors expect them to sit quietly in their desks, and adjust their behavior accordingly. I almost never observe students disrupt academic lessons. Rather than rebel, they detach themselves from the flow of classroom activity, filling space but not participating. Teachers do not seem to mind such inattention—or expect students to take an active role in the transmission of curricula. When I ask school employees to estimate how many of their pupils are likely to attend college, they offer figures between 10 and 20 percent.[6]

The responsibilities assigned to middle school teachers are more extensive than those for elementary educators. It is hard to disagree with the principal when he observes that "too much is expected of our teachers—they are overloaded." Though the average teaching load for full-time teachers at OMS is just under three classes per day, instructors spend long hours at the school. According to the school's guide to curriculum and responsibility, members of the faculty are assigned numerous extracurricular responsibilities—143, to be exact! These include things such as student guidance, serving as a representative to the PTA, and coordinating special school events. One teacher has been delegated twenty-one special duties. As this weighting of responsibility suggests, employees are required to devote a greater portion of their time to administrative duties than to instruction. Supervising club activities and athletic teams tends to demand the most of teachers, who regularly work on weekends when games or special events are scheduled. From the time they arrive on campus in the morning until the early evening hours, they devote themselves to a seemingly unending array of activities. The extensive administrative load leaves educators little time to prepare lessons.

Chuo Elementary School

There is no direct route from the town of Oka to central Nishiyama, where Chuo Elementary School (CES) is located. Descending from Oka, one must negotiate a combination of single-lane roads, highways, and narrow but busy streets to reach CES. On average, the trip takes about forty minutes. But these roads connect two areas that feel separated by vaster distances. Oka students tell me that they rarely venture to the city, other than for occasional shopping trips. In Nishiyama, one can find the large department stores, chain electronics stores, and sports emporiums that would not draw enough customers to survive in rural hamlets like Oka. CES is located in one of the oldest neighborhoods in town.

A nondescript building, CES is composed of two four-story wings connected by a hallway. The campus is squeezed between single-family homes, with a single-lane road demarcating its boundaries. Parking is sparse, forcing school employees to squeeze their cars into a lot designed for far fewer vehicles. Observing social studies lessons at the school, I learned that area immediately surrounding the school once functioned as a center for samurai families in the vicinity. Though many of the shops within walking distance of the school have changed owners and functions since that time, their squat wooden fronts provide a constant visual reminder of the city's historical roots. Many of the parents of CES students own those stores; others work as civil servants or salarymen for local businesses.

The atmosphere in the halls and classrooms of Chuo feels more formal than at Oka. This is partially a reflection of the larger number of students the faculty is responsible for: 415 children (compared to 108 at OES). Managing an institution of that size demands a higher degree of order than the smaller school in the mountains. But there are signs that the school has also made a conscious decision to create a more structured learning environment. For example, pupils at the school are required to wear uniforms, which is unusual for an elementary school in Japan. Although children spend most of the day in their gym outfits, they do arrive on campus each morning wearing navy-blue blazers, slacks, and skirts. Publicity materials for the school emphasize its strong commitment to moral education.

As is true at OES, the halls of Chuo are constantly buzzing with activity. As I walk through the corridors one morning, I am surprised by the sight of several first graders climbing on gymnastics equipment (a balance beam, tumbling mats, and uneven bars) that has been set up outside their classroom. Their teacher explains to me that the theme of an observation lesson scheduled for the following week will be "Things we learned to do in the first grade." To prepare for this, some of the students have decided that a review of their gymnastics skills is necessary. Inside the classroom, too, formality does not temper student enthusiasm. Teachers tend to use standard lesson formats more often than their counterparts at OES, but they also encourage children to invest fully in their studies. During the daily morning meeting, instructors routinely ask students if they are feeling well.[7] In response, young boys often yell out, "Yes, I am feeling well!" (*Hai, genki desu*) at the top of their lungs. Rather than scold these children for screaming, adults praise their enthusiasm. In upper-grade classrooms, teachers do not reprimand students for moving around the room or calling out answers. Even in the library, students who chat animatedly with their friends are not reprimanded; the list of rules posted on the wall does not include any references to appropriate noise levels. At Chuo, behavior tied to carelessness or unkindness is frowned upon; rowdiness, on the other hand, is treated as a natural accouterment of childhood.

The faculty room is no more tranquil. Approximately forty feet on each side, the room functions as a workspace, meeting room, and social lounge.

The desks of the principal, vice principal, and two head teachers are located on the wall furthest from the entry doors, facing those of the faculty. Employees' desks are organized into five clusters of four or six desks. Teachers work beside colleagues teaching either the same grade or the level just above or below. At CES, each young teacher is paired with a veteran educator working at the same grade level. Throughout the day, teaching teams meet at their desks to prepare lessons and discuss students. At other times, they work individually at their desks, planning, grading, and maintaining records. Interestingly, CES employees take recess periods more seriously than at any other school I observed. At 10:15 every morning, someone makes coffee and tea in a corner of the faculty room that has been set up as a kitchen, and most people in the room gather and chat over refreshments. Next to the kitchen area, a rectangular table is lined with ten chairs. At midday, employees who are not responsible for homerooms eat lunch together at this table. At other times of the day, the area is used for small group meetings.

The relaxed feeling in the faculty room flows from an emphasis on cooperation and peer support that pervades the school. Authority is distributed laterally more often than horizontally. The principal serves as the titular leader of the school, but teachers play a more active role in day-to-day administrative matters. Responsibility for leading the short faculty meetings that are held each morning, for instance, rotates among all teachers. Instructors also design and implement professional development workshops for their colleagues. During my period of fieldwork at CES, I observe few signs of conflict between teachers. Adults as well as children are expected to look after each other, and to ensure that the institution functions smoothly.

Although CES does tend to embrace rather traditional approaches to teaching and learning, signs of innovation and change are also visible. I am surprised to learn that students in the upper grades are divided according to ability for small-group lessons (*shoninzu gakushu*) in math. Just a few years ago, ability grouping of this sort was unheard of in Japan. The school also pays serious attention to children with special needs. When I taught in a Japanese school in the early 1990s, special education students received minimal attention from teachers, whose knowledge of their needs seemed quite limited. At CES, in contrast, a full-time special education instructor goes to great lengths to educate her colleagues about current research on categories of children with special needs and effective techniques for responding to those needs. She also creates regular opportunities for even the most low-functioning students at the school to interact with other children. Eleven students at CES receive special education support, although twenty-five qualify for such services.

When asked to describe changes they have observed in their students in recent years, teachers at CES do not, however, refer to increased numbers of students diagnosed as having special learning needs. Instead, most emphasize the impact of societal change on children's attitudes toward learning. A common lament among instructors is that students today have trouble concentrating. Although educators working in Oka express similar concerns, evidence of social change is more striking at Chuo, due to its location in the center of the city. Nishiyama is not confronted by challenges as serious as those in large metropolitan areas such as Tokyo or Osaka, but the proximity to karaoke boxes, electronics stores, and video arcades does provide children with more extensive temptations than can be found in Oka.

Increased access to the media has also raised consciousness about events that transpire in other parts of the country. This was most apparent during my second week conducting research at CES. In response to the abduction of an elementary school student in a city far removed from Nishiyama, CES altered its system of dismissing students at the end of the day. Previously, children were sent home at various times, depending on their grade level. In response to safety concerns generated by the abduction, the entire student body now meets in the gymnasium at the end of each school day. Children are organized into groups based on their residence neighborhood. Before allowing the groups to begin the trek home, a teacher holding a microphone instructs everyone, "Don't play too much on your way home. Watch the person in front of you. Older kids (*sempai*), keep your eyes on younger kids. Older kids, make sure that everyone is in your group before leaving." Threats to student well-being may be far removed from the CES campus, but this does not shield students from their effects. During my classroom observations, students strike me as remarkably energetic, enthusiastic, and academically able. Their teachers, however, are uneasy about the direction in which society is moving, and the subtle changes they have witnessed in their students' performance at school.

Chuo Middle School

Chuo Middle School (CMS) has an excellent reputation in the area. When I ask members of the community to share their impressions of the school, they emphasize the orderly learning environment and large numbers of graduates who matriculate to highly ranked high schools. The principal is regarded as an effective leader who sets a positive example for teachers as well as students. People tell me that CMS is one of the oldest and most stable schools in Nishiyama, and that I should enjoy my time there.

Throughout my period of fieldwork at CMS, the campus undergoes extensive renovations. New buildings are being erected next to existing edifices, most of which will eventually be torn down. This is necessary because the original school buildings no longer meet earthquake codes. The remodel creates extensive constraints for students and faculty. In effort to finish the new buildings as quickly as possible, construction crews work throughout the day. Only a sliver of the outdoor grounds is accessible to individuals without hardhats. Despite the enormity of the changes taking place outside, the school manages to prevent the renovations from disrupting scheduled activities. Teachers and students seem inured to the constant din of construction taking place outside their classrooms. I rarely see anyone acknowledge the workers laboring just a few feet from their desks. Sports teams that usually train outside make use of every available indoor space to conduct their drills. After school, groups of students regularly jog through the hallways, urged on by their team captains.

The CMS administration makes a concerted effort to emphasize scholastic achievement. Daily morning meetings in the faculty room typically begin with announcements pertaining to upcoming tests and events related to high school entrance admissions. The vice principal regularly distributes reports that document the performance of CMS pupils and asks faculty to analyze them in attempt to identify things the school could be doing better. Students, too, seem more concerned with their academic futures than their counterparts at Oka. During informal conversations I hold with second- and third-grade students, many describe school-related stress they experience. The heightened attention to schoolwork is not surprising, given that I collect data at CMS during the final quarter of the year, when final examinations are given and third-year students are preparing to apply to high school. Surprisingly, however, according to the student surveys I distribute, the percentage of pupils at CMS who attend cram school (*juku*) is the lowest of the three middle schools in my sample.[8]

Formulating generalizations about the characteristics, academic as well as personal, of Chuo is quite challenging—and becomes increasingly so the longer I remain at the school. This is partially due to the size of the institution: 493 students and 45 employees. It simply takes more time to get to know people at a school approximately four times larger than another. Further complicating this task is the multiple layers of behavior I observe among students on campus. Behavior among pupils varies noticeably—among first and third year students, high and low achieving kids, and even by individuals depending on context. In Oka, students more readily display their *honne*, or honest feelings. At Chuo, in contrast, pupils seem to invest greater effort in outwardly conforming to adults' expectations of them, while concurrently displaying subtle resistance to those expectations or shielding their feelings from public view. One result of the emphasis on academics at CMS is that students are adroit at putting on a facade of compliance in the classroom that disguises their disengagement. In every class I visit, several students appear to be paying attention to teacher lectures and taking notes, when in fact they are doodling, drawing on their notebooks, or writing notes to their friends. Roughly equal numbers of students make no attempt to appear engaged; they put their heads on their desks or chat with neighbors.

Another notable difference between Oka and Chuo students pertains to the level of resistance on display at the two schools. In both locations, students experiencing academic difficulties tend to withdraw, to disappear inside the classroom so as to minimize the amount of attention paid to them. At CHS, however, a number of students—mostly boys—actively challenge authority and flout school rules. Examples of such misbehavior include students throwing objects across the room to each other, wandering around the room during classes, beating on the windows, and leaving the room without permission. What I find most interesting about such activities is the reactions of teachers. When confronted by disobedient students, CMS teachers tend to look the other way or gently guide them back on track. One member of the faculty explains to me that teachers have been encouraged to avoid confrontations with students to minimize the chances that the students will exit the system. Although I do witness examples of student disobedience and teacher acquiescence to challenges of authority, it is important to note that the majority of students do follow school rules. Most are well mannered, polite, and compliant. First-grade students in particular display great enthusiasm in the classroom. When asked to describe their pupils, teachers emphasize the positive qualities of their charges. I also find that rebellious students are not necessarily rebellious in all their classes. Even the most unruly or disengaged students in core academic classes often come to life in classes that include fewer lectures and tests (such as art and physical education). Students' attitudes toward school vary significantly throughout the day, depending on their perceptions about the subject matter, the teacher, and their own abilities.

As is true in Oka, teachers at CMS spend long hours on campus. They do not hold as many different special assignments due to the larger pool of labor, but this does not translate into a lighter workload. I am surprised when a P.E. teacher informs me that he goes home at 9 p.m. most evenings and spends many weekend days on campus. Members of the CMS faculty display a greater commitment to enlivening lessons than educators at Oka, where parental expectations related to academic achievement are lower. Teachers' comments and actions indicate that they feel pressure to uphold the school's academic reputation. While all members of the faculty display impressive dedication to their work, their ability to engage and challenge students varies noticeably. Interestingly, younger teachers tend to use more traditional pedagogical methods than their *sempai*. Experienced teachers, in turn, lecture less frequently and show a greater propensity to enhance the written curriculum with innovative activities. Before initiating a discussion of a chapter in their textbook about artwork, a senior Japanese teacher, for instance, displays a handful of objects (woodblock prints, a box of tissues, and pencil boxes) to her third-year students and asks them to vote on whether each qualifies as a piece of art. Later, the same teacher shares a sense of concern that young teachers tend to teach "the old-fashioned way," emphasizing lecture and memorization. She worries about the plethora of young teachers who can be described as "manual teachers" because they approach teaching as a set of steps to be followed in sequence, the way that workers at McDonald's or Mister Donut do. When asked to account for this difference in approach to teaching, the woman tells me that in the early 1990s, the Ministry of Education encouraged teachers to experiment with new instructional approaches. Many new teachers, she says, have not had that experience. My classroom observations back up the teacher's comments. New teachers do show a greater inclination to lecture their pupils—and to have greater difficulty generating student interest in their lessons.

The vice principal explains to me that the school has an obligation to pull all students forward (*hipparu*) so that they will be prepared to enter society. Although that is officially the responsibility of the family, when parents don't accept that responsibility, the school has to take over. For example, there are currently two students at CMS who suffer from school-refusal syndrome (*hikikomori*). Teachers bring work to these students in their homes each week to ensure that they can graduate. Two other students come to school each day but have trouble attending their classes. To accommodate the unique needs of these students, the school allows them to spend the day in a special room where they work independently. One of these girls tells me that as soon as she graduates, she plans to move to Tokyo and become a pop star.

According to the vice principal, the number of CMS parents who have trouble carrying out their parental responsibilities has expanded rapidly in recent years, forcing the school to work more diligently to foster positive relationships with families and to offer more parent-education activities. The substantial energies devoted to these efforts appear to pay off. Despite the frequency of low scores on semester- and year-end tests, all students at CMS eventually graduate. Most earn places at well-regarded high schools in the area. In fact, the year when I conduct my fieldwork, thirty-nine CMS students are accepted to high schools without taking written entrance examinations, based on the strong letters of recommendation they received from teachers and their performance on interviews. CMS may be facing more complex and demanding challenges than in the past, but the school is doing its best to surmount the obstacles it faces, and has maintained its excellent reputation in the community.

Hama Elementary School

Although the Hama section of Nishiyama was absorbed into the city in the 1970s, inhabitants of the area emphasize its unique characteristics and separation from the city center. Administratively, it may be treated as one part of Nishiyama, but residents of the area continue to talk about their neighborhood as if it were an independent entity. Economically as well as culturally, Hama is oriented toward the ocean that serves as its eastern border. Most businesses in the area are connected in some way to fishing or shipping, although a hodgepodge of family-run stores and a small entertainment district also attract people to Hama. In the summer, an influx of beachgoing visitors from other parts of the prefecture adds energy to an otherwise sleepy locality. Sailors from Korea, China, and Russia also make frequent calls to the port. As is common of many beach towns, Hama is known for its leisurely pace and informality. While Hama residents point to this relaxed atmosphere with pride, outsiders often speak critically of what they perceive of as a less refined way of life.

Hama Elementary School (HES) is located just a few blocks from the shore. Like other schools in the area, HES does not enjoy a stellar reputation in Nishiyama. When I ask people to share their impressions of the school, the ideas most commonly mentioned are naughty students, discipline problems, and weak academics. Views about the education provided to students who attend schools in Hama are often coupled with opinions about the neighborhood. Adults living in other parts of Nishiyama tend to assume that parents in Hama do not adequately support their children's education. Differentiation among Japanese schools does not occur in any systematic way below the high school level, but impressionistic comments suggest that Hama schools are located at the bottom of the academic pyramid.

I am therefore surprised by the great enthusiasm for learning that I observe on the HES campus. Like many schools in the area, the size of the student body has been steadily declining for decades. A facility built to house approximately 1,000 students now serves only 170 pupils, with a single class at each grade level. Despite this low number, the halls of HES are constantly buzzing with activity. Children move through the building freely, undeterred by the walls constructed to segment classroom spaces. They seem equally comfortable in their homerooms, on the playground, and in the faculty room. Rarely are students required to remain seated in their desks for extended periods of time. As one might expect, first graders are constantly on their feet, moving around the room, the campus, and even the neighborhood. But sixth graders, too, are encouraged to physically engage in the learning process. During reading lessons, for example, a teacher directs students to recite passages from the textbook in five positions: (1) sitting down; (2) standing and facing the cherry blossoms outside; (3) standing and facing the entryway; (4) squatting on the ground; and (5) "sitting, in your hearts."

School employees use words such as "energetic," "enthusiastic," and "cheerful" to describe their students. Rather than attempt to curtail children's great stores of energy, HES teachers treat that vigor as a valuable resource that can be capitalized on to enliven learning activities. When students do not display sufficient enthusiasm for learning, instructors frequently ask them to repeat an activity with more excitement or in a louder voice. Interestingly, this emphasis on fervor rarely produces discipline problems. Pupils display excitement about what they are asked to do but also seem to understand the boundaries of acceptable behavior. When a group of children approaches that limit, most teachers quickly settle the students down. Based on the school's reputation, I expect to regularly witness acts of student defiance and rebellion at HES. Instead, I am impressed by the consistent dedication to learning on display at the school.

Of course, there are exceptions to this pattern. One young teacher struggles to keep his third-grade students focused in class. Though he has no trouble building excitement in his lessons, the man is unsure of how to react when pupils become so involved in an activity that they lose focus. Compared to other classes in the school, his room feels rather chaotic. During a conversation I have with the instructor, he explains to me that he began his teaching career at school with a total of only twelve students; his homeroom was composed of just three children. Although he works hard to improve his practice, working from eight to eight on most school days, he is frustrated by the slow progress he is making.

From time to time, the staff is also confronted with cases of student misbehavior that it finds disturbing. At one faculty meeting I attend, teachers spend approximately fifteen minutes brainstorming appropriate responses to a case of shoplifting that occurs during a school vacation. When I talk with the boy's homeroom teacher, she informs me that incidents like this occur every year at most elementary schools. She is not concerned about this particular episode because the child's mother immediately contacted her about the event, and the two adults worked together to develop an appropriate response. The teacher did not mind spending several hours over her vacation meeting with the boy's mother because "my job is to take care of situations like this." Such incidents, however, are rare. Most days at HES unfold without drama or conflict. The issues that trigger discussion during faculty meetings during my stay at the school are fairly mundane: pupils who do not greet teachers with sufficient enthusiasm, students who cross the street without looking both ways, changes in the daily schedule, acceptable ways for students to hold their umbrellas while walking to school, school cleanliness, and so forth.

As is true of the other elementary schools in my sample, students at HES seem consistently up to the challenge of mastering the curriculum presented to them. In first grade as well as fifth grade, in math and social studies lessons, children display great enthusiasm for what they are doing. In every class, I can usually spot one or two students who take a bit longer than the rest of the group to absorb new ideas, but the overall level of achievement is high. Furthermore, teachers do an impressive job keeping students—even those who lag behind their classmates—involved in their studies. The prevalence of hands-on activities, group work, and one-on-one support from instructors reduces the chances that an individual will disengage from what the rest of the class is doing. Because Japanese students do not take standardized achievement tests, it is difficult to compare the academic skills of HES pupils to their peers at other institutions. My lesson observations and review of test scores indicate that students are developing a solid academic foundation. They appear to have the literacy, math, and social skills necessary to meet the challenges that may face them when they advance to middle school.

Hama Middle

The corridors of Hama Middle School (HMS) are also constantly abuzz, although the source of that energy varies from room to room. This is partly due to the size of the student body: 471. But numbers alone do not explain the steady hum of activity in the classrooms and hallways. In first-year homerooms, student excitement about learning and being members of a middle school community bring to life even the most commonplace activities. Third-grade rooms, in contrast, can feel boisterous, unwieldy, or dreary, depending on the subject being explored and the teacher's ability to motivate students. Clearly, between the first and third year, pupils' attachment to the school undergoes significant modification and adaptation. By the time they begin their final year of middle school, many HMS students conform—at least in some respects—to the reputation that outsiders attach to the school.

The classrooms and offices at the school are organized into a three-story rectangle with an open courtyard in the center. Students are keenly aware of school space—who has claimed certain sections of a floor as their own and which areas are considered public. Homerooms are arranged hierarchically, with first-year students housed on the ground floor and third years on top. During breaks from classes, pupils tend to mill around the hallways outside their homerooms, rarely ascending or descending to the floor occupied by another grade level. They are also unlikely to venture into the central courtyard, which is impeccably maintained. From most locations on campus, the beach is not visible, although it is located just across the street. Only from the entryway and the faculty room are the sand dunes easy to spot. Teachers do occasionally take advantage of the school's location and facilitate learning activities outdoors. The lure of the beach can also be strong for students who feel that they need to take a study break.

The challenges that face members of HMS faculty are more complex and demanding than those I observe at the elementary school down the street, HES. This is partially tied to the curriculum: the volume of material that secondary teachers are expected to cover is much larger than at the elementary level. Yet when instructors discuss their work, lesson preparation is rarely mentioned as the most demanding aspect of their job. Instead, they underscore the long hours they are required to spend on nonteaching tasks (such as club supervision and committee work) and the stress associated with mentoring struggling pupils. According to school employees, the difficulties experienced by adolescents at HMS are multifaceted, and more severe than at other schools in the area. As one teacher observes, "It's a combination of things—problems at home, problems with classmates, and the difficult curriculum. It's all of those things." Students who misbehave or are deficient in basic academic skills tend to monopolize teachers' time, at the expense of the more academically capable pupils in their classes. In contrast to the general tendency in contemporary Japan to depict underachieving and disruptive children as a by-product of recent changes in society, teachers at HMS tell me that the school has a long history of such problems. One veteran teacher explains to me that "it's been the situation in this area for a long time—it's specific to the Hama community." Another instructor recalls that when he attended middle school in a nearby town, HMS students "had a reputation as being good at sports but rough."

A quick tour of the campus produces ample support for the faculty's claims about rebellious students. Most pupils wear school uniforms that meet the school's specifications, speak politely to adults, and follow directions given by teachers. But the number of students who consciously challenge school rules is greater than on other campuses I visit, and their acts of defiance more overt. It is easy to spot students with body piercings, hair dyed unusual colors, or uniforms that have been altered. More striking, though, are the regular challenges to teacher authority that I observe. While teachers are giving lectures, pupils often walk around the classroom, talk loudly with their friends, cover their heads, draw on their desks with markers, and sit in the hallway for entire class periods. At the two other middle schools in my sample, students who challenge authority tend to be ostracized or avoided. At Hama, on the other hand, displays of insolence appear to elevate a student's social status; rebelliousness is viewed as cool. Rule-abiding students regularly solicit the input or approval of their more defiant peers.

As one might expect, third-year students are more likely to question authority than first year pupils. Yet I am surprised by the extent of the changes that occur in students as they advance through the system.[9] The contrasts between recent enrollees and their *sempai* (seniors) at HMS are more obvious than at other schools I visit. During my entire stay at HMS, I do not spot any signs of rebellion among first-year pupils. Students in all four homeroom classes come to school clad uniforms that conform to specification: no shortened skirts, dyed hair, or face piercings. More significantly, they display an enthusiasm for learning similar to the elementary school students I observe. In all subject areas, first-year students earnestly follow the wishes of their teachers, listening quietly or participating in group discussions as directed. The learning environment has become more formal than in elementary school, but the students' commitment to learning remains constant.

By the time they begin their third year at the school, however, large numbers of students question the rules and practices that organize life at HMS; many do so quite brazenly. When I speak to such students, they commonly tell me that school is *yada* (awful, disgusting) and that there is nothing they like about it. In class, they broadcast their views without hesitation. Though I do not witness any acts of violence at the school, in third-grade rooms it is common for students to call across the room to their friends, refuse to follow directions given by teachers, and draw on their desks with markers. Student absenteeism is an ongoing problem at HMS. When individuals lack the motivation to attend classes, they frequently wander through the halls, spend instructional time in the nurse's office, or leave campus. Adults warn disobedient students that if they don't behave, their grades will suffer, but the targets of such threats are not often concerned about their academic performance.

The resistance displayed by HMS pupils compounds the stress experienced by an already overworked teaching staff. Instructors quite candidly express their frustrations with students whose needs are much greater than was true just a decade earlier. Furthermore, the iron-fisted techniques used to discipline misbehaving students are no longer considered acceptable. On an almost daily basis, I observe school employees struggle to find the appropriate balance between toughness and empathy, sticking to school rules and bending them. For instance, throughout the day, teachers patrol the halls, looking for absent students. When such pupils are located, they are rarely punished; instead, teachers attempt to convince them to return to class. Students take advantage of this tension between official school policies and their actual implementation, challenging the authority of teachers without fear of punishment. Some instructors do earn the respect of students and keep them focused during lessons. These tend to be veteran teachers who use the force of their personalities to maintain the attention of their charges. When I ask a group of third-year students if they study for the classes of teachers they like, they respond, "No, but we listen in class." For new teachers, learning how to successfully manage a classroom and carry out all their additional responsibilities can be overwhelming. During the year when I visit HMS, the principal relieves two staff members of their duties as homeroom teachers, and another teacher checks into the hospital for a month after experiencing a mental breakdown.

Students' motivation increases noticeably when they are convinced that a particular activity is worth the required investment of effort. Though teachers often struggle to keep their pupils engaged during academic activities, they skillfully gauge the morale of the student body, organizing events that provide students with relief from the academic grind when necessary. For example, they cancel classes one afternoon so that students can take part in a school-wide jump-roping competition, with homeroom classes jumping in unison under ropes that are fifteen or twenty feet long. Children who regularly challenge teachers leap alongside their more studious peers. And I never witness any discipline problems during afterschool club activities. During these meetings and practices, students willingly carry out even the most boring tasks, from repetitive drills to cleaning equipment. In these settings, traditional *sempai-kohai* (senior-junior) authority frameworks create a sense of order that is notably absent from many classrooms.

Activity in the Schools

Though located within close proximity to each other, the institutions described above offer distinct settings for teaching and learning. Surface similarities—a common national curriculum, the same textbooks, comparable daily schedules—obscure significant variation in human interactions on the six campuses. Individuals exert a powerful influence on the implementation and reconstruction of the activities that organize daily life. Over the course of the school year, the members of the learning communities mold activities to fit their unique needs and personalities. Rituals such as classroom meetings and graduation ceremonies may be held at all the schools, but the forms given to those events as they are enacted in their particular contexts look and feel quite different. Within a system often characterized as homogeneous, people create institutions that are anything but uniform.

My research methodology was designed to capture the richness of daily life in the schools I studied, and the manner in which members of those learning communities responded to *yutori kyoiku* policy guidelines. Although ethnography is best known as an approach employed by anthropologists use to produce empirical descriptions of the social organization of particular human populations (Ellen 1984, 7), researchers are increasingly using this methodological approach to study the effects of educational reform. As Sutton and Levinson (2001) posit, it is essential that we treat "policy as a complex social practice, an ongoing process of normative cultural production constituted by diverse actors across diverse social and institutional contexts" (1). Qualitative studies of reform initiatives can capture intricacies of policy implementation that may be overlooked in reports that do not adequately consider insiders' perspectives. According to Stritikus and Wiese (2006), "Ethnographic examination of the policy-to-practice connection shows the actual constraints and contradictions faced by ground-level practitioners and thus allows us to move beyond seeing practice in simplistic terms" (1109). Walford (2001) underscores this idea, noting that "looking at the positive results of policy change in isolation may lead to totally incorrect evaluations of its overall efficacy, but ethnography ensures that the wider context is examined and the effects of any change are observed within the whole culture of the school or classroom" (3). Focusing on meaning making at the school level is also consonant with the notion of policy analysis situated in embedded contexts advocated by McLaughlin and Talbert (2001).

I sought to capture that ground-level perspective on *yutori kyoiku*, which has been absent from most assessments of the movement. Eager to analyze relaxed-education policies "in relation to how they are practiced on a daily basis in people's lives (Kendall 2004, 24), I spent between two and three months at each of the schools in my sample. Acting as a participant observer, I adhered to the criteria for ethnographic research identified by Walford and Massey (Walford and Massey 1998; Walford 2002).[10] Inside the schools, I employed comprehensive selection strategies, interviewing all teachers and administrators at each site and observing each homeroom on multiple occasions. I conducted 307 formal observations of lessons at the six institutions (162 in the elementary schools and 145 in the middle schools) and interviewed a total of 80 teachers, 16 administrators, and 3 school counselors over the course of the year.[11] In addition, I administered questionnaires to students, parents, and educators;[12] analyzed school documents; and attended special events, such as in-service seminars, lesson study workshops, sports festivals, PTA meetings, and staff parties (*enkai*). Some of the most revealing details about the challenges that confronted teachers as they attempted to follow the MEXT's reform plans were shared with me at social events, when individuals could step back and reflect on their experiences. Conversations with students were less structured, but no less frequent: each school day I chatted with students about their studies and interests. Those discussions usually took place before school, after school, at lunchtime, or during club activities (*bukatsu*). Though students sometimes had difficulty articulating their precise thoughts about their education, conversations with youngsters provided a helpful balance to adults' assessments of changes taking place in the schools. The variety and depth of my interactions of members of these school communities allowed me to develop a thorough understanding of their routines, views about education, and relationships within and beyond the borders of campus. Throughout my period of research, I also made frequent trips to Tokyo to meet with education officials and professors of education, to compare local and national perspectives on the reforms I was studying.

In the chapters that follow, I present the results of my work—evidence of changes that have occurred as a result of the relaxed-education reforms, images of life inside six schools that are attempting to implement the MOE's policies, and analysis of the factors that have supported or impeded the goals of the relaxed-education movement. These ground-level perspectives on school reform will provide concrete examples of the repercussions that policies related to curriculum and assessment have on the daily experiences of students, teachers, and school cultures.

FOUR

The Teaching Force

The Ministry of Education maintained that introduction of the relaxed-education policies would make it possible for members of local school communities to play a more active role in decision making and delivery of the new curriculum. Students, parents, businesspeople, and community leaders were all offered expanded opportunities to provide input into curriculum and instruction. But ministry reports and statements indicated that the results of the relaxed-education reforms rested heavily on the shoulders of teachers. At each stage of the process of reform implementation, teachers played pivotal roles; they were expected to apply their skills as instructional planners, pedagogues, community liaisons, and program evaluators in support of the government's plans for change. Yet MEXT employees often lacked a clear understanding of how educators were responding to those opportunities. Because communication about relaxed education traveled primarily in one direction (from top to bottom), education planners made decisions with limited knowledge of how their decisions were affecting school practice.

This chapter will explore teachers' opinions about *yutori kyoiku* and their responses to MEXT policy directives. Particular attention will be paid to tensions between MEXT plans for teacher activity and deeply rooted expectations regarding the responsibilities of teachers. As I will show, the educators I observed and interviewed were keenly aware that central authorities were entrusting them with unprecedented levels of authority over the curriculum, yet rarely did those educators accept that power with enthusiasm. Rather, they assessed the autonomy that was offered to them by MEXT officials working in Tokyo in the context of established practices, expectations, and rewards specific to their school communities. The data I collected underscore the enormity of the challenges associated with modifying teacher practice, even when embracing change will augment educators' authority.

The Influence of MEXT on Teacher Behavior

Research on schooling in Japan tends to emphasize MEXT's pervasive and cogent influence over the nation's schools (Kida 1986; Schoppa 1991a). With authority to shape education policy, determine the national curriculum, and manage personnel, the ministry appears to wield almost unchecked power over the schools. Horio (1988), for instance, maintains that not only does the ministry work to control the actions of teachers through policy measures that reinforce its own administrative authority, it also employs the legal system to force adherence to its decrees. "In their attempt to recapture a privileged position within the new legal framework of Japanese democracy," he posits, "the Ministry's bureaucrats have been forced to invent a wide range of arguments which allow them to navigate their way around the notion that in a free society the State has no business telling teachers what to teach, textbook authors what to write, or students what to learn" (ibid., 381). Granting education officials extensive authority over the design and dissemination of curricula may streamline the decision-making process, but does not ensure smooth implementation of reform policies. Bureaucrats may undermine—consciously or inadvertently—the very policies they endorse publicly.

In administrative systems with power concentrated at the top, upper-level officials often interfere with decentralization plans that aim to empower local actors (McGinn and Street 1986). This raises the possibility that within a hierarchically organized, tightly controlled system, the degree of authority delegated to teachers to oversee *yutori kyoiku* programs could be limited.

Research on education-policy making in Japan published after the collapse of the economy, however, raises the possibility that the Ministry's influence over local educators has loosened. Studies that link policy formation with their implementation draw attention to the important role that subnational actors play in shaping educational practice. DeCoker (2002) observes that "although the Japanese education system has a rigid structure, a 'soft middle' level allows for modifications to take place in policy-making and implementation" (xvi). Shimahara (1998) describes Japanese schools as being "co-managed" by administrators and faculty, with minimal status distinctions between the two groups. Qualitative studies of Japanese schools confirm that teachers do indeed take an active role in shaping curricula to fit their instructional objectives and student needs (Cave 2007; Lewis and Tsuchida 1998). Such experience with curriculum design could prove valuable to teachers as they respond to relaxed-education policies.

Another feature that distinguishes the Japanese education system from many others that have experimented with curricular decentralization is the important role that collaboration plays in the professional lives of teachers (Bjork 2000a; Lewis 1995; Sato and McLaughlin 1992; Shimahara 1998). In Japan, instructors are expected to give up a degree of individual freedom in exchange for a strong group attachment. The contributions they make to the larger community, rather than personal accomplishments, tend to earn them recognition and respect. One notable illustration of this is the research lessons (*kenkyu jugyo*) that schools depend on to improve the quality of instruction offered to children. At all the schools I visited, a small committee of teachers—or the entire staff—set professional goals for the faculty and organized events designed to support those objectives. Teachers presented lessons to their peers, who supplied critical feedback designed to help the presenter polish her instructional skills. Stigler and Hiebert (2009) relate that "by working in groups to improve instruction, [Japanese] teachers are able to develop a shared language for describing and analyzing classroom teaching, and to teach each other about teaching" (123).

This raises the possibility that Japanese educators may be uniquely positioned to follow plans for curricular decentralization. Members of a system that provides them with a strong pedagogical foundation, ongoing opportunities to collaborate with colleagues, and a well-established professional development program, teachers appear to have the capacities necessary to assume the role of "change agent" delegated to them by MEXT.

Responses in the Schools

Throughout my period of fieldwork, I focused on the practical realities of what teachers were being asked to do, and how they were responding to policy directives. My goal was to produce "rich descriptive data about the context, activities, and beliefs" (Goetz and LeCompte 1984, 17) of the individuals MEXT was depending on to realize its goals. As Walford (2001) notes, "Ethnographic examinations of the policy-to-practice connection show the actual constraints and contradictions faced by ground-level practitioners and thus allows us to move beyond seeing practice in simplistic terms" (3). Yet the voices of individuals working in schools were conspicuously absent from the vast majority of previously published reports on relaxed education.

In this section, I detail the opinions about *yutori kyoiku* expressed by teachers. The data I collected indicate there was little consensus about the merits of the relaxed-education reform movement. Teachers' opinions varied widely, depending on factors such as grade and subject level taught, educational philosophy, and responsibilities held within a school. Furthermore, instructors tended to express ambiguous feelings about the changes they had been asked to make. I did encounter a handful of individuals who voiced firm support for or opposition to relaxed education, but most included numerous qualifications or contradictions in their reflections; as they formulated their responses to interview questions, many appeared to be attempting to solidify their own beliefs.

The MEXT strategy of entrusting schools to translate broad reform guidelines into concrete action plans augmented both teacher authority and workload. Instructors were given the authority to shape the new components of the Course of Study at almost every stage of the process. The schools I visited took that responsibility quite seriously. When the new Course of Study was disseminated, committees to oversee the new curriculum were formed at each campus. These groups conducted extensive research on the new topics they would be required to introduce in 2002. As is typical of Japanese schools, principals were not actively involved in this process (Bjork 2000b); the committees were comprised mostly of teachers, who assumed leadership for curricular development. Many of these committees visited "frontier schools" that had been designated by the government as sites that would begin experimenting with relaxed-education subjects prior to their introduction nation-wide, serving as models for other institutions. Teachers at each school (sometimes the entire faculty, sometimes the members of the special committees) studied the goals for Integrated Studies and elective courses, and established guiding themes for these subjects that would mesh with their pupils' interests and needs. One middle school in my sample distributed a questionnaire to all students and used that data to develop create frameworks for *yutori kyoiku* subjects. After that groundwork had been laid, faculty members worked in teams to develop the courses that would be offered at each grade level. The stacks of reports on preparation for *yutori kyoiku* that lined the shelves of faculty rooms at all the schools I visited attested to the serious attention they had paid to curricular revision.

Teachers' responsibilities did not end after they completed the initial research and planning process. Because relaxed education is driven by the idea that instruction should be dynamic and student centered, teachers were encouraged to regularly modify lessons in response to student performance and interest. As one informant noted, "Each lesson has a different aim. IS planning is done by each teacher by himself. I have to make a new lesson plan for every class. Each teacher has to decide on the goals. If the teacher makes mistakes about the aims, the students will be lost." In addition, because MEXT chose not to publish textbooks for IS or electives, teachers had to develop their own instructional materials. Reform guidelines also encouraged organized activities that connected students to their communities, such as field trips and presentations delivered by local citizens. On many levels, implementing the new subjects was more onerous than traditional components of the curriculum.

The teachers I interviewed spoke extensively about the additional demands that adoption of the relaxed-education policies placed upon them. In reflecting on the effects of the 2002 Course of Study, they tended to weigh the positive repercussions of the new curriculum against the stress tied with preparation and implementation of new courses. A middle school Japanese language teacher, for instance, stated, "It is very difficult for me and other teachers to prepare for and teach IS because it is so different from what we usually teach. We spend long hours getting ready. If schools did an excellent job teaching IS, it could have positive results, but I don't think that happens very often." A science instructor from a neighboring middle school remarked that teaching electives "requires a lot of preparation on the part of teachers. That is especially true of science because teachers are expected to come up with interesting hands-on activities that promote discovery learning for every class. That takes a lot of time and is expensive."

Most teachers tried to maintain a positive attitude toward the curricular changes that had been adopted and were willing to prepare original IS and elective lessons. But they also evaluated the reforms with a critical eye. As numerous researchers have noted, Japanese teachers work long hours (Stevenson 1991b; Shimahara 1986; Shimahara 2002). In addition to overseeing instructional activities on their campuses, they are also expected to carry out administrative duties that are often delegated to nonteaching staff in schools in the United States. At the schools in my sample, teachers were assigned between four and twelve special responsibilities.[1] These included activities such as serving as liaison to the PTA, coaching athletic teams, keeping track of school materials, and acting as grade-level coordinators. In addition, school employees were required to carry out an array of duties that were not recognized as special responsibilities, but which consumed large quantities of their time: at most of the schools I visited, teachers made home visits to each member of their homeroom at least once a year;

at designated times throughout the year, they fanned out to busy spots in the surrounding community to monitor student behavior and traffic safety; instructors even took turns cleaning the faculty bathrooms.

While I understand that educators in all countries are assigned special responsibilities, the cumulative hours that Japanese teachers devote to non-teaching activities is higher than in schools in other countries I have visited. Their weekly schedules are more intense, and they do not receive the extended summer vacations that are provided to educators in many other nations.[2] When I dropped my son off at soccer practice at his elementary school at 8 p.m. on weekdays, the teachers' parking lot was usually full. Middle school teachers regularly told me that they worked at their desks until 10 or 11 p.m. the previous night. I share this information because it demonstrates that Japanese were willing to work diligently—on matters that they felt worthwhile, or if required to by administrators.

As a result of the excessive demands on their time, teachers were sometimes forced to prioritize their responsibilities, concentrating on tasks that they judged of utmost importance and devoting minimal attention to others. So, when instructors were asked to prepare original IS or elective lessons, they considered the associated demands in the context of multiple activities that necessitated their attention. One instructor related that "Japanese teachers are extremely busy. They have to plan for regular classes and supervise club activities. They don't have time to carefully think about things like IS or what students' lives will be like up until they become grandparents. Even if they're told to think about those kinds of things, they can't. It's really hard. Teachers have so many responsibilities." Even enthusiastic proponents of relaxed education struggled to find the time to prepare original lessons.

One might have expected adoption of the 2002 Course of Study to reduce teachers' workloads, given that classes were no longer held on Saturdays and the conceptual material included in the curriculum was reduced. Yet most teachers felt that the new curriculum exacerbated the stress they experienced. As one informant observed, "It is called relaxed education, but I don't think people really have more time. More activities are compressed into a shorter amount of time, which actually creates more pressure on students and teachers. If things were really more relaxed, that would be a good thing, but in fact, things have gotten more intense. Too much is expected of teachers. We are overloaded."

Although teachers were aware of MEXT's commitment to reducing the stress experienced by children, that knowledge had not produced meaningful changes in their work habits. Instructional hours may have been reduced, but instructors continued to feel pressure to cover the contents of the pre-*yutori* curriculum—in fewer class periods. Doing otherwise was considered too risky. Well-established opinions about what their pupils needed for future success prevented them from adhering to MEXT reform guidelines. As a result, most of the teachers I interviewed reported that relaxed education had actually exacerbated job-related stress they experienced.

Shifting Expectations Related to Instruction

In the schools I visited, teachers displayed an awareness of MEXT expectations for classroom practice but did not organize their actions to fit those prescriptions. Instead, they made decisions with the following factors in mind: (1) notions of effective instruction that they had developed over long periods of time; (2) practical considerations related to students' academic futures; and (3) their impressions of local community priorities and how their actions might affect public opinion about schooling.

Notions of Effective Instruction Developed over Time

The factors that educators found particularly unsettling related to disruptions to established practices that the relaxed-education policies triggered. Teachers' sense of discomfort was especially apparent when they spoke about the Integrated Studies curriculum. Their reflections on the new subject raised some weighty questions about their roles in the classroom and the mission of the schools. MEXT's endorsement of relaxed education appeared to have set in motion a process of self-examination that extended beyond the confines of the new programs, forcing members of the school communities to reconsider ideas about teaching and learning that had anchored the education system for decades. In this way, *yutori kyoiku* programs served as the catalyst for debate about the direction of the schools at the same time that the education system was evolving in unpredictable ways.

As they approached other subjects, instructors were grounded in time-honored practices, curriculum outlines, and culturally constructed conceptions of how to teach a particular subject. When educators planned IS lessons, in contrast, they often felt as if a secure foundation had been pulled out from underneath them. This insecurity was manifested in a number of ways. In many cases, the instructional methods teachers had relied on to deliver other subject matter could not be easily applied to the new curriculum. In addition, because there are no disciplinary boundaries that limit the material that can be covered in IS lessons, a teacher whose specialty is, say, mathematics or music could be asked to oversee a study of environmental science or local arts. This discovery troubled teachers because it exposed limitations in their professional capabilities. In some instances, the limitations were intellectual: instructors were forced to confront the reality that they did not have a strong base of knowledge in all the topics that students investigated. As an elementary school curriculum coordinator pointed out,

MRS. KANAGAWA (FOURTH-GRADE TEACHER): Each teacher has different special knowledge. Some teachers are specialists in science, others in history. Sometimes young teachers cannot do what they should do in IS because they don't have the right curricular background. In my school, almost all of the teachers want to study the local area, so they want to teach IS, but some other schools have teachers who dislike IS because they have always learned and taught using textbooks. So of course they want to continue to teach using textbooks. Without a textbook they have trouble teaching what they need to teach.

Other informants communicated anxiety about the pedagogical methods MEXT was encouraging them to employ. The investigation-based, student-centered model of IS promoted by MEXT left many people confused about their function in the classroom. Because their students spent a significant amount of class time working independently on their projects, teachers were not always sure what they should be doing to assist their pupils. The following comments underline the uncertainties commonly experienced by teachers as they approached the IS program:

MR. WATANABE (FOURTH-GRADE TEACHER): Teachers are not sure what methods they should use to guide their students. When the students have trouble, they don't always know how to help them. Students and teachers both have to get used to the program.

MS. WADA (5TH GRADE TEACHER): IS is not a type of learning that is forced on children, but something they want to do. In regular subjects, when a unit of study ends, so does the children's learning. With IS, once the student starts investigating some material or question, that question is continuously broadened, and can produce further questions. So in IS, it's not like the teachers are directly conveying knowledge to their students, but the students themselves can expand their own knowledge.

MR. SHIRASAKI (MIDDLE SCHOOL VICE PRINCIPAL): I agree with the goals of *yutori kyoiku* policies—I would like kids to be more excited about studying. However, I think the schools are asked to do too much. . . . It's difficult for teachers to implement reform in schools when they come in such rapid succession. Teachers are not lazy, but they need more time to think about the changes. If they had five or ten or fifteen years to make sense of the reforms, they could do a better job implementing them.

Scholars such as Lewis (1995), Sato (1991), and Stevenson (1991b) have noted that Japanese teachers often minimize their own contributions to learning activities so that students will assume more responsibility for their learning. This commitment to facilitating discovery rather than feeding information to pupils is one of the reasons often given for the high level of student engagement in Japanese schools. But when instructors adopt the role of facilitator (as opposed to lecturer), they typically create a detailed plan of how learning activities will unfold; they have a vision of the endpoint toward which their students are moving. With IS, the boundaries and final products of lessons are more indefinite. This ambiguity made many teachers I spoke with uncomfortable. Though the government presented teacher autonomy as an empowering idea, instructors sometimes regarded the power over the curriculum that had been delegated to them as intimidating. Almost all the adults I interviewed were concerned about recent changes in Japanese children and felt that the schools needed to address those changes. But the implications of the reforms that had recently been adopted by the ministry proved disquieting to many teachers, for the practices they had relied on in the past did not always apply to the new curriculum:

MR. SAITO (THIRD-GRADE TEACHER): We have to make up lessons based on students' interests. That is hard. If we teach math, there is a textbook that outlines what we should do. There are also teachers' guidebooks we can use. But with IS, we don't have those resources. We have to decide what and how to teach by ourselves. . . . Teachers in Japan are used to teaching from a textbook. That allows them to relax. IS takes a lot more preparation time. Some people aren't exactly sure how they should be teaching.

MR. TAKEDA (ELEMENTARY SCHOOL VICE PRINCIPAL): IS is completely different from the previous curriculum and way of teaching. Now we decide what to study together, with the students. Also, we are studying with a problem-based learning approach. This is very difficult for the teachers.

Practical Considerations Related to Students' Academic Futures

To make room for the new Integrated Studies courses and the expanded elective offerings, the number of hours set aside for most academic subjects was reduced in 2002 (see tables 2.3 and 2.4). To underscore this point, one principal pulled out a copy of the new Course of Study and pointed out to me how many hours had been trimmed from the curriculum. As he noted, the extent of the cuts varied by discipline and grade level but affected all subject areas.

Although educators tended to agree with the goals of *yutori kyoiku*, concerns related to student mastery of basic academic skills weighed heavily on their minds as they considered the changes they were being asked to make. The combination of the reduction in total school hours and revisions to the Course of Study made many teachers uncomfortable. Almost all my informants were troubled by the difficult choices they were required to make about how to use limited preparation and instructional time. Educators frequently described relaxed-education programs and traditional academic subjects as competing for precious instructional time.

Despite MEXT assurances to the contrary, many teachers believed that relaxed education interfered with rather than complemented the core curriculum, and that adhering to the ministry's reform plans would lead to a lowering of academic standards. In the view of many of these educators, curricula associated with *yutori kyoiku* had displaced instructional time that had previously been devoted to more rigorous academic study. This shift, if not carefully implemented, could undermine the intellectual development of children. The following comments echo ideas shared by many of the educators I interviewed:

Mrs. Fukui (sixth-grade teacher): I had trouble answering the item on your questionnaire that asked about changes to the Course of Study because I agree with many of the ideas included in the new curriculum, especially those that have to do with learning and teaching styles. For example, I think that discovery learning is a good idea. But I don't think that the contents of the curriculum should have been cut and discarded. Instead, MEXT should have thought carefully about how to proceed from topic to topic.

Mr. Tanaka (middle school principal): Yes, the contents of the Course of Study have changed, the contents were reduced, but I think the changes have made things more difficult for students and teachers. The teachers have less material to cover, but they aren't sure how to deal with the changes. They have become rudderless, shifting from one direction to another. They can

> cover the material in the new Course of Study, but they want to raise students' academic abilities, which creates pressure and work for them.

When they felt compelled to choose between the new subjects and basic skills subjects, teachers usually opted for the latter. Very few instructors spent as much time preparing for IS or elective lessons than they did for more traditional subject areas. Although MEXT stressed the importance of reducing stress on students and promoting "twenty-first-century skills," teachers continued to make traditional academic subject matter their top priority.

In some education systems, individuals who do not adhere to curricular guidelines could receive poor evaluations from their administrators. The teachers I interviewed for this study were not concerned about such repercussions. During the 1970s, strong opposition to teacher-rating schemes undercut the influence of those instruments (Aspinall 2001).[3] Ever since, they have carried little weight in promotion trajectories, salary decisions, or professional development. Instead, administrators tended to rely on collegial mentoring systems and school-based professional development activities (*kenshu*) to maintain high instructional standards. That system of lateral accountability did encourage the teachers I interviewed for this study to take their professional responsibilities seriously. Core academic subjects, however, were treated as more deserving of attention than topics not included on entrance examinations. This tacit ranking of curricula shaped the behavior of teachers and reduced the incentive to focus on integrated studies and elective courses.

Impressions of Local Community Priorities

Underlying the factors mentioned above was a pervasive, often imprecisely articulated unease about parental opinion related to *yutori kyoiku*. Although the vast majority of teachers interviewed mentioned that they had not received any negative feedback about the relaxed-education reforms, they remained unconvinced that the community supported their efforts to reduce academic pressure. Even when parents expressed satisfaction with the 2002 Course of Study, teachers often continued to worry about the negative effects that attention to "soft" subject matter might have on their students' mastery of basic academic skills:

Mr. Hata (middle school science teacher): We have not prepared a survey and distributed it to parents, so I will have to guess. I think that most parents are not really sure what relaxed education is. They didn't have that kind of curriculum when they were in school. There are probably both people who support and dislike the program, but I can't give you exact percentages.

MRS. KAWAMURA (MIDDLE SCHOOL HOME ECONOMICS TEACHER): Parents did not directly express their opinions about IS, but they do like seeing their children perform in front of people. Students rarely get a chance to do that. I think that was a good thing. We haven't formally asked parents for their opinions, but I haven't heard anything negative from parents. We no longer have classes on Saturdays. They were cut at the time IS was introduced. I think parents would rather have their children spend more time on subjects like math or Japanese, but they have not said that to me directly.

Although parents did not directly communicate their views about relaxed education to employees of the schools I visited, teachers were highly sensitive to external opinions about their actions. Many had trouble committing themselves to lessons not explicitly designed to develop basic academic skills, assuming that parents would find fault with such learning activities. Underlying decisions made by both parents and teachers were concerns about student preparedness for high school entrance examinations. This consideration tended to override other factors related to curriculum and instruction. Teachers generally assumed that parents were more focused on the scores their sons and daughters received on entrance examinations than they were on more idealistic objectives promoted by MEXT, such as developing a love for learning or the ability to solve problems. My interviews with parents reveal that teachers were correct in drawing this conclusion.

When I asked parents to identify the strengths and weaknesses of relaxed education, the opinions they expressed were equally ambiguous. Like teachers, parents generally concurred with the goals of reform, but their enthusiasm diminished when they began to talk about the specific implications for their own children's academic futures. The following comments by the parents of elementary school students captures this tension:

MRS. YAMAGUCHI: I am all for *yutori kyoiku*. Teaching it is valuable. But a lot of pressure is also being placed on teachers. Kids have to learn more kanji in less time. They have to study more at home. If they are going to teach *yutori kyoiku* at school, they have to give more time at school. I want the five-day school week abolished and make it a six-day school week to make Japan more competitive academically at the international level.

MR. TAKEUCHI: I think it's good for kids to develop thinking skills, to discover things, but kids have to make some effort, to be challenged to get to the next level. It's very difficult. It depends on their level of maturity. The five-day school week sounds nice, but not if the curriculum is cut.

Conditioned to accept the demands associated with entrance examinations, parents had trouble imagining a system immune to such pressures.

My interviews confirm observations made by scholars of Japanese education in recent years that portray parents as strategic consumers of educational services. Goodman and Phillips (2003), for example, state that "when the chips are down and parents are given the option of taking their children out of the pressurized atmosphere of the education system, very few are willing to take it. Indeed, those who are most vocal about the pressures of the system are often those whose children are most likely to attend *juku* (cram schools) several times a week" (21). Hood (2003) also underscores the important role that parents play in determining the success or failure of educational change initiatives in Japan: "If I had to point to the most significant 'party' in the resistance to the reforms, what would it be? It was not the Ministry officials. It was not the teachers either. I believe it was the parents. Even those parents who claimed to support certain aspects of the reforms, often, on closer examination, supported the proposal in principle for other people's children, but not for their own child" (76).

Both parents and teachers carefully assessed their ideals about what students should be learning in relation to the specific factors that determined future academic opportunities. When asked for their opinions of the relaxed-education movement, most emphasized the positive aspects of its underlying goals. Individual decisions, however, were molded to fit the realities of an examination driven system. Drawing distinctions between idealism and pragmatism minimized the potential for conflict to emerge.

Education systems in the West do not yet appear to have internalized the demands of high-stakes testing to the same extent. Because the testing regimes were put in place more recently, teachers and parents are in the process forming opinions about how to respond to the new demands placed on children in school. Many are still making sense of the long-term implications of No Child Left Behind and Race to the Top. Interviews I have conducted with American teachers establish that, like their Japanese counterparts, many feel they have no option other than to emphasize the language arts and mathematics curriculum, and to devote extensive class time to test preparation. In chapter 10, I report on those interviews, which document the adjustments teachers are making so as to satisfy recently adopted accountability procedures.

Broader Questions about Teaching and Learning

The difficulties teachers experienced as they attempted to follow MEXT guidelines reform forced many of the people I interviewed to reconsider ideas about education that had become deeply ingrained and accepted over many years. Reflecting on the goals and results of relaxed education, teachers contemplated their relationships with students, the methods they relied on to prepare lessons, and the tools they utilized to measure student achievement. Shimahara and Sakai (1995) use the term "ethnopedagogy" to describe this locally constructed approach to teaching. They describe ethnopedagogy as "a cultural theory of teaching shared among Japanese teachers as a frame of orientation. . . . It is intrinsic to the craft of teaching invented by practitioners and reproduced through self-discovery, casual conversations, and inservice education" (168).

As instructors implemented the 2002 Course of Study, ethnopedagogical considerations had a more direct impact on their decision making than did concerns about following ministry guidelines. In many cases, educators found that strategies advocated by MEXT did not mesh with their established routines or values about teaching and learning. For example, government publications recommend that teachers make independent student investigations a core component of IS classes. Some instructors, however, viewed the independent investigations as less valid than lessons focused on the dissemination and recall of predetermined content. As a fifth-grade teacher explained to me,

> The aim is to get students who hate school interested in their schoolwork, to motivate them to study. That is the goal. There are many elementary school students who do not like school, but who are interested in using all sorts of materials to conduct investigations. They work very hard because the lessons are based on investigations. Sometimes when I watch that happening, I think they are really learning something, but sometimes I worry that after the students conduct their investigations they won't go any further. With regular subjects, the instructor teaches the classes, gives homework, pushes the information into their heads. Students say they don't like that, but they remember the information.

A sixth-grade teacher working at a different school referred to similar concerns, noting that

> every student has different interests. I want to meet every child's needs and that is difficult with a subject like this [IS]. Also, in the school, all of the teachers have different ideas. It's hard for us all to agree what to do. With [relaxed education], teachers are supposed to make decisions based on the interests of students, but there are still some teachers who feel like they should decide what is taught.

The tensions described by these and other teachers I interviewed raised a range of complex issues related to the parameters of learning: Is it valuable if it cannot be measured quantitatively? Are learning activities worthwhile if they do not prepare students to pass a written examination? Are certain types of knowledge more valuable than others? The absence of definitive answers to such questions put many teachers in an uncomfortably precarious situation as they responded to MEXT decrees. Educators' comments suggested that the introduction of *yutori kyoiku* had set in motion a process of self-examination that left unanswered some fundamental questions about their roles in the classroom and their professional responsibilities:

MRS. KAWAMURA (MIDDLE SCHOOL HOME ECONOMICS TEACHER): The students conducted individual investigations. They were really impressive. But I'm not sure that really qualifies as studying. . . . IS eats up a lot of class time. I'm not sure if the students get enough out of those classes to justify the large amount of time it takes. I can see the results of mathematics and Japanese classes much more quickly. During IS classes, I sometimes wonder if it is valuable to use class time when I could be teaching math or Japanese. Because of that feeling, I have trouble devoting myself to IS.

MR. NAKAMURA (SIXTH-GRADE TEACHER): If I teach math or science, I have to teach formal lessons. With IS, it isn't really teaching, so it's different from teaching a regular subject. Rather than teaching, IS instructors provide students with a variety of situations and get those students to act. The meaning is a bit different. It's not really the same thing.

Remarks such as these indicate that some educators believe that to qualify as instruction, a lesson must be prepared and delivered by a teacher with a clear vision of its objectives, structure, and final products. From this perspective, the ministry's promotion of student-centered, constructivist learning not only represented a revision of the status quo, it also forced teachers to allocate class time to activities that they did not consider educationally valid. Uncertainties about the boundaries of teaching and learning made it difficult for some informants to commit to the government's plans. Following reform guidelines beyond a surface level demanded that educators contemplate weighty questions about the purposes of education. The answers they formulated in response to those questions sometimes necessitated serious revisions in the way they approached their work and interacted with students. Many were hesitant—for philosophical as well a practical reasons—to embark on that journey.

The Role of the Teacher in Policy Implementation

Published accounts of relaxed education are often premised on the supposition that teachers faithfully followed policy guidelines disseminated by the MEXT. This should not surprise us, given the prevalence of policy analyses that portray teachers as rational actors who adhere to decrees communicated to them by their superiors. Yet, as McLaughlin (1987) has noted, analyses of reform policies often fail to capture the complexity of policy translation. At each point in this process, she states, "a policy is transformed as individuals interpret and respond to it. What is actually delivered or provided under the aegis of a policy depends finally on the individual at the end of the line" (174). McLaughlin calls this a "bargaining model of policy implementation," and contrasts it with studies anchored in notions of rational choice. She underscores the importance of examining "individual actors' incentives, beliefs, and capacity" (175) when studying the results of a reform effort. Policy success, McLaughlin emphasizes, depends on two crucial factors: local capacity and will.

The Japanese teachers I studied clearly had the capacity necessary to realize Ministry plans for relaxed education. As I document in chapters 5 and 6, most teachers initially approached the new curriculum with an open mind and a spirit of cooperation. All the schools I visited carefully studied reform guidelines and attempted to revise curricula to fit MEXT's vision of change. They spent extensive hours conducting research on project-based learning and refining the strategies they used in the classroom. Of course, I occasionally witnessed lessons that could have been more engaging—especially at the middle school level—but the overall level of instruction was high. I am convinced that if teachers were truly committed to MEXT's reform agenda, they possessed the pedagogical skills needed to implement the reforms according to plan.

The question of will is another matter. While some teachers firmly supported *yutori kyoiku*, the majority remained skeptical about the new curriculum. Their reservations were multifaceted. Some teachers attempted to reconcile the discovery-oriented instructional approaches advocated by education officials with lecture-and-test methods on which they had relied in the past. Others thought that student-centered activities had the potential to increase children's motivation, but, lacking quantitative evidence of student learning, they were unsure about the concrete benefits of those activities. Such skepticism usually diluted—or extinguished—educators' commitment to the reform. When that was the case, teachers tended to revert to practices that had produced more dependable results in the past. Those activities were supported by an "implicit cultural logic that, because it is implicit and deeply cultural, is resistant to change" (Tobin, Yeh, and Karasaw 2009, 242). Individuals who faced obstacles revised policy guidelines to fit their own priorities.

Yet such resistance was usually camouflaged by surface-level compliance with ministry guidelines. Teachers and administrators in all of the schools I visited skillfully manipulated the public representation of *yutori* programs so as to avoid scrutiny or criticism from education officials. Weekly schedules and official reports tended to reflect an idealized version of the instructional program provided to students. On paper, it appeared that they had modified the curriculum, when in actuality little change had occurred, or alterations enacted in support of MEXT policies had been retracted. Displaying *tatemae* (public politeness to avoid confrontation) rather than *honne* (true behavior and opinions) made things easier for people operating at all levels of the system.

Shimahara (2002) has asserted that "Japanese teachers identif[y] their accountability in terms of their responsibility to fulfill national mandates—common national goals and materials stipulated in the course of study" (143). The data I collected do not support this observation. Teachers rarely expressed concern about how their own actions might be viewed by central authorities. Instead, when explaining their reasons for making decisions about curricula, instruction, and guidance, they cited locally situated influences. MEXT may have provided the broad framework of educational policy that circumscribed the teachers I interviewed and observed, but as those teachers carried out their professional duties on a daily basis, their focus was local rather than national.

This evidence confirms previous research on the Japanese education system that captures the essential role that local educators play in implementing education reform (Azuma 2002; DeCoker 2002; Rosegaard 1998).

Within what looks like a rigidly hierarchical authority structure, teachers have the latitude to modify centrally crafted policies to fit their own objectives. The educators I interviewed had clearly received that message and understood that they were free to use their professional expertise to shape the 2002 Course of Study. Instructors were aware of MEXT's expectations regarding curriculum and practice, but they also realized the limits of ministry oversight of activity in the schools. Although the formal system in which they operated encouraged them to display autonomy, educators' perceptions of what they thought society expected of them often prevented them from fully investing in programs introduced in support of relaxed education.

This suggests that the Japanese education system does allow for teachers to display autonomy, as scholars have previously emphasized, but that their ability to do so is often restricted by broader, intangible pressure to conform to established practices. In other words, the "soft middle" described by DeCoker (2002, xvi) seems to be encircled by a more rigid casing that is molded by public opinion and historical precedent. Teachers may have made some slight adjustments to the curriculum, but their core activities and the principles that anchored decision making in schools were not altered in any significant way; new segments of the curriculum were modified to conform to priorities that had become institutionalized over decades.

FIVE

Nurturing Enthusiasm in Elementary School Students

Adoption of the relaxed-education reforms created challenges for all educators, but teachers internalized the repercussions of the reform differently, depending to a great extent on their location within the system. Although research on Japanese education has drawn attention to contrasting features of elementary and secondary schools, the acuteness of those differences has been underemphasized, in my opinion. One explanation for this is that scholars tend to focus on a single level of the system. While it is usually possible to compare the conclusions articulated in a study of practices in elementary schools with those offered in a separate study of secondary schools, distinct research methods or lines of inquiry can make that exercise difficult. This study was designed to investigate the course of students' academic careers as they moved through the system—and how *yutori kyoiku* policies affected that journey.

As I conducted the fieldwork for this study, the contrasts between schools of different levels were more striking than I had remembered. Driving from an elementary to a secondary school, I often felt as if I were entering a completely different realm. Teachers may have been employed by the boards of education, but their professional lives were organized to fit unique goals and conditions. Those distinct institutional realities shaped instructors' responses to reform policies—and the resulting learning activities offered to students.

In this chapter, I examine the enactment of *yutori kyoiku* policies in the elementary schools. As is true throughout the book, I include detailed descriptions of classroom activities I observed and excerpts from interviews with educators so as to ground discussion of relaxed-education policies in the experiences of the people most directly affected by them. Two instructional activities described in this chapter support MEXT claims that relaxed education would bolster children's interest in learning, at least at the elementary level. Contrasts between those lessons, however, raise questions about the academic benefits of the relaxed curriculum. My analysis also compares instructors' opinions about their work and their students to my own observations of life inside their classrooms.

One of the guiding objectives for this research was to carefully document the effects of relaxed education on actual schools; to capture the "'lived realities" of those involved in the implementation and reception of policy decisions at the local level" (Walford 2001, 2). Rather than use those data to build a case for or against *yutori kyoiku*, I sought to identify the strengths and weaknesses, as well as the "tensions, contradictions, and incompatible aims" of MEXT policies (Finch 1988).

First Impressions

During the time of my data collection (2003–2009), the "academic achievement crisis debate" (*gakuryoku teika ronso*) was raging, and teachers were keenly aware of heightened public concerns about Japanese youths. According to a vocal group of critics, too many children were passing through the system without acquiring the skills or dispositions necessary to become productive members of society. Such publicly voiced condemnation of the school system reinforced troubling developments instructors had observed in their own classrooms. Children came to school with more extensive social, emotional, and cognitive needs than had been true only a few years earlier. There was broad consensus among educators that schools had no choice but to face that reality and devise new, more effective strategies for educating their pupils. Most teachers, however, appeared ambivalent about how to accomplish that goal. Identifying the problem was much easier than devising appropriate solutions.

Teachers at all the elementary schools I visited believed that their professional lives had become more complex as a result of recent changes in their students and the national Course of Study. Rarely did I talk with an educator who did not lament the deteriorating academic capabilities, social skills, or attitudes they had observed in Japanese youths. One fifth-grade teacher related, "We need to find ways to get kids more excited about learning. Students don't know what do when they have difficulties. They tend to give up. We need to help them find ways to get over those difficulties." Another instructor observed, "Today's kids want to study, but their communication and presentation skills are weak." Addressing these deficiencies was even more complicated, teachers explained to me, because many parents failed to provide their children with the support necessary to meet the challenges they faced in school.

These conditions created a sense of obligation among most teachers to seek new ways of connecting with students so as to motivate them to invest in school. In the United States and Europe, teachers have been grappling with similar challenges for decades; creating learning activities that will engage students with a range of academic and social needs has become an accepted facet of their work. For Japanese educators, however, the increasingly complex lives of pupils required them to reconsider the instructional approaches they relied on.

The Ministry of Education presented relaxed education as a remedy to the problematic changes referred to by the teachers above. Instructors, however, were often unsure about the suitability of the policies endorsed by MEXT. Teachers frequently struggled to reconcile changes in the new curriculum with their own opinions about what was best for children:

Mr. Takagi (vice principal): There are many students today who have trouble finding a sense of direction. They aren't sure what to do with their lives. If kids don't have clear goals, they need to be counseled. They need help finding their pathways. That's why relaxed education is necessary—to help students develop *ikiru chikara* (zest for living) and plans for their futures.

Mr. Inoue (fifth-grade teacher): The idea of *yutori kyoiku* was a good one, but what is important for children's education and the entire society—parents, teachers, the mass media—the entire society needs to think very carefully about those things. Japanese people need to develop a better understanding of what is important for children to learn and how they should learn it.

Mr. Suzuki (sixth-grade teacher): Relaxed education is supposed to be for children, but, to be honest, I wonder if it is really good for them. . . . I think the new curriculum is too easy, although it depends on the subject. The math is too easy for most of my students. They can finish it quickly and then they start talking or playing. But Japanese language (*kokugo*) is about right. Their ability to express themselves is weak, so they need to spend a lot of time on language.

As these statements capture, educators struggled to reconcile their desire to make learning more exciting and relevant for students with questions about the rigor of the 2002 Course of Study. As they implemented the ministry's plans for change, concerns related to their students' mastery of core academic skills constantly seeped into the decisions they made.

I conducted my most extensive fieldwork four years after the new curriculum was implemented nation-wide. At that point, elementary teachers had already observed some benefits of the time and effort they had invested in the program. Most reported that students were enthused about the new curriculum; they were also developing the skills and attitudes that, according to MEXT, had been underemphasized in more traditional lessons. This was most apparent in Integrated Studies (IS) learning activities, which required students to initiate and manage independent research projects, to express what they learned orally and in writing, and to make connections across disciplinary boundaries. IS also made it possible for children who might not have excelled in regular academic subjects to obtain positive feedback for their accomplishments. As one teacher recounted,

> In my class, students researched lizards, and when they gave their oral presentations, they showed what they had learned. When they were talking in front of everyone, they not only solidified their own knowledge but also received praise from their peers. After being told, "You are the lizard king!" a student might become motivated to do even more research, to work harder.

Reflecting on the IS curriculum, another educator observed that

> children's consciousness (*ishiki*) is put in the front. They get to study the things that they really want to learn about. That makes them happy. Also, we spend a lot of time studying the local community. That's good for the community. They feel important. For example, we have people from the community come to school and act as guest teachers. In my class we did a unit on plums. We studied how they are grown, how to make plum juice, and so on. We are going to have a plum festival and invite the second graders. We will teach them what we have learned and give them some plum juice.

Teachers hesitated, though, to draw firm conclusions about the effects of the reform. One reason for their tentativeness was an absence of quantitative information that measured student progress. Lacking test scores, they were required to make judgments based on their subjective evaluations of what students had done; that made several teachers uncomfortable. Another qualification interviewees offered was that it was too early to make meaningful assessments of the IS program. Several teachers posited that it would be a number of years before it would be possible to ascertain the impact of IS on their pupils.

The consensus among elementary teachers was that IS demanded more of their time than other subjects. Yet even those that expressed reservations about the subject set their concerns and worked diligently to realize the government's change plans. One teacher stated that "Integrated Studies does not have a long history. In IS, I need to be open to many new ideas, to know many things. I have to get excited about the subject or I cannot do a good job teaching it. I need to have the attitude that it is a special event, like a festival." Another commented, "Basically, many teachers still don't have strong opinions about IS, but each school has some experience now, successes and failures, and we are gradually starting to feel more positive about IS." Remarks such as these revealed that elementary teachers regarded the IS program as a long-term project, and if they continued to invest in the reform, it would eventually meet the objectives MEXT had established for it.

Effects on Student Learning

At the time I conducted my yearlong study of implementation of the relaxed-education initiatives in Kita Prefecture, teachers may have felt that they were still adjusting to a reconfigured educational landscape but the reflections they shared with me suggested they had actually developed a concrete sense of the curriculum's strengths and weaknesses. Most interviewees had experimented with a range of learning activities and had begun to fine-tune the pedagogical approaches they used to support relaxed education. In the following sections, I report on the learning activities facilitated in the elementary schools I studied. My analysis will focus on three key questions: (1) Did the 2002 Course of Study instill in students an excitement for learning, as MEXT expected it would? (2) To what extent were teachers able to meet the Ministry's goal of promoting the "new academic abilities" (*shin gakuryokukan*)? (3) Had reductions in the topics included in the Course of Study undermined children's intellectual development, as critics of *yutori kyoiku* claimed?

Student Motivation

Simply put, the Japanese elementary schools I visited were exhilarating settings for learning. Teachers delivered lessons that sparked student excitement about the unfamiliar or unknown. In other words, they cultivated the "zest for living" (*ikiru chikara*) identified in MEXT planning documents as one of the key objectives of relaxed education. On an almost daily basis, I observed children throwing themselves into their studies, and being rewarded for their efforts: fourth graders shouting "*sugoi*" (Wow!) as they returned to their classroom to describe the shadows of the sun they had just observed through darkened microscope slides they had created; second graders singing a morning song with such vigor that I covered my ears in self-defense; first graders sprinting across the playground in search of flowers to observe and sketch. The energy and enthusiasm for learning displayed by students was truly infectious. How did schools generate such palpable enthusiasm for learning?

Teachers strategically organized the school day to fit the children's natural rhythms and interests. In stark contrast to the images of Japanese classrooms often distributed abroad, the elementary schools I studied implemented instructional programs that nurtured what John Dewey described as "the child's need of action, of expression, of desire to do something, to be constructive and creative, instead of simply passive and conforming" (Dewey 1900, 80). Lessons required students to actively participate in their learning—physically, intellectually, emotionally, and socially. IS, science, and social studies lessons, in particular, incorporated physical activity into lesson procedures. And learning frequently extended beyond the walls of the classroom. Adhering to MEXT guidelines, teachers scheduled IS field trips into the communities that surrounded elementary schools. Students were regularly sent on expeditions to collect materials or observe objects that could be found on campus. Children were not often required to remain seat at their desks for extended periods of time.

In 1987, White noted that "Japanese elementary school teachers usually don't find themselves laying down the law, and instead spend time trying to create ways to engage children emotionally" (182). My observations indicate that decades later, teachers continue to follow this approach. The instructors I studied tended to interpret noise and activity as evidence that students were absorbed in learning; they encouraged rather than clamped down on student displays of enthusiasm. For example, after reading a story in the social studies textbook about the Great Buddha, a sixth-grade teacher had his students form their own version of the Buddha on the floor of the gym using twine, colored traffic cones, newspapers, and basketballs. He provided little direction to pupils, who collectively decided how to determine the size of the life-size Buddha using the proportions of a small picture in their textbook. At several points in the lesson, three boys assigned the task of creating the Buddha's head with basketballs could not resist the temptation to throw the balls at one another. The teacher chose not to respond to this short lapse in concentration, and after two or three minutes of play, the children got back to work. By the end of the period, the class had constructed a portrait of the Buddha that spread across the entire gym floor and generated spontaneous applause and gasps from its young designers.

This lesson illustrates how the elementary school educators in the schools I studied designed lessons with both student interest and cognitive growth in mind. It is important to recognize that the learning activities—rather than examinations—motivated children to invest in their studies. Assessment was integrated into the fabric of daily activities without creating stress for children or instructors. Teachers crafted lessons that appealed to children's innate curiosity—and capitalized on the enthusiasm generated to challenge students intellectually. Teachers structured activity in their classrooms to provoke students' physical, social, and intellectual engagement in learning. This augmented children's interest in learning and encouraged them to explore important questions they came across in their daily lives. As one teacher observed, "Our students do have *ikiru chikara* (zest for life). They are happy and come to school with a lot of enthusiasm, although each child is different."

New Academic Abilities

Elementary children in Japanese schools are constantly on their feet, moving through the classroom, the playground, and the school. I was also fascinated by the techniques instructors employed to facilitate mental engagement with the curriculum. Teachers working in primary schools used transmission-oriented pedagogical methods sparingly. More commonly, they designed lessons that required pupils to formulate their own explanations for phenomena they observed. Children regularly presented their ideas to the class and to challenge assertions made by their classmates. Teachers, in turn, avoided labeling student responses as correct. For example, during a math lesson I observed, a fourth-grade teacher encouraged her students to "think of ways of doing this that are different from the way you usually do it. You can think of more than one different way. Math is really interesting because there are so many different ways to solve a problem."

This is just one example of instructors promoting what Wiggins and McTighe (1998) term the "uncoverage" of knowledge: "A curriculum designed to develop understanding would uncover complex, abstract, and counterintuitive ideas by involving students in active questioning, practice trying out ideas, and rethinking what they thought they knew" (21). This pedagogical approach, which was consistently on display in the elementary school classrooms I visited, encouraged pupils to think deeply about the topics they explored. It also communicated to children that they had the capacity to devise solutions to problems without the input of adults. Such attention to pupil engagement produced countless "aha" (or, in the Japanese context, "*sugoi*") moments of discovery in the classroom.[1]

Teachers working at all grade levels challenged children to come up with their own solutions to problems instead of depending on adults to lead them through procedures. Although the absence of a detailed set of procedures created frustration for some students, it also created the impetus to persevere when faced with difficult tasks. Even the youngest students were expected to solve problems independently, with limited input from adults. For instance, during the first week of school, a first-grade teacher assigned her students to make chains of paper dolls. Rather than provide them with a detailed set of instructions to follow, Mrs. Utsumi simply modeled the process of folding the paper, cutting out a single human figure and then expanding the paper to reveal a string of identical dolls. After observing this presentation, one girl asked, "How do you make them connect?" But the teacher would not offer any specific guidance, instead responding, "Well, ask your friend."

Most of the children in the room failed on their initial attempts at this task. The most common approach they employed was to draw a single figure in the middle of the top square of paper, which produced a set of identical but disconnected dolls. This led to numerous cries of "I made a mistake again!" Mrs. Utsumi's response to such expressions of frustration was, "Making mistakes is our specialty" (*Shippai wa watashi-tachi no senmon desu*). After twenty minutes of independent work, only four of the twenty-six children in the room had successfully constructed a chain of dolls. Still, the instructor refused to provide further direction. Finally, after approximately thirty minutes, students began to realize that the sides of the figures had to touch on both sides to create a continuous string of dolls. By the end of the period, all but three boys had successfully completed the task. After the period ended, when I asked Mrs. Utsumi why she refrained from offering more scaffolding to her young students, she explained,

> If I showed them how to do it, they would immediately know exactly what to do, which would be boring. I want them to watch and learn from each other. If they make mistakes, that is okay. Today is not the only day they will do this. They will continue to make paper chains in the future, and eventually they will all figure it out.

From the time they enter the first grade, students at this school were encouraged to devise their own solutions to problems they encountered, and to see tasks through to completion.

The combination of student autonomy in the classroom and emphasis on creative problem solving promoted the "new abilities" that, according to MEXT, are essential to both personal development and to Japan's international competitiveness in the twenty-first century. Children were constantly challenged to apply their creativity and critical thinking skills to real-life problems. Prodded by their teachers to investigate provocative questions and to examine those questions from multiple vantage points, they sharpened their ability "to learn and think by themselves . . . and develop the attitude to solve and explore problems independently and creatively" (MEXT 2003, 27). In all the elementary schools I visited, students acquired both enthusiasm for learning and the "new abilities" that MEXT believed would help them achieve personal satisfaction and professional success.

Relaxed Education in Action: Sample Lessons

Fourth-Grade River Ecology

The themes for Integrated Studies at Oka Elementary School have changed every year since the subject was introduced. This year, teachers decided to focus on local environmental issues:

Third grade: our hometown
Fourth grade: the local river
Fifth grade: the local mountains
Sixth grade: individual choice/independent projects

Fourth graders at OES have been investigating the condition and impact of the local river in multidisciplinary fashion: examining the history of the river, writing stories about its relevance to local culture, and studying about the effects of pollution. Today a scientist who works in the area gives a presentation about the science of water pollution. Clad in a white lab coat, he distributes a handout with information about the properties of water to students. After succinctly reviewing the handout, he moves to the front table of the science laboratory. There, he adds some green food coloring to a beaker filled with water and informs the group that he is going to teach them how to determine the pH level of a liquid. Next, he adds an eyedropper full of soft drink to the water in the beaker, which turns yellow. This, the man explains, indicates that the liquid is acidic; the color of the sample indicates the liquid's pH level. "Now you will have a chance to test the acidity of liquids," he announces.

Students, working in small groups, conduct several pH tests on samples. Each team has drawn water samples from five different locations around the school. The energy level in the room is high; children animatedly chat as they test their samples. As they do so, the guest teacher circulates through the room, offering assistance and talking about different things that add odor to water (such as plankton and bacteria), which prompts much sniffing. I notice one boy is sitting by the window, focused on what is going on outside rather than the experiment. The rest of the class is actively engaged in the activity, clearly enjoying this opportunity to explore and extend a topic they have been studying for several weeks.

After twenty-five minutes of testing, the guest instructs students to clean up and return to their stools. When they do, he gives a brief lecture that distills key information from the activity they have just completed. The energy level drops, but most students are listening. I am impressed by the man's knowledge—and his ability to communicate difficult material to a group of ten-year-olds. After completing his remarks, the guest passes out a worksheet and asks everyone to respond to the following prompts: things you discovered, things you saw, and things that surprised you.

Fifth-Grade Rice Planting

When the fifth-grade homeroom teacher, Mrs. Maeda, invites me to join her class on a field trip to plant rice, I immediately accept. She informs me that the class has been studying rice since the beginning of the year and has already made several visits to a nearby rice field. The class assembles in the school entrance hall. Each student carries a cutting tool, a thermos, a towel, and a pair of large rubber boots. Five mothers have come along to help. The class forms a line and follows the teacher down the hill to the *tambo* (rice field). There, the caretakers of the field, a man and woman who appear to be in their mid-70s, are waiting to greet the children. Almost everyone present is sweating under the hot sun, although the physical activity has yet to begin.

Mrs. Maeda makes some brief comments about the growth of the rice plants since their last visit, and assigns jobs to the students, who immediately fan out across the field. Several groups trudge through the muddy field and begin cutting mature rice stalks. Others collect the severed stalks and carry them to a corner of the field, where the caretakers prepare to hang and dry them. A handful of fifth graders climb up a tower of bamboo poles and tie the recently cut stalks to the rods. As I work with students in the field, I ask them their opinions of this activity, and almost all respond that it is more fun than studying at school. I wonder how many children are harvesting rice for the first time, considering the large number of families in this area who work as farmers or grow rice to supplement their primary income.

The activity continues for three hours. After all the plants have been prepared for drying, Mrs. Maeda gives a short lecture, emphasizing the hard work that is involved in growing rice. This rice is 150 percent more delicious than rice that is grown using machines, she tells them. Students listen politely but look as if the labor they completed sapped them of their energy. The female caretaker follows with her own thoughts about rice. She tells the children it is important to appreciate food. When she was younger, just after World War II, many people didn't have enough food to eat. She hopes they understand how lucky they are to have rice to eat every day. With this thought fresh in their minds, the group of fifth graders walks back up the hill to campus, tired but talkative.

I share these two activities to give readers a sense of the approaches some elementary school teachers used to translate plans for *yutori kyoiku* into concrete learning experiences—and how different those activities could look. The water-analysis and rice-planting activities highlight some compelling questions about the goals and effects of relaxed education that educators across the country were grappling with as they attempted to follow reform guidelines. The fundamental question guiding my analysis of these and other IS lessons I observed is: Do the activities constitute valuable use of instructional time? Of course, responses to that question depended on one's views about the curriculum. MEXT documents emphasize that Integrated Studies was designed to increase student motivation to learn and develop skills of inquiry and analysis. To what extent did children's participation in the water analysis lesson or the rice-harvesting activity support those goals?

Both of the lessons bolstered students' interest in their studies. All the students I spoke with shared positive assessments of the activities. Children thought that conducting science experiments and playing in a rice field were far more exciting than practicing *kanji* at their desks. As table 5.1 shows, IS scored near the top of student rankings of their favorite subjects. When asked to explain what it was about IS that appealed to them, pupils related that they valued opportunities to select the topics they would study,

Table 5.1. Student rankings of their favorite subjects

Rank	Elementary school	Middle school
1	Physical education	Physical education
2	Art	Art
3	Integrated Studies	Science
4	Music	Music
5	Science	Integrated Studies
6	Math	Social studies
7	Social studies	English*
8	Japanese language	Japanese language
9	—	Math

*English was not yet a required subject in most elementary schools.

the freedom to move beyond the confines of their classrooms, and the more relaxed study environment. Another attraction of IS was its uniqueness. From the students' perspective, IS represented a welcome addition to the curriculum. It also supported one of the ministry's priority strategies that guided reform: "Improve the learning environment to one which is enjoyable and free of worries" (MEXT 2002, 7).

Students may have enjoyed IS, but what academic benefits did they derive from participating in these activities? Did the above lessons improve students' basic scholastic proficiency, as MEXT hoped they would?

The guest instructor began the river-ecology lesson with a formal lecture during which he presented key concepts related to the topic. Students then used the knowledge they had acquired to conduct a clearly defined laboratory investigation. Finally, they filled out a worksheet that required them to synthesize their findings. The instructional methods employed by the instructor conformed to those MEXT encouraged teachers to use as they enacted the 2002 Course of Study. The laboratory component of the lesson was hands-on and student centered; pupils drew their own conclusions based on the evidence they collected. Third, students investigated an issue directly relevant to the community in which they resided. The instructor's attention to scientific content knowledge would appease critics who argue that relaxed education lacks intellectual rigor. From my perspective, the river-ecology activity was both more stimulating and cognitively demanding than simply reviewing the contents of a textbook chapter. Not only was the visitor qualified to speak about river ecology, his understanding of the topic was deeper than that of the homeroom teacher. He augmented both student enthusiasm for science and their knowledge about water.

The academic benefits of the rice-planting field trip were more ambiguous. Students did enjoy spending the afternoon in the field with their classmates, but what did they learn from the experience? The activity contrasted with traditional academic lessons more sharply than the river-ecology laboratory did. Students spent the entire time outside, engaged in physical labor. They did not pick up a pencil or take any notes. Measuring the knowledge students acquired over the course of the unit, however, was challenging. There was no established body of factual knowledge that pupils were expected to master. In their informal comments and oral presentations, children did share insightful comments about rice planting, but the teacher's assessment of those observations was more subjective than for subjects like math and Japanese language. The fifth graders had been studying rice harvesting for several weeks and had visited the *tambo* at each stage of the process. The teacher organized the unit in this way so that her pupils would develop an understanding of the stages of rice cultivation, a sense of ownership for the rice field, and an appreciation of the efforts of local farmers. Rather than simply read about rice production in a social studies textbook, they explored the concept through active engagement with the land and members of their community.

Relaxed education was conceived of as an antidote to the negative repercussions of systemic overemphasis on standardized testing. Both of the lessons described above met the objectives for IS established by MEXT. According to one policy document, "Experiences in natural and social contexts are vital for enhancing mental and physical activity. Children gain a hearty 'zest for living' through both mind and body as they undergo moments of excitement, surprise, frustration, and success during their interactions with nature and society" (MEXT 2004). Students who tested water samples and worked in the rice field deepened their knowledge of the topics they were investigating through hands-on explorations. Children's comments and actions confirmed that the activities also aroused the types of emotional responses described in the MEXT report. Not all the IS activities I observed were as experiential as the two analyzed here. But at the three elementary schools I studied, teachers consistently implemented lessons that followed MEXT guidelines related to the focus, structure, and delivery of IS curricula. And students felt that IS was more exciting and engaging than core academic subjects, which was how education officials hoped they would react.

Reports published over the past decade by the USDOE in support of data-driven instruction and school accountability measures suggest that high-stakes tests are an essential component of school reform. The NCLB relies on examinations to enhance teacher investment in their work. Japanese elementary schools offer another perspective on how to motivate educators. Those institutions used teacher autonomy rather than a set of test-based rewards and sanctions to augment teacher investment in their work. The elementary educators in my sample consistently capitalized on that autonomy to design lessons that fit the unique needs of their students. There is no guarantee that teachers working in other settings would behave similarly, but the evidence I collected calls into question the notion that high stakes are an essential component of academic excellence. In the elementary schools I observed, which downplayed the significance of quantitative measures of achievement, teachers worked diligently to challenge and motivate their pupils.

Children's Intellectual Development

That is not to say that primary school employees wholeheartedly embraced *yutori kyoiku*. Though I did not witness any overt resistance to reform at the elementary level, many teachers remained skeptical about the merits of relaxed education, even as they faithfully followed the government's plans for change. Consonance between curriculum guidelines for IS and their implementation in the schools masked underlying tensions experienced by educators. Even as they oversaw events such as excursions to rice fields, many teachers wondered if relaxed education was the appropriate antidote to the difficulties experienced by their students, as the following conversation with a teacher from another school in my sample illustrates:

MRS. ARAKI (FIRST-GRADE TEACHER): A lot has changed since I started teaching. As the Course of Study was revised, we had to delay introduction of many concepts until later in the years. For example, kids used to study three-dimensional shapes in 6th grade, but now they do that in middle school. The curriculum has gotten too easy. Kids barely have any homework. They don't spend a lot of time in their desks studying. This is not only a result of changes in the curriculum. There are many influences. But it is an important factor.

CB: Is that a good thing or a bad thing?

MRS. ARAKI: Well, it's easier for the kids, but they need a strong academic foundation. For example, do you know about Integrated Studies? I really like IS, but the idea was that students would apply what they learned from other topics, using discovery learning. That's a good idea, but if you don't have good basic academic skills, it is very hard to do. Sixth graders study rice fields for IS [at my school]. This would be a good opportunity for them to use math skills in a real-life situation. They could calculate the area of a rice field

> or figure out how much rice a field of a certain size would produce. But if they haven't learned the formula for finding the area of a parallelogram, they can't do that. Also, IS takes up time in the schedule that used to be set aside for math and Japanese. So there is less time to teach that material.

Mrs. Araki's reflections capture a general sense of unease shared by elementary school educators working in all the schools I visited. Their concerns often overlapped with those expressed by public critics of *yutori kyoiku*. According to those critics, Japanese children had been set on a journey that was leading to a steep cliff, with no alternate route in sight; as a result of cuts to the Course of Study, students would be deprived of the solid academic foundation that had driven the nation's economic progress during the postwar economic boom. Such anxiety about academic preparedness had clearly affected teachers like Mrs. Araki. When they spoke broadly about the challenges confronting contemporary children and schools, their comments were tinged with concern and skepticism.

Yet when educators shifted from general remarks about the state of Japanese youths to more specific descriptions of the students in their classes, they usually described their students' capabilities in more positive terms. Prompted to clarify the particular difficulties their pupils exhibited or to point out children who were struggling, teachers often added qualifications to criticisms they had expressed previously. For example, after a fourth-grade teacher told me that her students' mathematical skills were weak, I asked her what kinds of problems they found most difficult. She responded that "everyone can do the skills, but not all of them are fast. That is why I am going to spend some extra time with long division until they improve." In a discussion that explored similar territory, a sixth-grade instructor told me that he had seen a steady decline in students' math skills. When I encouraged him to say more about this decline, the man said, "Well, there are a couple [of children] I am worried about. The problem isn't their intelligence but their ability to concentrate." A third instructor observed that "Japanese schools focus on bringing everyone up to a basic level, spending a lot of time on the basics. That is a strength, but it sometimes doesn't meet the needs of advanced kids."

These comments point to an unacknowledged duality in the opinions about flexible education articulated by many elementary school educators. Most interviewees conveyed concerns about the scholastic performance of contemporary children; but when pressed to identify the particular weaknesses of their own students, teachers conceded that their apprehensions were confined to a small number of pupils—and that those children's difficulties were often more psychological than academic in nature. Furthermore, while such comments were shared in response to questions about *yutori kyoiku*, it was not clear that changes in the Course of Study were responsible for the changes that troubled them.

The absence of achievement test data made it difficult to analyze educators' claims about the academic performance of their students or to compare the performance of the pupils in my sample schools to those in other parts of country. At the time of my fieldwork, MEXT encouraged—but did not require—schools to administer norm-referenced tests for mathematics and Japanese language, and many school districts opted out of this process. In addition, the schools that distributed the tests were not willing to share the results with me, citing privacy concerns. I did, however, observe students in the classroom on a daily basis. I conducted a total of 162 formal observations of lessons in elementary schools, and countless informal short visits to classes and nonacademic activities.[2] The extensive time I spent in classrooms gave me a good sense of the demands placed upon the children in those rooms, as well as their academic strengths and weaknesses.

I was impressed by the consistently high level of work produced by elementary school students. One of the most difficult challenges I faced as a primary school teacher in the United States was accommodating students with vastly different academic needs and capabilities; those were already visible in the first grade and became more pronounced as children moved up the grades. Within a group of twenty-five second or third graders, there were likely to be a handful of students who scored two years above grade level, and an equal number of pupils two or more years below grade level. In the Japanese classrooms I visited, the spread between high- and low-achieving students was much narrower. More important, almost all students at each grade level had developed a solid basic foundation in literacy and numeracy that allowed them to participate in daily instructional activities without special assistance. For example, by the end of their initial year of school, all the first-grade students enrolled at the three elementary schools in my sample had mastered *hiragana* (the first of three alphabets introduced to Japanese children) and could read simple stories with confidence; they also had a good grasp of their addition and subtraction facts. It was quite unusual to meet a fourth grader who had not memorized the multiplication tables or could not complete long-division problems with accuracy.[3]

One limitation of this project is that I observed the students at my core schools for only a year. I did not track their academic development over the course of their elementary school careers. It is possible that the demands placed on students at those schools—as well mastery of the curriculum—were greater prior to introduction of the 2002 Course of Study. A longitudinal study might shed light on this issue. Nevertheless, the students I studied were challenged to complete exercises that were, from my perspective, developmentally appropriate. At each grade level, teachers assigned cognitively demanding assignments and structured learning activities so that even students who may have lacked confidence could succeed. Instructors exposed students to a range of concrete experiences before moving to abstract concepts. The supportive learning environments they created made it possible for children to feel a sense of accomplishment in all curricular areas, without experiencing test-related pressures.

In addition, the teachers I observed adeptly responded to the challenges presented by individuals whose academic or social skills were not at the level of their classmates. Through careful planning and monitoring of student behavior, educators kept even the most demanding children engaged in the daily flow of classroom activity. They created learning environments in which students were constantly challenged—but also received the support necessary to complete demanding tasks. Learning was active and social. When children struggled, their classmates usually offered assistance. Teachers hovered at the perimeter and stepped in when individuals did not receive the support they need from their peers.

Would additional quantitative data have allowed me to draw more precise conclusions about students' academic progress? Yes. But requiring schools to administer standardized achievement tests annually—as is now required in the United States—would consume valuable instructional time. It could also undermine the autonomy that allows Japanese teachers to experiment with innovative instructional approaches. Proponents of increased accountability in US schools frequently take a "more is more" approach to educational reform. Their arguments are premised on the idea that generating larger sets of data will lead to more effective instructional planning. As one Teach for America instructor once announced at a panel I had organized, "I don't know how I would get to know my kids without data." But the performance of Japanese elementary educators problematizes that assumption. The teachers I observed developed a deep understanding of their students that was not informed by standardized test scores. Instead, they shaped the curriculum to fit the needs of pupils that became apparent to them through close observation, ongoing conversations, and attention to children's participation in daily classroom activities.

As a result of this carefully woven support net, the overall level of success in elementary school classrooms was quite high. Even students whom teachers expressed concern about managed to keep pace with their classmates. The sense of accomplishment these students derived in school encouraged them to continue investing in their studies. The combination of motivating instruction and careful oversight from teachers allowed most elementary school students to meet or exceed their potential. Adults may have found fault with changes in the instructional program they had observed in recent years, but I was struck by the high percentage of children who acquired the core academic skills identified by MEXT as perquisites for future success.

Factors Influencing Teachers' Investment in Reform

Most of the elementary school instructors in my sample displayed steady commitment to relaxed-education reform plans. They were often critical of certain facets of the government's plans for change—but they set aside those reservations when asked to implement the new Course of Study in their classrooms. Downplaying any concerns they may have had about the new curriculum, teachers implemented learning activities that supported

Table 5.2. Teacher opinion of integrated studies

Based on your experiences teaching Integrated Studies, how satisfied are you with the IS program?	Elementary school	Middle school
Completely dissatisfied (1)	0%	13%
Not very satisfied (2)	29%	33%
Neutral (3)	36%	33%
Fairly satisfied (4)	36%	20%
Completely satisfied (5)	0%	0%
Average Score	**3.07**	**2.60**

Table 5.3. Comparison of current and previous curriculum

How do you feel about the current curriculum, compared with the curriculum prior to the introduction of the Integrated Studies program?	Elementary school	Middle school
Completely dissatisfied (1)	0%	13%
Not very satisfied (2)	22%	33%
Neutral (3)	41%	47%
Fairly satisfied (4)	33%	7%
Completely satisfied (5)	4%	0%
Average Score	**3.19**	**2.47**

the goals of *yutori kyoiku;* they consistently enhanced student enthusiasm for learning through hands-on investigations of topics relevant to the communities in which they lived.

What factors explain the elementary school teachers' willingness to follow MEXT plans for change, despite the uncertainty most of them felt about reform? Interviewees described in detail the challenges created by introduction of the 2002 Course of Study. However, educators working at the primary level tended to focus on logistical issues related to program implementation. The difficulties they found most taxing often related to scheduling, planning lessons, and obtaining instructional materials. Such concerns, though troublesome, could be overcome without disturbing the teachers' core beliefs about instruction. This helps to explain why, as tables 5.2 and 5.3 indicate, elementary school educators shared more positive assessments of IS than secondary teachers: they were more likely to discover that objectives of the IS program coincided with their own educational philosophies. In addition, the informal support they received from their colleagues, as well as more-directed professional development opportunities and primarily lesson study activities, helped them overcome the difficulties they faced. More experienced in interdisciplinary instruction, not as constricted by daily schedules, and more distanced from the entrance examination system than their counterparts working at the secondary school level, elementary instructors demonstrated steadier commitment to the IS program.

The ministry may have packaged *yutori kyoiku* as a significant departure from the status quo in schools, but in actuality, the extent of the changes elementary school teachers were required to make has been overstated in many reports on relaxed education. Applying Cuban's (1992) conceptualization of reform to this situation, the policies adopted by MEXT in support of *yutori kyoiku* qualified as *incremental reform* at the elementary school level. Cuban explains, "The premise behind incremental reform is that basic institutional structures are sound but need tinkering to remove defects and make their operations more effective and efficient" (228). *Yutori kyoiku* did not necessitate fundamental changes in the administrative structures or existing educational programs in the primary schools I studied. Instead, flexible education policies could be appended to the schools without disrupting established practices. Adjusting to a curriculum that had been trimmed did require some effort on the part of teachers, who were already quite busy. But relaxed education did not require them to master content or pedagogy that diverged significantly from what they were familiar with. In fact, I would argue that MEXT's prescriptions for reform could be regarded as validation of established practices in the elementary schools. Relaxed education was philosophically consonant with the principles that had guided elementary education for decades.

As DeCoker (2013) comments, research conducted from the late 1970s to the early 1990s produced "what is arguably the most sophisticated English-language body of comparative scholarship on the educational system of any country in the world" (5). This scholarship captures in detail the goals and structures of Japanese elementary schools, and highlights great continuity over the past thirty years (Hess and Azuma 1991; Lewis 1984; Shimahara and Sakai 1992; Stevenson 1991a; White 1987). Also apparent are the linkages between deeply rooted practices in the primary schools and MEXT prescriptions for *yutori kyoiku*. The "new academic abilities" (*shin gakuryokukan*) that MEXT presented as a critical element of relaxed-education reform may not have been so new after all. Elementary schools have a long history of encouraging students to form their own opinions about complex issues and to devise solutions to real-life problems. In 1995, for example, Lewis observed that instruction in Japanese elementary schools has traditionally been guided by "a view of children as active learners rather than simply passive recipients of information. This view recognizes that children have their own powerful ideas about how the world works—scientifically, socially, morally—and that learning must engage and shape those ideas, not simply superimpose information or procedures that children memorize and then forget" (176). As they followed the guidelines for relaxed education, elementary school instructors could draw from a trove of practical experience. Their familiarity with pedagogical methods that require students to take an active role in the construction of knowledge was invaluable as they translated MEXT plans for change into concrete learning activities.

My research calls into question the assertion that adoption of the relaxed-education policies triggered a system-wide state of crisis. The elementary schools I studied cultivated the academic abilities and mental dispositions identified by both conservative and progressive critics as those required for success in contemporary society. Students learned to think critically, to conduct investigations of compelling questions, to solve problems collaboratively, and to apply their knowledge to real-life problems. Furthermore, teachers promoted those skills through learning activities that were both challenging and appealing to children. Introduction of the 2002 Course of Study did create some logistical challenges for instructors, but they could proceed without reconceptualizing their views of teaching and learning. Neoconservative critics might be surprised at the enduring nature of the elementary school in the midst of widespread social change. As I illustrate in the next chapter, however, middle school teachers approached reform plans with experiences and expectations that differed from elementary educators in several key respects.

SIX

Responses to Change in the Middle Schools

Plans for reform as well as analysis of education change initiatives implemented in Japan should give serious consideration to the multifaceted nature of what is often regarded as a unified, highly centralized system. Few reports on relaxed education have examined the effects of the reforms on different levels of schools. Yet elementary and secondary schools are organized to fit distinct goals, institutional structures, curricula, and students. Cognizant of this situation, I studied pairs of schools in each of the three communities included in my core sample. Each day, I spent half of an instructional day in an elementary school and the other half in the middle school that served the same neighborhood.[1] In this chapter, I examine the influences that shaped middle school teachers' responses to the relaxed-education reforms. As I will show, middle school instructors often struggled to reconcile the actions they were being asked to perform with practices that had been in place for decades.

As was true at the primary level, some middle school teachers agreed with the goals of *yutori kyoiku*; many did not. The institutional contexts in which they worked created obstacles that made it difficult for even those in agreement with the reform objectives to fully support the policies that had been adopted. Designing hands-on, student-centered lessons created extensive challenges for middle school instructors. Deeply rooted notions about the role that secondary education plays in the trajectory of a student's career—as well as practical considerations that organized instructors' daily lives—conflicted with the plans for change MEXT had established for them. During the six years I conducted fieldwork for this project, I did not visit a single middle school where a cadre of teachers committed to relaxed education provided the leadership necessary to produce long-lasting change. Instead, what I witnessed was a combination of unenthusiastic compliance with MEXT directives, confusion, frustration, and resistance.

New Components of the 2002 Middle School Curriculum

The demands the relaxed-education policies placed on middle school teachers resembled those exerted on their counterparts working in the elementary schools in several respects. The most significant change for them, too, was the requirement that they create and enact new Integrated Studies (IS) courses. To make room for IS, instructional hours were trimmed from other subjects. Although the number of hours allocated to IS instruction at various grade levels differed slightly, the process of curriculum design was similar: groups of teachers studied MEXT reports about the objectives of IS, surveyed students to determine possible themes of IS units, and developed broad curricular outlines. As MEXT advised, they did not develop those units in great detail. Instead, they were encouraged to consider the unique interests of their students and features of the surrounding community as they outlined the IS curriculum. Although all the teachers I interviewed understood the goals of IS, not all were assigned to teach the subject. That responsibility was one of many that could be assigned to faculty members. In theory, those duties would be balanced so that everyone had roughly equal workloads.

At the institutions I visited, the themes of middle school IS units frequently overlapped with those selected by elementary school teachers. This is not surprising, considering that (1) elementary and middle school educators rarely shared information about what they taught; and (2) all schools were encouraged to shape the IS curriculum to fit local industry, culture, and history. Schools located in a fishing village were likely to include fishing-related topics in the IS curriculum, regardless of the age of their students. Many of the IS themes mentioned in the previous chapter (noodle making, rice cultivation, ecology) were also investigated by middle school students. One notable addition, however, was the topic of career exploration. In either their second or third year of middle school, most students spent some time conducting research on potential career pathways.

An additional change introduced in conjunction with relaxed education was the expansion of the elective subject curriculum (*sentaku no jugyo*).[2] Although electives were already a standard feature of the secondary curriculum, beginning in 2002, middle schools were required to increase the number of instructional hours set aside for electives. As was the case with

IS, not all members of a faculty were required to teach electives. At all three middle schools in my sample, students could select from a menu of elective offerings.

The structure of the elective courses I observed varied noticeably, depending on the goals, capacities, and personalities of the instructors. At the beginning of the semester, for instance, a math teacher explained to her second-year students enrolled in an elective course, "We will focus on reviewing concepts introduced in regular math classes and on test preparation. We will do lots of drills and problem-solving practice, go over strategies for approaching different types of problems . . . This is a class for people who would like to be challenged." At the same school, another teacher assigned the students in her elective course to create photo albums that could be used to introduce the school to visitors; students spent most of their time walking around the school taking pictures and writing captions to accompany those photographs.

The system of assessing learning in IS as well as elective classes was different from that used to evaluate their progress in core academic subjects. Instead of being graded on a scale of 1–5, students received letter grades, which did not factor into high school admissions decisions.

Responses to *Yutori Kyoiku* in the Middle Schools

Middle school teachers' opinions about the overarching goals of relaxed education did coincide with those expressed by elementary instructions in many respects, but the issues they found most challenging as they attempted to implement the new curriculum were different. Although logistical details complicated the work of secondary educators, they tended not to focus on matters related to scheduling or instructional materials when they reflected on the impact of relaxed-education policies. They were more eager to discuss issues connected to instructional practice and their relationships with students that recent curricular changes brought to the surface. Middle school teachers' comments revealed that adoption of the *yutori kyoiku* policies had instigated a process of self-examination and interrogation that many found troubling. The challenges triggered by recent reforms fell into three broad categories: intellectual, pedagogical, and philosophical.

Intellectual

Though MEXT presented teacher autonomy as an empowering idea, instructors sometimes regarded the increased responsibility over the curriculum that had been delegated to them as intimidating. In contrast with primary teachers, secondary instructors generally viewed themselves as subject specialists. Educators working in middle schools were grounded in time-honored methods, curriculum outlines, and culturally constructed conceptions of how to teach a particular subject. Social studies instructors, for instance, could consult the Course of Study and textbooks as they prepared for their core classes. The concepts students were expected to master at each grade level were thoroughly identified in the Course of Study and reinforced in textbooks. That combination of clarity and uniformity provided the individuals I interviewed with a sense of security as they approached their work.

When educators prepared for IS courses, in contrast, they often felt as if they were operating on shaky ground. As mentioned earlier, because there are no disciplinary boundaries limiting the material that can be covered in IS lessons, a teacher whose specialty is mathematics or music might be asked to oversee a study of environmental science. Teaching IS courses frequently forced instructors face the reality that they did not have a strong base of knowledge in all the topics that students were investigating. In some cases, their knowledge of a topic was no deeper than that of their pupils. As one interviewee observed, "Sometimes I cannot answer their questions or provide them with the information they need." This discovery upset many teachers, who were confronted by questions about their intellectual capabilities, which was not usually the case they when they taught their primary subject.

Overseeing elective activities also required extensive subject-level mastery and pedagogical flexibility, for those lessons frequently pushed educators into unknown territory. Middle school teachers, who were inclined to rely on more transmission-oriented instructional approaches, tended to find this reality more troubling than their colleagues working in elementary schools. Some of the secondary instructors used their broad intelligence or self-confidence to overcome the obstacles that surfaced in the course of teaching electives. Others struggled to follow MEXT plans for the new curriculum; they might have had the capacity to skillfully implement a lesson outlined in a textbook, but coming up with an original learning activity that challenged and engaged students was another matter. The product of such uncertainty was often independent study periods or hastily organized review of previously introduced concepts. (See chapter 7, "Curricular Reform, Academic Achievement, and Educational Opportunity," for more detail.)

The intellectual insecurities provoked by introduction of the 2002

Course of Study were compounded by the individualistic orientation that many instructors applied to IS and elective curriculum development. Scholars such as Lewis (1995) and Fernandez (2002) have lauded Japanese teachers' mastery of the subjects they teach and the attention they devote to honing their instructional skills over time. Stigler and Hiebert (1999) also underscore the benefits that flow from collaborative planning and professional development, especially in the area of mathematics. However, for logistical as well as personal reasons, most of the middle school teachers I observed worked primarily in isolation as they developed and implemented elective curricula. This seemed counterintuitive, given the extensive demands associated with teaching elective subjects. But only rarely did multiple instructors teach the same elective subject matter, and school professional development activities—such as lesson study—generally focused on the core curriculum. As a result, elective instructors had few resources to draw from when things did not go according to plan.

Pedagogical

Middle school teachers also expressed apprehension about the instructional methods advocated in reform guidelines. The inquiry-based, student-centered model of learning MEXT was promoting in support of relaxed education left many people confused about their roles in the classroom. Scholars have noted that Japanese teachers often minimize their contributions to learning activities so that students will assume more responsibility for their own learning (Lewis 1995; Sato 1991; Stevenson 1991b). That research, however, focuses primarily on practices in elementary schools. In addition, when instructors facilitate student-centered learning activities, they often follow an outline of how learning activities might unfold. With IS and electives, the boundaries and final products of lessons were more indefinite. This ambiguity made many teachers I spoke with uncomfortable. The implications of the reforms recently adopted by the ministry proved disquieting to many interviewees, for they could not always apply practices they had used in the past to the 2002 curriculum. Scholarship on pedagogical reform suggests that the challenges they experienced were not unique. According to Cohen and Spillane (1993), when educators attempt to make the shift from pedagogue to "coach or conductor," they often experience "unusual difficulty, for teachers must manage complex interactions about complex ideas in rapid-fire succession. The uncertainties of teaching multiply phenomenally, as does teachers' vulnerability" (70).

In the middle schools I studied, relationships between students and teachers were visibly asymmetrical: instructors were treated as experts responsible for delivering knowledge to their pupils. IS units, on the other hand, tended to center on independent student research projects. According to MEXT recommendations, adults were expected to support—not lead—students as they searched for information relevant to their topics. Teachers did not always welcome this reconfiguration. Many were uneasy about relinquishing authority over learning activities. Because students spent such a significant amount of time in IS classes working independently, instructors were not always sure how they should be assisting their pupils. Encouraging teachers to shift from a disseminator of knowledge to a facilitator of student discovery may have seemed like a laudatory goal to outside observers, but middle school teachers who were used to controlling the flow of information often struggled to keep their input to a minimum.

MEXT emphasized that elective offerings should be tailored to fit the interests and academic needs of students at a particular school. Teachers who took that advice seriously often became frustrated when the approaches recommended in policy reports did not produce their desired outcomes. Translating MEXT's plans for pedagogical innovation proved challenging for the instructors I observed, and the institutional cultures in which they operated did not always offer the support or rewards necessary to impel lasting changes in their behavior. As was true with IS, elective offerings sounded much more appealing on paper than in practice. When teachers experimented with pedagogical techniques and were met with disappointing results, they tended to revert to methods that had brought them success in the past. As a result, a section of the curriculum designed to bolster student enthusiasm for learning actually reinforced the belief among most secondary teachers that highly structured, teacher-directed instruction was the most effective way to organize their classes. The lesson described in the next section captures the sense of frustration many middle school instructors experienced as they implemented the new curriculum.

A Ninth-Grade Science Elective

Mr. Takahashi bursts into the room and announces to the thirty-one ninth-grade students (twenty-seven girls and four boys) that he hasn't quite finished preparing for this class, but he will be ready soon. Seven minutes later, he returns carrying a plastic tub loaded with materials, which he places on the table in the front of the room. As he organizes the materials, Mr. Takahashi informs the class that although electives are fairly new in Japan, "some people think they will end next year. Sometimes electives become a time to play, not to study. Some schools have replaced elective time with Japanese and English classes. We need to protect the electives. Today I am going to show you how to use chemical reactions to make some traditional Japanese sweets." The eight students sitting in the back row chat through the entire introduction.

After writing the directions for the activity on the front board, Mr. Takahashi models the procedure for students. He fills a beaker with water and holds up all the materials they will need. Throughout the room, students converse as they fill their beakers with water. It becomes difficult to make out Mr. Takahashi's words. Frustrated, Mr. Takahashi announces, "I am trying my hardest today, so please listen." The volume of chatter, however, does not go down. After surveying students, he decides to end his introduction early.

The room is composed of ten lab stations, each with a black slab top and a sink. Three or four ninth graders are seated at each station, heating sugar over a flame to create caramel lollipops. Mr. Takahashi checks on each group and gives advice as necessary, which is often. At several points he stops to prod students, physically as well as verbally, in attempt them to make them focus on the activity. The procedure is not complicated, but most of the students seem more interested in socializing than in science.

I leave my seat in the back of the room and circulate through the room to see how the students are doing. Almost all of them have successfully completed the task. I ask one group of girls what they think of this class. They all tell me they like it. I ask them why they chose this particular elective course, and they respond that they wanted to do experiments. Another group informs me that they signed up for this class because they like science. Next, I proceed to the group made up of four boys. The boys reflect that they do not find science particularly interesting, but they like the idea of completing hands-on experiments. They like this class because they do not have to take any tests and do not receive grades like in other classes, which reduces the pressure they experience.

Thirty minutes into the period, almost all the students have finished working on the activity and are now chatting about other things. It appears that about two-thirds of the students successfully created lollipops and are enjoying the fruits of their labor. One group of boys, I notice, made a mistake and did not produce lollipops. They do not appear upset about this. They are laughing and talking about a recent school basketball game. The atmosphere in the room is light and carefree. But what exactly have the students learned? A majority of them did produce the assigned product, but it is not clear that they understood the scientific reasons for what occurred. If students were truly motivated, they could have extended their understanding of chemical reactions, but I do not witness any evidence of such intellectual probing. Instead, they appear to have followed the steps of the procedure like they would a recipe, without considering why the sugar changed form.

I join Mr. Takahashi, who is perched at the front of the room, and ask him about the lesson he delivered and about electives in general. After pausing to think, he explains,

> The idea of electives is good—that students interested in a particular topic can study them in more depth. But what usually happens is that the time is not taken seriously and kids just fool around. I think it would be better to use the time for regular subject instruction. Electives are not a good use of time. Also, they require a lot of preparation on the part of teachers. This is especially true of science because teachers are expected to come up with interesting hands-on activities that promote discovery learning for every class. That takes a lot of time and is expensive. The preparation demands are not as extensive as for other subjects . . . but I think teachers of those subjects would agree that it would be better to use elective time for regular classes.

Mr. Takahashi adds that some kids get a lot out of these classes—the ones interested in the subject—but others do the minimum amount of work required and use the rest of class time to play. Next year, he informs me, his school will use the time currently set aside for electives to provide additional instruction in basic academic skills. He thinks this will be a positive change.

Despite these words of optimism, Mr. Takahashi teacher seems deflated at the end of this lesson.

Consequences of Teacher Uncertainty

Although, as I note above, middle school teachers tended to agree with the goals of the new curriculum, they were often hesitant to make changes that had the potential to undermine students' mastery of basic academic skills. "I think elementary school teachers are very enthusiastic about IS," one middle school teacher told me, "but it's more difficult for us. There's so much pressure to develop the academic abilities of our students." Tensions between their ideals about the purposes of education and the realities of the academic hierarchy in which they worked made it difficult for many instructors to fully invest in a reform agenda that depended on their commitment and labor. For educators like Mr. Takahashi, initial enthusiasm for *yutori kyoiku* dimmed as their efforts to implement the new curriculum created additional work and stress, yet did not produce clear benefits.

Adoption of the 2002 Course of Study produced an initial surge of interest among middle school teachers, who were intrigued by MEXT's plans for reducing academic pressure. In all of the middle schools I visited, teachers spent long hours examining the relaxed-education policies and constructing IS and elective curricula. At a hypothetical level, the changes recommended by the ministry made sense. Instructors were concerned about a wide range of disconcerting changes in Japanese children, which ranged from a lack of interest in studying to poor interpersonal skills. The idea of creating a more relaxed and engaging curriculum may have appealed to teachers when discussed abstractly, but their enthusiasm often faded after they began translating curricular guidelines into concrete learning activities. Rarely did their plans produce the desired outcomes. Furthermore, offering IS and electives consumed time that could have been devoted to activities with more tangible results and rewards. These discoveries produced a steady erosion of support for *yutori kyoiku* in the middle schools. Educators who had once displayed an openness to change began to question, resist, and subvert flexible education policies.

Loyally adhering to reform guidelines was not likely to bring middle school teachers tangible rewards or raise their status. Most secondary school instructors believed that providing test-driven instruction was the most dependable way of satisfying parents and administrators. As a result, while some middle school teachers remained determined to surmount the challenges associated with relaxed education, they were outnumbered by colleagues with serious misgivings about the changes they had been encouraged to make. When this was the case, teachers revised policy guidelines to fit their own objectives or followed curricular guidelines at a surface level. In some locations, teachers blatantly ignored MEXT decrees.

Although the Course of Study specified the number of hours that should be allocated to each subject in the curriculum, teachers found ways to subvert this direction and use time ostensibly set aside for IS and elective courses to cover more explicitly academic subject matter. The autonomy entrusted to Japanese instructors made it possible for them to do this without provoking criticism or punishment. Teachers did not hesitate to adjust the schedule to fit personal and institutional goals. In some middle schools IS units were only scheduled intermittently during the year, when time permitted; on other campuses, class hours designated as IS or electives on the official schedule were actually used for other purposes, as one interviewee admitted:

> Mr. Aoyama (seventh-grade English teacher): To be honest, we don't always teach what we're supposed to. We don't have enough time in the schedule to teach math, so we use that morning IS time for math. If we don't use that time for math, we have to find other time to teach math. We can also use cleaning time for instruction—fifteen minutes a day adds another hour to the schedule.

At another middle school, IS instructional time disappeared from the weekly schedule prior to major examination periods.

When their plans for the expanded electives curriculum did not produce their desired results, two of the three middle schools in my sample instituted changes that signaled that elective courses, as defined by MEXT, were no longer a priority. At one institution, the faculty discarded its menu of elective choices in favor of an approach it called "worksheet studies" (*printo gakushu*). Teachers no longer facilitated hands-on activities designed to kindle student interest in those subjects; instead, they distributed worksheets that reviewed concepts previously covered in the regular curriculum that were likely to appear on high school entrance tests. At another middle school, teachers used time ostensibly set aside for electives to offer additional mathematics, Japanese, and English classes. Although the curriculum was not altered on paper, the elective program effectively ceased to exist.

At these two schools, I did speak with teachers who were dismayed by the changes to the curriculum that had been instituted. For example, one veteran teacher remarked, "I don't like this new system. It doesn't follow the spirit of the reform program because kids don't get to pick their elective subjects." Dissonant voices, however, were in the minority. Most of the educators I interviewed felt that modifying the Course of Study was justified. As one instructor commented, "Although the school will still offer a subject called 'electives,' the school—not the students—will decide how the time will be used. That time will be used for the regular curriculum. It's a creative way to get around the rules. I think it will be a good change." In my interviews with middle school instructors, complaints about the difficulties associated with following the MEXT's reform plans drowned out expressions of support for relaxed education. The vast majority of educators working at this level focused on their teaching responsibilities in their core academic areas, and invested minimal effort in IS and elective courses.

Idealism Meets Reality

The middle school teachers I studied clearly understood MEXT's goals for relaxed education. When speaking about educational reform abstractly, most concurred with the rationale put forth by the ministry in support of *yutori kyoiku*. But when challenged to implement reform policies in their schools, educators' views about change often shifted. While some middle school teachers firmly supported MEXT's reform agenda, a sizeable majority remained skeptical about the policies that had been adopted. Many had trouble reconciling the discovery-oriented instructional approaches advocated in reform guidelines with the lecture-and-test methods they had relied on in the past.

Few of the middle school instructors I observed were as well versed in student-centered learning techniques as their counterparts working in the elementary schools. Whereas many primary school teachers instinctively turned to hands-on activities to introduce new concepts, for middle school instructors, teaching in this way did not come as naturally. In the context of the Japanese secondary school, such emphasis on student discovery of knowledge constituted "teaching against the grain" (Simon 1992). Seventy-three percent of all academic lessons I observed in middle schools were teacher centered, with no attempt made to encourage group work or student discovery. At the elementary school level, in contrast, fifty-five percent of the lessons were student centered (See table 6.1).[3]

The prevalence of teacher-centered instruction may be surprising to some readers, given the emphasis on group activity in Japanese culture (Nakane 1986; Moeran 1986). In the middle schools I observed, students were frequently assigned to work in groups. Such collaboration, however, most often took place during homeroom meetings, extracurricular activities, and special events (such as class trips or school festivals). Teachers may have recognized the benefits of having pupils work in teams, but their support for collaboration did not extend to all aspects of school life. In the core academic subjects, instructors often hesitated to take pedagogical risks. Their primary concern was covering material clearly and efficiently, and direct instruction was the most reliable method of delivering that material.

Research published prior to adoption of the relaxed-education policies indicates that the instructional practices I observed in middle schools have deep roots. Based on fieldwork she completed in Tokyo during the 1980s, Fukuzawa (1994) relates that Japanese middle school teachers "rarely deviated very far or very long from the text. Unlike teachers in the United

Table 6.1. Instructional approaches in academic lessons

	Student active/ group work	Teacher-centered/ lecture
Elementary school	55%	45%
Middle school	27%	73%

Table 6.2. Instructional approaches in IS/elective lessons

	Student active/ group work	Teacher-centered/ lecture
Elementary school	100%	0%
Middle school	75%	25%

States, who often tailor texts to local needs and their own teaching style, Japanese teachers are forced to adhere to the text because (1) the pace required to cover the material does not leave time for extras and (2) the national curriculum is the basis of high school entrance exams" (297). To support this assertion, Fukuzawa notes that in only one out of the 103 lessons she observed did a teacher assign students to work in small groups to discuss the relevance of a reading; in academic subjects, only science labs included "student-centered or experimental teaching methods" (300).[4]

It was not always clear to me whether a teacher I observed had the capacity to design and implement a lesson that emphasized the student acquisition of knowledge rather than the transmission of facts—or if that instructor had reservations about the value of that instructional approach. For most middle school instructors, will and capacity were tightly linked, and the lack of will frequently undercut an educator's disposition to experiment with unfamiliar pedagogy.

Individuals may have had the potential to become effective facilitators of student-centered learning if they were offered sufficient incentives. Yet, due to their skepticism about the wisdom of what they were being asked to do, very few individuals were willing to invest the time and effort necessary to surmount the difficulties they experienced as they implemented the new Course of Study. When faced with either logistical challenges (e.g., lack of sufficient planning time) or disappointing results in the classroom, teachers revised policy guidelines to fit their own objectives for students or followed plans for *yutori kyoiku* at a surface level. In some locations, educators blatantly ignored MEXT decrees.

Incremental versus Fundamental Reform

In chapter 5, I posit that in the elementary school context, relaxed-education policies constituted an incremental reform that required only minor adjustments to existing structures and programs. The situation was quite different in the middle schools. The resistance to reform displayed by middle school educators underscored the acuteness of the changes they were asked to make. Realizing MEXT plans for *yutori kyoiku* at the secondary level required much more than adjusting the weekly schedule or ordering a new set of books. As I have documented, adoption of the relaxed-education policies forced middle school teachers to confront thorny questions about their responsibilities in the classroom, relationships with students, and identities as educators. Informants found this process intimidating—sometimes troubling. Instructors often discovered that the philosophies and instructional approaches that the ministry was promoting clashed with their own visions of effective instruction. Established practices in their schools presented additional barriers to change.

The depth of the change required of educators working in these schools suggests that relaxed education constituted a *fundamental reform* at the secondary level. Fundamental reforms "aim to transform and alter permanently . . . institutional structures. The premise behind fundamental reforms is that basic structures are irremediably flawed and need a complete overhaul, not renovations" (Cuban 1992, 228). MEXT endorsed a set of changes (eliminating Saturday classes, reducing the contents of the Course of Study, expanding elective offerings, introducing Integrated Studies to the curriculum, and encouraging teachers to alter their pedagogical practices) in the attempt to instigate critical changes in the way the curriculum was organized and delivered. On many levels, *yutori kyoiku* challenged principles that had anchored middle schools for decades. And MEXT was depending on the commitment and effort of teachers to realize its vision for change.

Fullan and Miles (1992) maintain that for an education reform to produce systemic change, it must meet two conditions: (1) the initiative must focus on the development and interrelationships of all the primary components of the system simultaneously; and (2) it must also address deeper issues related to the culture of the system. More specifically, the individuals responsible for implementing reform should be supported as they adjust to the new structures and modifications to their professional responsibilities. Neglecting either of these factors can result in symbolic rather than substantive change. According to Fullan and Miles (1992), "individuals faced with something new need to assess the change for its genuine possibilities and for how it bears on their self-interest" (748). Convincing teachers to alter their pedagogical practice is unlikely to prove successful unless the core structure of the system in which they operate also undergoes both "restructuring" and "reculturing" (ibid., 751).

This scholarship sheds light on the responses to the relaxed-education policies among the middle school teachers I interviewed and observed. After the *yutori kyoiku* policies were adopted, educators carefully studied the implications of those policies on their own work and on student learning. They evaluated the prudence of the plans crafted by education bureaucrats with reference to conditions on their school campuses and attitudes in the surrounding communities. Rather than adjust their behavior to fit MEXT guidelines, middle employees continued to shape decisions to fit practices that had proven, over long periods of time, "consistent with the stable web of beliefs and assumptions that are part of the culture" (Stigler and Hiebert 1999, 87). Those beliefs and assumptions were tied to the exigencies of entrance examinations rather than to ideals about children's love for learning.

The result was, as Fullan and Miles might have a predicted, symbolic rather than substantive reform. Teachers in all three of the middle schools in my sample succeeded in repelling the changes MEXT was encouraging them to make. They may have conformed to ministry guidelines at a surface level, but their core activities and guiding principles were not altered in any significant way. New segments of the curriculum were modified to conform to priorities that had become institutionalized in the middle schools over decades. Those institutions continued to offer IS and electives, but the contents of those courses were revised so as to focus on material previously included in core academic subjects or homeroom activities. Students did not develop increased enthusiasm for learning or a deeper connection to their schools as a result of *yutori kyoiku*. Like most fundamental reforms, the relaxed-education policies did not gain the widespread support necessary to produce long-lasting change (Cuban 1992).

Differences across Levels

It is logical that the relaxed-education reforms provoked such different responses in elementary and middle schools, considering the distinctions that mark the different levels of an education system. LeTendre (2000), for example, has remarked that in both the United States and Japan, "there are significant changes in curriculum, instructional style, and norms of behavior associated with the transition from elementary school to middle school" (25). I concur with this observation—but would add that the changes LeTendre refers to are more severe in Japan. As students progress from elementary to middle school, they are expected to reorganize their behavior to align with new institutional contexts. The structure, pedagogical practices, and approaches to student guidance common to Japanese elementary schools are replaced by a markedly different set of practices in the middle schools. This is symbolically illustrated at the elementary school graduation ceremony, when pupils parade before the community in dark military-style middle school uniforms for the first time. This exchange of clothing foreshadows deeper changes to come. When they enter middle school, students must negotiate a new set of behavioral, academic, and social expectations. In other words, they must learn to function within a different institutional culture.

During the first year of middle school in Japan, those contrasts are not as apparent; the schools I studied treated the year as a liminal period during which students need extensive academic and emotional support. But in the following grade, most educational activity undergoes an abrupt shift. Instruction as well as guidance becomes firmly focused on preparation for high school entrance examinations. Teachers tend to employ instructional strategies that allow them to quickly cover large bodies of information. The group activities so common to elementary classrooms become increasingly rare. Instead, lecturing consumes a large percentage of class time, and students are advised to review concepts they don't understand at home. Instructors place greater emphasis on the recall of factual information—especially material that might appear on entrance examinations—than on student engagement in lessons. I was surprised at how frequently and explicitly instructors communicated this curricular hierarchy to their pupils. They often prefaced the introduction of a new concept with the words, "Pay attention because this might appear on an entrance examination." Concepts unlikely to be included on those examinations tended to be deemphasized or skipped.

The extent to which the contents of entrance examinations shapes curriculum and instruction in Japanese middle schools should be taken seriously to educators working in the United States, where the expansion of standardized testing requirements has begun to influence the behavior of teachers in similar ways. Although examinations are not yet as deeply engrained in the psyche of American educators, the hours allocated to instruction in language arts and mathematics has steadily increased over the past decade. As I describe in greater detail in chapter 9, since 2002, teachers in the United States have reduced the amount of time they devote to subjects such as history, science, foreign languages and the arts since 2002 (Groen 2012; McMurrer 2007; Sunderman et al. 2004). One study found that districts reduced the percentage of instructional time allocated to subjects not included on accountability tests by an average of 32% (USGAO 2009). Evidence collected in Japan and the United States underscores the strong influence that the contents of high-stakes examinations exerts on curricular planning. In both contexts, test-related pressures often lead teachers to make decisions that conflict with their professional knowledge and experience.

Another clear contrast between levels of the Japanese education system relates to the expectations assigned to students. In the elementary schools, teachers work closely with individual students and attempt to provide them with the academic and emotional support deemed necessary. In the middle schools, the role of the teacher shifts from supportive ally to respected authority figure. After instructors present knowledge to pupils, it becomes their responsibility to use that information appropriately. According to Fukuzawa (1994), "both compared to early elementary school in Japan and many American middle schools, instruction in Japanese middle school classes is soberingly intense, fact-filled, and routinized. Motivation must come from the student and self-discipline is at a premium" (66). For example, homework assignments are rarely collected or graded; it is up to students to gauge their progress and to review concepts that are not clear to them. Teachers convey to students—through practices such as this as well as explicit statements—that the effort they invest in their education will determine their academic opportunities.

Reducing academic pressure and enlivening the curriculum may have sounded appealing when discussed abstractly, but accomplishing these noble tasks proved arduous because of an inescapable reality: secondary schools are organized around a single focal point—the entrance examination. Individuals may not agree with the heavy influence that these tests exert on education decision making in Japan, but the priorities of secondary schools are clear to everyone. Compared to the process used to determine admission to boarding schools and colleges in the United States, the Japanese approach is more streamlined and unambiguous. That clarity makes it easier for students, parents, and teachers decide how to invest their energy and resources.

Yet within that system, not all individuals can succeed. The entrance examination process is organized to ensure that students are sorted into appropriate slots. If acceptance to a prestigious high school or university is to have any cache, the process must identify losers as well as winners. If all students were to pass the high school entrance examinations, the system would be thrown into disarray. Interestingly, when I was conducting fieldwork, education pundits regularly warned the public that due to the declining population, there would soon be enough places in institutions of higher education to accommodate all students who complete a high school education. The resulting alleviation of competition was viewed by many as a troubling development.

In this context, it makes a great deal of sense to shape one's behavior to fit the demands associated with seemingly omnipotent entrance examinations. The relaxed-education policies, however, were not aligned with the priorities of the middle schools. Indeed, efforts to reduce pressure and competition in the schools represented a challenge to the traditional secondary education system. And the responses to *yutori kyoiku* I have presented in this chapter accentuate the entrenched nature of that system. Elementary teachers managed to overcome the challenges they faced as they implemented the 2002 Course of Study because consonance between the goals of relaxed education and established practices in their schools allowed them to proceed with a sense of cautious optimism. Middle school teachers, on the other hand, were urged to invest time in designing and delivering courses disconnected from the core function of their institutions. Education officials maintained that investing in relaxed-education reform would enhance student enthusiasm for learning as well as their academic capacities, but middle school teachers tended to frame the two goals as in conflict. The individuals responsible for realizing reform plans often viewed those changes as undermining the academic mission of middle school education. This tension diminished teachers' commitment to relaxed education.

Yutori kyoiku was envisioned as a counterbalance to heavy emphasis on test-driven instruction. But the ultimate barometer of student success at the middle school level continues to be the scores they earn on high school entrance examinations. The secondary teachers I observed tended to set instructional priorities based on what was and was not included on those tests. As a result, goals related to personal growth and development were often set aside so that the schools could concentrate on test preparation. IS and elective lessons may have provided benefits to students, but those gains were unlikely to improve their chances of gaining admission to the high school of their choice. Because student mastery of concepts covered in IS and elective courses was not a factor in the admissions process, teachers did not worry about the possible negative ramifications of de-emphasizing these subjects.

SEVEN

Curricular Reform, Academic Achievement, and Educational Opportunity

In this chapter I continue to explore the effects of adoption of the *yutori kyoiku* policies on teaching and learning in the middle schools. More specifically, I consider the implications of teachers' questions about the links between relaxed education and academic achievement. The new Course of Study delegated unprecedented authority to educators to shape curricular content to fit the unique characteristics of their schools and communities. Teachers were encouraged to use that autonomy to enliven the curriculum so as to make studying more exciting for students, especially those who had been struggling in school.

MEXT asserted that the prevalence of problems experienced by Japanese youths necessitated reforms that could alleviate the pressures experienced by their students and to enhance their interest in learning. *Yutori kyoiku* initiatives also promoted "new academic abilities" (*shin gakuryokukan*)[1] required for success in contemporary society (Tsuneyoshi 2004a). Of particular concern to MEXT were the "considerable numbers of children who do not feel they can understand school lessons" (MEXT 2002, 20). To better meet the needs of low-achieving students, teachers were encouraged to implement "lessons that are easy to understand" (MEXT 2002, 27). Ideally, learning activities created to support *yutori kyoiku* would spark an interest in learning that would allow all students achieve success in school.

Yet, as I observe in chapter 6, middle school teachers rarely implemented the new curriculum according to plan. How did their translation of ministry reform guidelines influence student learning in the middle schools? And how did middle school students react to the relaxed-education curriculum? What were their perspectives on *yutori kyoiku*? Reports on the relaxed-education reforms rarely address the implications of the 2002 Course of Study on the opportunities delivered to different segments of the student population. Yet, as I document below, a set of initiatives crafted with the needs of underachieving students in mind exacerbated achievement gaps between high and low-performing students. To illustrate this pattern, I include descriptions of two middle school lessons—one IS and the other an elective—that I observed.

Education and Opportunity in Japan: A Historical Perspective

Questions related to the role that education plays in creating opportunity for Japanese citizens have interested researchers, domestic and foreign, for decades. Tominaga's (1969) analysis of the effects of parental education on the educational attainment of their children was one of the first such studies. Since then, scholars have explored the influence of a wide range of factors (e.g., educational background of parents, father's occupation, investment in supplementary instruction, ethnic background, referrals made by high school teachers) on an individual's future academic and employment opportunities (see, for example, Cummings and Naoi 1974; Dore 1967; Kariya 1985; Okano 1993; Rosenbaum and Kariya 1991; Stevenson and Baker 1992; Treiman and Yamaguchi 1993). This scholarship invigorated ongoing debates about whether the education system expanded or constrained the opportunities afforded to Japanese youth (LeTendre 1995; LeTendre 1998). Some studies emphasized the meritocratic features of the schools and the benefits that public education provided to all students, regardless of their background (Cummings 1980; Dore 1967; White 1987). Research on these topics confirmed that (1) Japanese schools treat children as equals, regardless of their background; (2) teachers are encouraged to "teach to the center"; and (3) students generally develop strong academic skills, especially when compared to their peers in other countries. Cummings (1982), for example, observed that "[an] educational system, given appropriate conditions, can produce egalitarian incomes in young people. . . . Postwar Japan provides an interesting example of the power of education for social transformation" (34). This view of teaching and learning meshed neatly with the common representation of Japan as a middle-class society, with small percentages of citizens either acquiring vast wealth or living in poverty.

Other scholars noted that the system was not as egalitarian as it might appear on the surface. Researchers who questioned the depiction of schools as social levelers noted the powerful influence that a family's socioeconomic background often had on the educational pathways followed by children (Kariya 1985). For example, in his study of Japanese high schools, Rohlen (1983) concluded that the rank of the school attended by a student was a reliable predictor of his future employment and social status.

In the late 1980s and 1990s, researchers paid increasing attention to issues related to "issues of meritocracy, egalitarianism, and the role education plays in determining social status" (LeTendre 1995, 150). The nation's rapid economic development attracted short- and long-term visitors from around the globe. The resulting influx of workers from other countries augmented diversity in schools that served what had frequently been characterized as a homogeneous, predominantly middle-class population (Gordon 2008; Nabeshima 2010; Okano and Tsuchiya 1999; Tsuneyoshi, Okano and Boocock 2011). These demographic shifts motivated some scholars to examine the experiences of marginalized groups, such as the Ainu, longtime residents from Korea and China, Okinawans, Buraku,[2] and guest workers from developing countries (Okano and Tsuchiya 1999, 110). Analyses of the treatment that children from these groups received in Japanese schools revealed widespread evidence of discrimination. Tsuneyoshi (2001) observed that "it has become difficult to maintain the belief that treating everyone the same is identical to equality. It is starting to seem like not everyone benefits equally from the same benefits and treatments" (113).

The collapse of the economic bubble in the late 1990s created conditions that made it increasingly problematic to cling to the notion of Japan as an egalitarian society "composed of wafer thin status distinctions" (Rohlen 1983, 135). A prolonged recession combined with the adoption of neoliberal reforms created instability in the workplace and exacerbated disparities between different segments of the population (Itoh 2000).[3] Researchers as well as the popular press highlighted the challenges experienced by citizens struggling to maintain the standards of living to which they were accustomed. Widespread use of the phrase "gap society" (*kakusa shakai*) suggested that views about economic opportunity in Japan had undergone significant revision.[4] Just as the topic of economic stratification was capturing the attention of the public, the results of a series of international achievement tests fueled concerns about the state of public education. Data from the 2003 and 2006 versions of PISA indicated that Japanese students' performance was declining, relative to their peers in other industrialized nations (Takayama 2007; Tsuneyoshi 2004b).

Complicating the pictures was a handful of studies that rigorously examined the assessment data, with careful attention to the distribution of scores. These analyses noted that the aggregated test scores masked important variability in student performance: drops in median scores were disproportionately affected by steep declines in the achievement of students located at the lower ends of the score distributions (Kariya et al. 2002; Nomi 2006; Park 2008). In other words, high-performing students continued to do quite well, while low-achieving students were falling further and further behind their peers. The timing of the release of this test data was also significant because evidence of the apparent decline in achievement appeared soon after the relaxed-education policies were introduced nationwide in 2002.[5] This led to a barrage of claims that *yutori kyoiku* was responsible for the plunge in achievement, as well as for the growing disparities between high- and low-achieving students.

In addition to analyzing test score data, Kariya and his colleagues examined trends in students' attitudes toward school. Kariya et al. (2002) replicated a survey originally administered to 1,375 second-year high school students living in Osaka in 1979 and found that students' interest in and commitment to their studies dropped between 1979 and 1997. Data from this survey drew attention to links between mothers' educational background and their children's attitudes toward school (See table 7.1). Furthermore, the motivational divide between students with university

Table 7.1. Influence of mother's level of education

Students who agreed with the statement: "What I learn in class sometimes make me want to know more about something."	1979	1997
University-educated mother	65.9%	57.8%
Middle school–educated mother	56.4%	37.0%
Difference	9.5%	20.8%
"I think I need to study to meet the expectations of my teachers and parents."	**1979**	**1997**
University-educated mother	71.8%	57.2%
Middle school–educated mother	64.2%	40.7%
Difference	7.6%	17.5%
"I think it's enough not to fail."	**1979**	**1997**
University-educated mother	27.1%	29.4%
Middle school–educated mother	33.8%	55.6%
Difference	6.7%	26.5%

Source: Kariya 2000

educated mothers and those whose mothers had earned only a secondary diploma expanded substantially since the original study was conducted. As Kariya and Rappleye (2010) noted, students "whose families assisted or modeled the positive effects of obtaining an education excelled, while those with few positive examples of the incentives of education became increasingly difficult to motivate" (31) in Japan's post-boom years.

These studies add valuable, often overlooked perspectives on educational reform and academic achievement in Japan. First, they establish that high-achieving students in Japan continue to perform quite well, compared to their peers in other countries. The performance of low-achieving students, in contrast, has declined steadily and is primarily responsible for Japan's lowered rankings on international league tables. Second, this scholarship draws attention to links between socioeconomic status and widening gaps in student achievement and attitudes toward school. For a society that has long emphasized its egalitarian nature, this evidence is significant.

Yet statistical analyses of test score data provide limited insights into changes in student performance in schools. As Kariya (2002) remarks, "Just looking at whether academic performance has fallen is no help in improving education. Only by combining this with research into students' daily lives and study patterns and by taking into account changes in these areas is it possible to conduct analysis that contributes to educational reform" (11–12). The study of students' attitudes about learning that Kariya and his colleagues conducted enhances our understanding of Japanese students' attachments to school—but omits the critical factors of classroom practice and school culture; the conclusions they draw are based on self-reported questionnaire data collected from high school students. Research that documents how changes to the curriculum and new prescriptions for instructional practice is influencing everyday activity in the schools remains elusive. As a result, assessments of the impact of *yutori kyoiku* are frequently made on philosophical rather than empirical grounds.

In the sections that follow, I describe and analyze the effects of the relaxed-education policies on the learning opportunities supplied to middle school students. Building on the work of Kariya, Nomi, and Park (2002), I explore the implications of educational reform on the academic performance of children with diverse socioeconomic and educational backgrounds. My analysis examines the new curriculum in embedded context, connecting education stakeholders' opinions about *yutori kyoiku* to everyday activities and decision making in schools. This focus on school-level action moves discussion of educational reform from the hypothetical to the concrete. Framing analysis in this way also shifts the spotlight from policy formulation to the learning experiences offered to children. The perspectives of local actors directly involved in the reform process also helps to explain *why* policies meet or do not meet their objectives.

Enlivening the Curriculum for Middle School Students

Tensions between the goals of the relaxed-education reforms and the demands associated with entrance examinations created challenges for teachers as they enacted the 2002 Course of Study. The educators that I interviewed could describe MEXT's reform plans accurately and in great detail. They understood the rationale driving the proposed changes, as well as the reasons MEXT was pressing them to alter their instructional practice. Among the teachers in my sample, there was a perception that the ministry was particularly concerned with students who were struggling academically in school. In their reflections on relaxed education, instructors often referred to subtle pressure they felt to raise the achievement levels of their most needy students. One interviewee, for instance, told me that "the aim is to get students who hate school interested in their schoolwork, to motivate them to study. That is the goal." Middle school instructors were generally sympathetic to the idea that schools should promote what have been termed "new abilities" (*shingakuryoku*) through learning activities that encouraged students to "identify problems for oneself, think for oneself, make independent judgments and actions and solve problems well" (Tsuneyoshi 2004a, 10).

Despite assurances from MEXT that embracing its reform agenda would supply students with a sturdy academic foundation, instructors had trouble supporting proposed changes if they were not convinced that those alterations were in students' best interests. As I observe in chapter 6, educators tended to view *yutori kyoiku* as in conflict with the core curriculum. In response to the multiple, sometimes overwhelming responsibilities assigned to them, they often felt compelled to ration their preparation time, investing extensive effort in certain activities and devoting minimal attention to others. This response to the new Course of Study had important implications for student learning.

MEXT emphasized that elective courses should be tailored to fit the interests and academic needs of students at a particular school. Rather than publish textbooks for elective subjects, the ministry encouraged instructors to create original materials for their elective courses. That expectation created additional demands for instructors who already felt overworked. The teachers I observed tended to treat IS and elective courses as an unwelcome burden on their time. Constrained by the limited amount of time they were prepared to invest in relaxed-education subjects, they employed instructional methods for IS and electives that proved least disruptive to their other professional responsibilities.

As one might expect, the structure and objectives of courses created in response to the relaxed-education reforms varied significantly, depending in large part on the actions of the instructors. At each of the middle schools in my sample, a few teachers followed MEXT's exhortation to make the transition "from guidance to support" (*shido yori shien wo*). These instructors facilitated interactive learning activities that both engaged and challenged pupils. Of the middle school instructors that I observed, English teachers at Chuo Middle School most adeptly nurtured both students' enthusiasm for learning and intellectual growth. Building on concepts they had introduced in regular English courses, they created simulations and games in which students were encouraged to apply grammar points to real-life situations. In preparation for one such lesson, one teacher constructed a list of questions that incorporated grammatical points students had been studying in their textbooks (e.g., "Can you _____?"). Using the questionnaire, students worked in pairs and interviewed their classmates. In another English elective, half of the class took on the role of shop owners and attempted to sell their goods to their classmates, who pretended to be shopping. In both situations, the teacher circulated through the room and rewarded students who were following directions. These activities reinforced challenging material from the core curriculum—and bolstered pupil enthusiasm for the subject. And because adults actively supervised the activities, the level of student participation was high.[6] The combination of thorough lesson planning and careful oversight of student performance resulted in high levels of pupil engagement and academic growth; this was true for all students, regardless of ability level. English teachers told me that limited instructional time would have made it difficult for them to introduce many of the communication-based activities in their regular courses.

In other elective courses, however, teachers struggled to achieve this balance of academic rigor and student engagement. Free of the pressure to master content that might appear on an examination, students relaxed and socialized with their friends as they completed elective projects. It was not always clear what skills they were acquiring as they conducted that work. In the science lab described in chapter 6, for example, students clearly had a good time making caramel lollipops, but few of them appeared to have considered the scientific concepts that grounded the activity. The individuals who did make such connections were those who also excelled in regular science courses.

In other elective periods I observed, teachers emphasized the affective rather than the cognitive goals of *yutori kyoiku*. In such classrooms, pupils spent a great deal of time chatting or working on projects at a leisurely pace. When I talked with the teachers in charge of those classes, it often became clear that the instructors had not formulated clear learning objectives and frequently lacked confidence in their ability to guide student learning. Many used elective class time as an opportunity to prepare students for entrance examinations. Review sessions were rarely structured to support struggling students or to augment interest in the subject matter, as the following excerpt from my field notes illustrates.

Third-Grade Social Studies Elective—Chuo Middle School

9:50 Mr. Nobuchi announces that today's geography lesson will be devoted to independent work. He passes out two worksheets, which have been copied from a book, to each student. Pupils immediately form groups—all of which are segregated by gender—and start working on the exercises cooperatively. The worksheets ask students to find the longitude and latitude of various locations in the prefecture. Mr. Nobuchi sits at the teacher's desk in the front of the room, correcting papers. All of the students in the room are filling in the worksheet. This is really unusual—a group of third graders showing such control and self-direction in class. I wonder what factors explain the students' positive attitude—the elective aspect of the course, the small size, or the kids who happen to have enrolled in this class.

10:00 A group of girls has stopped filling in the worksheets and is now talking about the size and shape of the snowflakes that are falling outside the window. One of them opens the window, leans out, and tries to catch snowflakes on a piece of paper. Mr. Nobuchi does not seem to notice—he has not looked up from the papers he is grading since the beginning of the period.

10:15 A group of three boys sitting in front of me has set the worksheet aside and begun chatting. It feels much more relaxed in here than in most academic classes. Mr. Nobuchi is now reading the newspaper.

10:20 A handful of girls have finished the worksheets and, without any prompting from the teacher, are now completing enrichment exercises in a workbook. Mr. Nobuchi continues to read the newspaper.

10:25 The instructor stands up and announces, "Let's go over these pages." After reading each question on the worksheet aloud, Mr. Nobuchi points out clues in the phrasing that can assist students as they work through the problem, then supplies the correct answer. He does not call on anyone or solicit student input. Members of this class could either: (a) study this material carefully and expand their knowledge; (b) fill in the answers as the teacher reads them out; (c) copy the answers from a friend; or (d) do nothing. Mr. Nobuchi says that one of the questions on the worksheet often appears on entrance examinations. I notice that a boy sitting in front of me has doodled all over his paper. He has not answered any of the questions.

10:35 The period ends before the class gets to the final question. It's not clear how well student did on these questions because they have not shared any of their answers with the rest of the group, and Mr. Nobuchi does not collect the worksheets. Before I can stop to ask him some questions about the lesson, he slips out of the room.

Teachers who made any serious attempt to follow MEXT guidelines for the new and expanded elective program were in the minority. Most of the instructors I observed approached their elective course assignments similarly to Mr. Nobuchi, the social studies teacher profiled above. Rather than create hands-on activities that bolstered student enthusiasm for learning or *ikiru chikara* (zest for living), they used class time to review concepts previously introduced in academic courses. Most commonly, they copied exercises or exam questions from previous years' textbooks and instructed pupils to complete as many of those sheets as possible by the end of the period. While this approach did have the potential to strengthen students' mastery of basic academic skills, it was antithetical to the goals of relaxed education. It's hard to imagine an activity less stimulating than sitting at a desk for fifty minutes completing exercises from old textbooks. In addition, teachers provided minimal direction to students as they completed the handouts. Mr. Nobuchi did deliver a lesson to the students in his class, but he did not identify any difficulties the pupils faced, answer their questions, or assist individual students as they attempted to solve challenging problems. Using worksheets to anchor his elective course reduced stress for Mr. Nobuchi, who experienced none of the angst that Mr. Takahashi went through as he struggled to bring science alive for his students.

Like most teachers at Chuo Middle School, Mr. Nobuchi frequently remained at school until ten or eleven o'clock at night, correcting papers, completing reports, or attending to committee work. In a strategic sense, the worksheet approach generated some obvious benefits—to the teacher. The demands placed upon Mr. Nobuchi were minor: make copies from an old textbook, distribute the worksheet to students, and supply the answers at the end of the period. Conducting the lesson in this way actually alleviated the pressure experienced by the teacher, who could use class time to catch up on his work for other classes and read the newspaper.

But the worksheet review lacked the intellectual substance or exchange of ideas that characterize inspiring teaching. Rather than enhance student enthusiasm for learning, it added to the number of hours the third-year students were required to sit at their desks absorbing information. Few of the pupils in these elective classes displayed any interest in what they were doing. Filling in worksheets certainly did not nourish their zest for life or bolster their motivation to study. Furthermore, students who struggled in school rarely applied themselves to elective courses. In all the middle schools that I visited, this type of worksheet review was the most prevalent approach used to present the elective curriculum. As a result, a reform intended to expand and enliven the curriculum had the opposite effect: large blocks of instructional time were devoted to test preparation.

Expanding Student Autonomy in the Classroom

Teachers at all the middle schools I visited invested long hours developing IS curricular frameworks that fit the unique characteristics of local communities, yet the instructional methods they relied on were remarkably consistent. As was true in the elementary schools, student-directed research projects anchored IS lessons in most middle school classrooms. At both levels, instructors typically presented a broad theme to pupils, directed them to pick a more specific topic within that theme to investigate, and established a set of project deadlines. As they moved from the planning stage to implementation in the classroom, however, middle school educators approached their work to fit goals and expectations distinct from their elementary school counterparts. Rather than form student research teams, teachers tended to assign middle school pupils to work on individual projects. In recognition of their students' limits as researchers, elementary school instructors offered extensive support to their pupils as they collected information related to their topics; teachers carefully monitored student progress and usually stepped in when they observed signs of struggle. Middle school educators, in contrast, generally adopted a hands-off approach to student investigations. They operated under the assumption that by the time children reached the secondary level, they had acquired the skills and discipline necessary to complete an extended research project.

In all the middle schools I visited, instructors followed MEXT's advice of organizing IS lessons so as to maximize student independence. Not all middle school pupils were prepared to make the most of that autonomy. The excerpt from my field notes below describes an IS meeting for third-year middle school students who were investigating potential careers:

1:50	All third grade students meet in the computer room. Mrs. Kato is in charge. The head teacher, a student teacher, and the school nurse stand behind her. Ms. Kato writes the following information on the board:
11/4 (today):	Use the entire period to work on your worksheets. Start preparing for your interviews at local businesses
11/4:	Contact workplaces
11/18:	Discuss manners for visits

Mrs. Kato holds up pages that someone left behind last time and advises the group to "be more careful about the use of paper. Visits to workplaces are coming up soon. We will only meet three more times before then. I want you to work really hard on finishing your worksheets and your interview preparation today. Last time, I noticed that many of you seem to be falling behind. If you haven't decided what you are going to write about yet, you better adjust your pace. We don't have time to chat today. Any questions?"

After pausing for several seconds but not receiving any questions, Mrs. Kato circulates through the room and quickly checks in with several students. The other adults in the room follow her lead. Mrs. Kato stops beside one boy who does not appear to be working and asks him what he is supposed to be doing. The boy does not respond. Mrs. Kato asks him what he is going to do next. Again, he does not answer. Mrs. Kato tells him to look for the information he needs on the computer. After checking in with one more student, she leaves the computer lab.

2:05 All the adults have exited the room. Some students begin to work on the computers, looking up websites and taking notes. Others chat with their friends. I notice that three boys appear to be sleeping.

This episode is notable for a number of reasons. First, it captures the accommodating approach to managing student investigations taken by the vast majority of middle school teachers I observed. Rather than work alongside pupils to address the specific difficulties they were experiencing, Mrs. Kato made vague suggestions and directed students to find solutions to problems on their own. When a student did not reply to her inquiries about his work, Mrs. Kato gave him the generic advice to search for information on the computer. She did not check to see if he followed up on this advice or if he needed additional help.

Research on problem- and project-based learning highlights the benefits of allowing students to complete projects designed to explore questions that interest them—but also draws attention to some challenges associated with this approach (Bell 2010; Marx et al. 1997; Thomas 2000). In their synthesis of research on this topic, Barron et al. (1998) identify four elements of effective project-based instruction: (1) defining learning-appropriate goals that lead to deep understanding; (2) providing appropriate scaffolds for students; (3) incorporating formative student self-assessment and revision into curricular planning; and (4) developing social structures that promote active pupil participation and a sense of agency (271). When a teacher neglects to attend to any of these elements, the chances that students will benefit from project-based learning decrease.

In the Japanese middle schools I studied, the absence of the four elements of effective problem-based learning identified by Barron et al. (1998) was more conspicuous than their presence. Occasionally, I did observe a teacher assist individual students who needed assistance with their investigations. More commonly, a teacher or group of teachers began an IS period by making some broad announcements about research projects and quickly proceeded to the faculty room to complete other tasks. An adult usually returned to the room at the end of the period and brought the lesson to a close, but I rarely observed anyone closely monitor student work in IS.

Teachers were careful to provide enough direction to students to demonstrate compliance with MEXT guidelines—but their behavior did not reveal a sense of obligation to carefully plan IS lessons so as to maximize student performance. Many of the educators I interviewed were quite open about their lack of attention to this component of the curriculum. The explanations that teachers gave for not investing more time in IS indicated that the multiple demands placed on them required them to ration their time, and that new subjects introduced to support relaxed education were not considered a priority. Instructors were willing to follow MEXT guidelines—but not at the expense of the core academic subjects.

Second, both teachers and students expected the other party to accept primary responsibility for IS projects. When pupils struggled to complete an assignment, Mrs. Kato—like many instructors I observed—responded with prompts that redirected responsibility back to the students. In such situations, pupils tended to continue to wait for more concrete assistance from a teacher. One consequence of this deflection of responsibility was that low-achieving students frequently entered an ongoing cycle of inactivity. Instructors regularly assigned homework and assigned tests in core academic subjects; they almost always remained in the room until the end of those classes. That was not the case with relaxed-education subjects. Both teachers and pupils were aware that performance in IS and electives had little impact on students' academic opportunities. The most salient assessment tool used to monitor student progress in IS was the self-evaluation form that pupils were regularly required to complete. Adolescents tended to rate their efforts highly, regardless of their actual use of class time.

Third, in the middle schools I visited, students worked individually rather than in groups. Teachers assumed that middle school pupils were capable of planning and carrying out research projects without extensive support from adults. Due to the emphasis on individual activity, the benefits derived from independent investigations varied noticeably among students—and were heavily dependent on the research skills and motivation a pupil brought to the task. The people who took IS assignments seriously tended to display initiative in all aspects of their education—the model students. These individuals showed impressible initiative in designing and carrying out IS projects. With limited guidance, they developed compelling research questions, used a variety of strategies to obtain information, and skillfully synthesized their findings in oral presentations. In the same classrooms, a number of students displayed ongoing difficulties making headway with their projects. These students did not often draw attention to themselves. Instead, they tended to withdraw—sitting silently through study periods, doodling, or sleeping. For them, IS did not make school more exciting or meaningful; it just expanded the number of subjects that generated homework and exposed their academic inadequacies.

At the assemblies during which children presented the findings of their work (*happyokai*), disparities in student ability and performance became strikingly apparent. Students were typically given ten to fifteen minutes to present their projects to an audience of teachers, parents, and pupils. At one such assembly I attended, a handful students made multimedia presentations that were sophisticated both in terms of content and appearance. Among the topics they explored were: the effects of decreasing population on the local community, the causes and effects of global warming, the effects of rainfall on a local river, and society's dependence on petroleum-based products. One third-grade student compared carbon dioxide emissions in different parts of the world and shared a thoughtful analysis of the reasons certain nations pollute more than others. At the same assembly, less-capable students struggled to read their own notes and had to be assisted by teachers; others read essays that sounded as if they had been copied word-for-word from encyclopedias or websites. The inferior quality of those presentations was even more notable given that students had spent seven months working on their investigations.

When asked to comment on the presentations, teachers responded with broad statements that avoided judgment. One instructor, for example, volunteered that "I think the quality of the presentations was about the same as last year, but the topics were different." Another told me, "Students worked on their projects for forty hours, from May to November. I think the contents are better than last year, but the delivery wasn't as good." Tellingly, no one I spoke with drew any connection between the quality (either positive or negative) of student work and the instructional methods used to support students as they investigated their topics. When interviewees made critical remarks, they tended to emphasize the lack of student effort. This framing of responsibility diverted attention from the actions of teachers and reduced their obligation to carefully evaluate the IS programs on their campuses.

Student Opinions about Relaxed Education

Students' opinions about the new curriculum afford another perspective on the relaxed-education reforms. As table 5.1 shows, IS and electives appeared near the top of student ratings of the subjects in the middle school curriculum. When asked to explain what it was about IS that appealed to them, pupils related that they valued opportunities to select the topics they would study, the freedom to venture beyond the borders of their classroom in search of information, and the more relaxed study environment. "I like IS because I like working on my own and I can focus on things that interest me," a middle school student told me. Another attraction of IS was its uniqueness: the subject represented a clear break from the more traditional components of the school day.[7] The projects that students completed were more open-ended and less demanding than assignments for academic subjects. As was true in classes such as art and physical education, middle school pupils often appeared more energetic and enthusiastic than they did during their core academic studies.

The generally positive reviews of elective and IS courses, however, obscured critical differences in the way that subgroups of students responded to the instructional opportunities granted to them. Pupils may have enjoyed elective courses, but that did not mean that they worked hard in those courses or developed the "new academic abilities" referred to in MEXT policy reports. Students emphasized how much fun it was to take part in hands-on science activities. During such lessons, they interacted animatedly with their classmates. But the process usually overshadowed the content of a lesson. During these activities, I always circulated through the room and observed pupils as they worked. Rarely did student conversations center on the concepts they were exploring. They were more likely to talk about their social lives or television shows, or to simply horse around. In elective courses, students did not feel the level of accountability they did in nonelective subjects.

The reduced pressure associated with electives appealed to pupils—but frustrated teachers. Even when elective instructional periods were allocated to academic review, students enjoyed great latitude to decide how they used class time. Highly motivated, achievement-oriented students tended to capitalize on the opportunities provided in elective courses to enhance their skills, while students most in need of extra support used class time to chat with friends, doodle, or sleep. The benefits derived from activities depended in large part on the internal drive of individual pupils.

The grades students earned in elective courses and IS carried little weight in the high school admissions process. The absence of meaningful consequences for poor performance in these subjects reduced the pressure placed on students—but it also undercut the sense of responsibility they felt to invest in those courses. The primary impetus for investing in elective coursework was individual initiative, which a significant percentage of middle school students seemed to lack. As one might predict, pupils who were determined to gain admission to competitive high schools capitalized on class time to augment their mastery of the concepts covered; individuals who lacked a track record of academic success exerted minimal effort. In all the lessons that I observed, there was a strong correlation between student performance in electives and in core academic subjects. Weak students may have been attracted to the less intense structure of elective and IS lessons, but the factors that fed into their satisfaction also helped explain their less than stellar performance in those courses. Rarely did I observe students with a history of academic difficulties apply themselves to elective lessons. As a result, students with ambitious academic aspirations moved further ahead of their classmates who lacked such commitment to learning. Very few teachers attempted to alter this pattern.

The Role of the Family in a Relaxed-Education System

The interview and survey data I collected establish that parents had ambiguous opinions about the goals of the MEXT reform agenda and the direction in which the schools their children attend are heading. In analyzing those data, it is difficult to identify consistent patterns or underlying logic in parents' thinking. Rather, what stands out are the inconsistencies and contradictions in their opinions. As table 7.2 illustrates, the parents I surveyed were generally happy with the quality of education their children are receiving: only 10% stated that they were "dissatisfied" with their schools and none picked the "extremely dissatisfied" option. In addition, when asked to assess the level of difficulty of their children's studies, 60% chose "just right." These positive assessments are rather surprising, given the supposed state of crisis plaguing the education system.

But when it came to items on the questionnaire that focused more specifically on recent changes to the curriculum, parent enthusiasm dimmed. Only 25% of respondents rated the relaxed-education reforms "good" or "very good," compared with 48% who judged them "bad" or "very bad" (see table 7.2). These figures seem to indicate solid opposition to *yutori kyoiku* among parents. But, again, this apparent accord is undercut by data from subsequent questions on the parent survey. For example, the percentage of parents opposed to the five-day school week was the same as that of parents who supported the change. And significantly more parents had a positive opinion about Integrated Studies those with negative views of the new subject (46% and 10%, respectively). These figures suggest that although parents were generally pleased with specific policies introduced to promote relaxed education, they remained skeptical about the general thrust of the MEXT's reform agenda. The large number of respondents who expressed indecision about the changes that had been introduced is also significant. Almost a third of all parents surveyed were not sure how they felt about the shorter school week and 44% had not formed a strong opinion about IS—four years after it was introduced.

Table 7.2. Parent survey results

1. How happy are you with your children's education? ($n = 69$)				
Extremely satisfied	Satisfied	So-so	Dissatisfied	Extremely dissatisfied
1%	38%	51%	10%	0%
2. How difficult is school for your children? ($n = 69$)				
Very easy	Easy	Just right	Difficult	Very difficult
0%	22%	70%	9%	0%
3. What is your opinion about relaxed education? ($n = 71$)				
Very bad	Bad	No change	Good	Very good
7%	41%	30%	21%	1%
4. What is your opinion about the five-day school week? ($n = 71$)				
Approve	Against	Not sure		
34%	34%	32%		
5. What is your opinion about Integrated Studies? ($n = 70$)				
Approve	Against	Not sure		
46%	10%	44%		
6. What is your opinion about the academic preparation that students in this area are receiving? ($n = 70$)				
Not a problem at all	I'm not worried	No change	Small problem	Big problem
0%	13%	7%	56%	24%

This information highlights the unique position that parents occupy in the educational hierarchy. Though they experience the effects of decisions made in the schools quite acutely, parents are removed from everyday activity on campus. As Okano and Tsuchiya observe, "Schools in Japan are considered to be relatively closed to parents and the local community, in that their views are not well reflected in the running of schools. This is partly because parents and the community do not have a formal channel for participation in their children's schooling" (Okano and Tsuchiya 1999, 161). Family members are invited to attend special events, such as sports festivals or graduation ceremonies, but culturally constructed boundaries prevent them from participating in the academic facets of schooling. Almost every school in Japan has a PTA, but its members spend most of their time fund-raising and organizing social events; they are not involved in decision making about curriculum or instruction. And there is no tradition of parents volunteering in the classroom, as is common in many other parts of the world. Very few of the adults I spoke with felt comfortable approaching teachers to discuss curricular issues.

Because they had little direct experience with *yutori kyoiku,* parents tended to form opinions about the new curriculum based largely on media reports and informal gossip. Accordingly, discussions among parents often echoed debates that pervaded television and newspapers at the time, and focused on the potential pitfalls of reducing pressure in the schools:

MR. HIROSE (ELEMENTARY SCHOOL PARENT): *Yutori kyoiku* is not necessary. Kids don't need more *yutori* . . . . Teachers today are not strict enough. Their effort is poor. Integrated Studies is okay, but not for everyday. It's just like playing. There must be a balance.

MRS. TABUCHI (ELEMENTARY SCHOOL PARENT): It is more important for kids to enjoy studying.

MR. HIROSE: That's true, but you can do that without *yutori kyoiku* . . . . The five-day work week sounds nice, but not if the curriculum is cut.

Another item on the parent questionnaire asked respondents to select the three things they felt were most important for their children to learn in school. As table 7.3 shows, parents appear to want schools to support their children's academic and socio-emotional development. Cultivating pupils' "basic academic skills" does appear at the top of the list of the fifteen items parents could choose from, but the second item on that list is "making friends," followed closely by "learning to be part of a group." Not a single respondent selected "exam preparation" as one of areas that schools should emphasize! Again, it is challenging to identify any clear message from this data. One possible interpretation is that parents want balance in their children's education; while they are concerned about basic academic skills, they do not believe that the three Rs should not dominate the instructional program. A second reading of table 7.3 would be that families count on the schools to focus on academics—but the line dividing academic instruction and exam preparation should not be crossed. A third is that parents are conflicted about the core function of the public school during an era of great change, inside and beyond the schools.

Very few of the parents I interviewed communicated concerns about their children's education directly to teachers or school administrators. Rather than sharing their criticism of relaxed education with the schools, they took responsibility for filling perceived gaps between what their children learned in school and what they needed to know to gain acceptance

Table 7.3. Parent priorities

Question: What do you think are the most important things for your children to learn in school? (Pick 3.)	
Basic academic skills	60%
Make friends	53%
Learn to be part of a group	33%
Cooperation	27%
Critical thinking	14%
Good manners	13%
Independence	11%
Creativity	10%
Zest for living	9%
Love of learning	7%
Life-skills preparation / learn live a good life	7%
Self-confidence	7%
Self-expression	0%

Note: $n = 70$

into a desirable high school or university. My interviews confirm observations made by scholars of Japanese education that portray parents as strategic consumers of educational services (Goodman and Phillips 2003; Hood 2003; Tsuneyoshi 2013). Parents were willing to add new products to their shopping carts—as long as those items did not take up space reserved for the basic staples they relied on for sustenance. Adults understood that not all subjects in the curriculum had equal value. When forced to make decisions about their children's education, idealism tended to give way to the recognition that test preparation was more likely to bring rewards than student explorations of topics they found exciting; more immediate considerations related to high school admission overrode concerns about the personal growth or well-being of their sons and daughters.

This tendency to assume responsibility for perceived gaps or weaknesses in the curriculum rather than attempt to initiate changes in school practice protected families from suffering any negative consequences of reform—but also widened the gaps that separated high- and low-achieving students. In the communities I studied, introduction of the relaxed-education reforms has nourished a shadow education system that has long functioned in tandem with the public schools (Baker and LeTendre 2005; Bray 2009; Dawson 2010; Rohlen 1983). Parents worried about the academic preparedness of their children frequently enrolled their children in cram schools (*juku*) or hired private tutors to fill in perceived gaps in their education.[8] Thirty-two percent of students I surveyed reported that they attended supplementary academic lessons in the evenings. *Juku* operators capitalized on public anxiety about declining academic skills. The manager of one of the largest *jukus* in the area where I conducted my fieldwork showed me brochures that underscored the necessity of supplementing daily instruction in the schools with private lessons in the evenings and on weekends to counter the diluted standards associated with the relaxed-education movement. He also explained, "Science and social studies are not affected by relaxed education . . . so we don't focus on those skills here."

Of course, not all parents were in a position to fill in the gaps in their children's learning. As one would expect, adults with higher levels of education and income were more likely to enroll their children in supplemental classes. As the mother of a middle school student explained,

> I think Integrated Studies is a good chance for children, for students to study something new, but I don't agree with the policy because reducing the curriculum means that families must support the curriculum at home. Some families can do that, but some cannot. Some families cannot afford to send their children to cram school, so it increases the gap. . . . Some families are picking private schools because they don't have to follow the ministry curriculum.

Another hole that families were expected to fill was the free time made available when Saturday classes were eliminated. According to MEXT documents, reducing the number of hours children spend at school would allow them to lead more meaningful and fulfilling lives. During the expanded time they spent outside of class, children could relax with family members, interact with nature, read books, participate in community activities, volunteer, and play with friends, among other things (MEXT 2002b). However, such forecasts were premised on the idea that families would take advantage of the additional time made available to them with the end of Saturday classes. Many of the supposed benefits of the five-day school week would bear required adult supervision or involvement. Few of the children who struggled in school enjoyed such parental support. As one teacher pondered, "I wonder how students use the Saturdays now they don't have school. There are probably kids who spend time doing interesting things with their families, but there are also kids who are left by themselves." Although I did not formally document students' use of free time, informal reports they shared with me indicated that those whose parents were heavily invested in their education tended to use weekend time more productively than those whose parents whose parents were less academically oriented or economically stable. In this way, cuts to the curriculum and instructional hours disproportionately affected students who already struggled academically. Lacking the extensive resources that many of their peers enjoyed or the motivation to succeed in the classroom, they were left to function on a more precarious academic foundation.

Deflection of Responsibility at the Local Level

The evidence presented in this chapter underscores the conflicts experienced by education stakeholders as they responded to reform policies crafted to support personal objectives that were not well aligned with the goals of *yutori kyoiku*. In the middle schools that I studied, initiatives intended to reduce the stress experienced by pupils provoked countervailing pressure to maintain long-established academic practices. The autonomy delegated to teachers made it possible for them to support, resist, or modify policy directives, even within a vertically organized system overseen by a central ministry of education. Tensions between MEXT's plans for change and locally rooted expectations about academic achievement made them hesitant to fully commit to relaxed-education policies. Instead, educators continued to concentrate on their core instructional duties—and employed strategies for implementing the "relaxed" portion of the curriculum that required nominal effort on their part.

The limited role that middle school instructors carved out for themselves reduced their workload—but created additional demands on students, many of whom were unprepared to accept increased responsibility for their own learning. In middle schools, the concept of *individualization* was usually translated as *individual* (student) *responsibility*. This interpretation of student-centered learning essentially removed teachers from the list of factors that determined the success or failure of the activities they managed. Pupils who had acquired strong academic skills, intellectual curiosity, and the drive to expand their knowledge usually thrived under these conditions. Those who lacked the ability or discipline to work independently, on the other hand, struggled to meet teacher expectations in environments that demanded increased self-initiative. In this way, modifications to the curriculum designed to reduce pressure in schools actually created additional stress for adolescents who lacked strong academic records.

This was especially true of students who did not enjoy strong support at home. Those who did not receive assistance from family members were dependent on teachers to help them complete independent projects. Yet, as I have detailed in this chapter, adults in secondary schools tended to deflect that responsibility. Even instructional time set aside for academic review often created disadvantages for underachieving pupils, who were frequently assigned to complete a series of worksheets without the assistance of an adult. For these reasons, students who lacked the resources or commitment to fill in the gaps between the slimmed-down 2002 curriculum and the previous version fell further behind their peers whose parents who took an active role in their children's education.

Commonalities between the quantitative studies that highlight bifurcation in the performance of Japanese students on international achievement tests (Kariya 2000; Kariya 2002; Nomi 2006; Park 2013) and the evidence presented in this qualitative study suggest that links between socioeconomics and educational opportunity in Japan have tightened. They also call into question the long-accepted view that Japanese schools provide equal opportunities to all children. Once distinguished for its commitment to egalitarianism, the education system appears to be following in the path of other countries where the adoption of neoliberal policies has raised the barriers confronting families with limited economic resources and social capital. Rather than create conditions in which all students can succeed, *yutori kyoiku* policies exacerbated gaps between high- and low-achieving pupils. Children were granted new opportunities to act independently—and to succeed or fail on their own as well.

EIGHT

Shifting Student-Teacher Relationships

As is true of many reform initiatives, assessments of *yutori kyoiku* tend to draw conclusions based on a rather narrow set of factors, primarily quantitative measures of academic performance. This is understandable, given the complexity of educational change and the challenges associated with analyzing multiple layers of teaching and learning. But, as I document in the sections that follow, education reform involves much more than simply the acquisition of facts. Students, teachers, administrators, and parents are all affected by modifications to the curriculum. Furthermore, redesigning a curriculum may exert a powerful influence on interactions between teachers and students. In this chapter, I discuss changes in the characteristics and attitudes of middle school students, teachers' responses to those alterations, and the role these factors played in implementation of the relaxed-education policies.

The social and moral development of children has always been a central component of the mission of Japanese schools (LeTendre 2000; Shimahara and Sakai 1995). In addition to providing a solid base of knowledge to their graduates, teachers are responsible for developing in students the attitudes and dispositions necessary to function in society. As Fukuzawa (1994) relates, in Japan "the very definition of teaching encompasses not only the transmission of knowledge but counseling, guidance and discipline" (62). During the heyday of Japan's economic expansion, the foreign press—eager to explain the nation's ascension from vanquished debtor to global leader—drew attention to orderliness and discipline in the schools. The prevalence of this storyline had a strong impact on outside observers' impressions of Japanese schools and continues to shape views of the education system. Images of adolescents clothed in military-style uniforms standing obediently next to their wooden desks have proven difficult to erase from the popular imagination, regardless of how accurately they may have captured conditions in actual schools.

Yet changes in relational dimensions of education have transformed the learning atmosphere in many Japanese schools. As one teacher told me, "From my point of view, students are changing year by year. Every year when I come to school, it seems like they are different. Now students do not hesitate to say what they are feeling. In a way, that is good; but if they talk too freely, they might become selfish. It is difficult to find the right balance." At the same time that instructors were attempting to establish such a balance, they were also responding to new expectations for student guidance.[1] According to MEXT, the nature of interactions between students and teachers needed to change so that schools would become nurturing, motivating sites for learning. Many of the practices relied on by school employees were no longer deemed acceptable by MEXT. This combination of unpredictable student behavior and more restrictive rules about discipline and class management created formidable challenges for teachers.

The data I collected in Japanese middle schools reveal changes in the flow of life in those institutions that have been overlooked in previous reports on *yutori kyoiku*. Shifts in student-teacher relationships were intricately connected to the implementation and effects of the relaxed-education curriculum. My analysis of the dynamics of *yutori* approaches to student guidance raises a number of questions tied to the issue of how to balance academic rigor and student engagement in learning. These questions are relevant not only to Japan, but to any nation experimenting with accountability in its schools. Drawing conclusions about the effects of an education policy based solely on assessments of academic achievement is limiting. To fully understand the implications of any educational reform, it is helpful to carefully consider the effects of the proposed change on student-teacher interactions, class management procedures, and the exercise of authority in the classroom.

Approaches to Student Guidance and Their Historical Foundations

In Japan, middle school is regarded as a pivotal stage in the child's advancement toward adulthood, for during these years the potential for individuals to "fall into a state of unworthiness" (Yamamura 1986, 36) increases. When they advance from elementary to secondary school, children must quickly adapt to strikingly different expectations at the two levels. Teachers continue to take responsibility for their pupils' moral development, but the strategies they use to facilitate such growth are modified to fit the maturity levels of their students. Nurturing children through the challenges that confront them can help them develop positive dispositions and relations with others, but unchecked indulgence can produce egocentric, undisciplined individuals (Bjork and Fukuzawa 2013). To avoid this pitfall, Japanese secondary schools have traditionally embraced the notion of "intimacy coupled with severity" (Rohlen 1983, 201). The culturally accepted ideal for teachers is to act as both understanding ally and demanding authority figure. White notes that in Japan there is "a notion that the child benefits from experiencing hardship. . . . *Kuro* (suffering or hardship) is believed to have a beneficial effect on the self, deepening it and maturing it, removing self-centeredness. Without *kuro* a person cannot be said to have grown up" (White 1987, 29). Learning to function within rigid, hierarchically organized institutions is seen as critical preparation for adult life.

This explains the traditional respect accorded to teachers who support their pupils but do not hesitate to wield a firm hand when necessary. Students are provided with more extensive responsibilities—but that autonomy is undercut by institutional norms that reduce the range of acceptable behavior. The routines and rules that organize school life become more prescriptive. As will be the case throughout their lives, secondary school students are required to read complex signals regarding their position within the group and use that information to make appropriate decisions about language, dress, and comportment.

To someone educated in other settings, the emphasis on controlling student behavior in Japanese middle schools may seem excessively punitive. The idea that individual autonomy and freedom is reduced as one gets older conflicts with notions of child development accepted in many Western countries. In the United States, for example, the tendency is to loosen the strings that bind adolescents as they mature (LeTendre 2000). It is widely accepted that individuals should earn freedom as they gain experience and demonstrate that they can make wise decisions on their own. But the practices described above evolved over long periods of time, molded to mesh with ideas about selfhood and human relations reinforced in Japanese society.

The restrictive aspects of Japanese middle school life provide pupils with a preview of what they will face in the coming years. In their workplaces and neighborhoods, citizens are subject to a greater degree of regulation than is common in Western democratic societies (Nakane 1986). In a society that has historically stressed group harmony (*wa*), the needs of the individual must often be sacrificed for those of the larger group. Middle school students experience this reality on a daily basis—in the classroom, in the corridors, and on the playing field. Following rather than questioning rules is valued, and less experienced members of the community (*kohai*) are expected to show respect for their seniors (*sempai*), even when they find fault with the leadership provided. Surrendering a degree of personal autonomy serves to "create an internal organization which will tie the individuals in the group to each other and then to strengthen this organization" (Nakane 1986, 177).[2]

In sum, middle school represents a key transition period in the lives of Japanese youth, bridging the worlds of childhood and adulthood. During this three-year period, shifts in the social and academic expectations signal that their lives as students are taking a sharp turn. Instruction becomes more teacher centered and tightly linked to exam preparation. Student guidance procedures encourage students to regulate their own behavior to fit the needs of the institution. To increase the likelihood that pupils will meet the increasingly narrow definitions of acceptable behavior, an "intensive program of social control" (Fukuzawa 1994, 83) is implemented. The key components of this program are daily routines designed to create order in school life, extensive rules related to student appearance and behavior, and a system of senior-junior (*sempai-kohai*) relations that entrusts upper-level students to oversee a wide range of activities on campus. If the system fails to produce its desired outcomes, teachers step in and address transgressions as they see fit; potent displays of authority communicate to all members of the community the importance of adhering to school rules. And, as is frequently reported in the media, the overzealous exertion of authority by teachers has sometimes led to abusive behavior (Miller 2010). In general, though, Japanese society has accepted the tight monitoring of students as a reasonable price to pay in exchange for safe and orderly middle schools.

Of course, not all educational institutions adhere to a single student-guidance model. My description of the mechanisms relied on to mentor middle school pupils is designed to serve as a point of reference that will be relevant throughout this chapter. Although research conducted in middle schools indicates that the guidance approaches described above are widespread (Fukuzawa 1994; Hill 1996; LeTendre 1998; LeTendre 2000), the degree to which teachers emphasize school rules and the consequences for breaking them vary from campus to campus. In addition, the practices summarized above are specific to a particular period in time: they were documented by researchers who studied middle school practices common during the1950s to 1990s. As I will show, students, teachers, and schools have all undergone substantial changes since the collapse of the economic bubble. Outside of Asia, these changes have not been thoroughly documented or widely disseminated. Many non-Japan specialists continue to assume that middle schools are highly regimented institutions filled with students who compliantly adhere to school rules. One visit to a Japanese secondary school today would quickly dispel that notion. Adolescents come to school with very different ideas about appropriate forms of behavior, dress, and responsibility than pupils who graduated just a few years earlier. Confounded by these shifts in youth culture, teachers are revising their methods, searching for the appropriate mix of discipline and acceptance. Few are succeeding.

Conditions in Contemporary Schools

At first glance, it might appear that little has changed over the past twenty-five years in terms the structure and expectations that anchor Japanese middle school life. Lessons begin with the same formal greetings and bowing; all members of the community are expected to participate in daily school-cleaning activities (*soji*); younger students should approach their senior classmates and teachers with appropriate levels of deference; and at the start of every physical education class period, pupils conduct elaborate stretching routines similar to those followed by their parents, and possibly their grandparents. Anyone who has been educated in or spent extensive time in Japanese schools is familiar with these activities. Their continued existence attests to a dependable regularity to the rhythm of school life.

The rituals that organize middle schools may not have been altered significantly, but their implementation has. In the 1990s, responding to criticism that middle schools were excessively rigid and intense, the MEXT encouraged teachers to display more empathy to their students. In May 1994, the ministry issued a directive that spelled out the implications of the UN Convention on the Rights of the Child for schools (MEXT 1994). Using the rhetoric of international human rights, the ministry emphasized the need to eliminate all forms of physical punishment in schools. MEXT reports emphasized the need to makes the school "an emotional resting place" for children (MEXT 2003, 52). The shift to more compassionate approaches to student guidance was regarded as one way of reducing bullying and in-school violence. This attention to the affective aspects of learning meshed with the curricular revisions that formed the core of the relaxed-education reform movement. Regulations related to hair length were not eliminated, but responding to transgressions with harsh remedies was discouraged.[3]

Corporal punishment and public humiliation of students was no longer permitted.

Over the last twenty years, the balance of "intimacy coupled with severity" appears to have been recalibrated. Increasingly, teachers are refraining from exerting their authority over students who misbehave. Rather than admonishing or disciplining pupils who cross the line of acceptable behavior, educators are using *amae* (indulgence) to steer them back on the right track. Presenting themselves as allies rather than authority figures, they gently encourage students to follow school rules and procedures. On the campuses I visited, students even called some teachers by their first names. In every school I visited, there were veteran teachers who presided over classroom environments that were highly ordered and formal. But even the most assertive instructors were careful not to use disciplinary tactics that could be construed as harsh or abusive. In all three middle schools, indulgence was more commonplace than severity. The following episode, which I observed at Hama Middle School, highlights the struggles that teachers are experiencing as they attempt to apply *yutori* ideals to student guidance.

Establishing a Sense of Order?

In the gym at Hama Middle School, Mr. Hori and Mrs. Sakamoto co-teach a physical education lesson during the second week of the academic year. The class is a composed of two classes of third year students, who straggle in at the beginning of the period and spread across the gymnasium. All the students are wearing warm-up suits, but most of their outfits have been altered. Several girls have cut lines in their pants, starting at the ankle and continuing up to the knee, creating flaps that hang like curtains in a window; others have removed the elastic cuffs from their sleeves. The boys have not invested as much energy into modifying their clothing as the girls, but still managed to communicate a sense of defiance. For example, it is rare to spot a boy whose pants or shorts reach up to his hips. The current fad is for boys to pull their pants down to their thighs, just covering the bottom hem of their shirts. I'm surprised that the droopy pants do not make it difficult to run, but the boys do not seem concerned. All the young men are wearing the requisite sweatpants, but I spot several who are not wearing the matching jacket.

Mr. Hori does not appear upset by the visual nonconformity displayed by these students. He stands in front and informs the group that today they will practice bowing and saying *"onegai shimasu"* (a greeting, loosely translated as "please teach us," which students typically recite in unison to begin all formal lessons). After demonstrating the proper bowing technique, he divides the class into groups of four and tells them to rehearse the action he just modeled. At this point, Mrs. Sakamoto, who has been observing from the opposite side of the gym, joins Mr. Hori in inspecting students as they practice bowing. Mrs. Sakamoto tells one girl to hold her buttocks together more tightly as she bows. Both instructors pay close attention to the angle of students' backs as they bend forward.

During these inspections, most of the participants listen carefully to the suggestions shared by their teachers and modify their performances accordingly. But as soon as a teacher moves on to another group, students tend to lose interest in the bowing exercise. One group of boys moves to a basketball hoop and takes turns trying to jump up and touch the rim; the members of another *han* initiate a shadow-boxing match; on the far side of the gym, a combination of boys and girls run across the floor and slide on their knees, enthusiastically engaging in a contest to see who can propel themselves the furthest.

The teachers continue to conduct the inspections but begin to look frustrated by the antics occurring around them. Thirty minutes into the period, Mr. Hori announces that the independent practice time has ended. He calls a group composed of two boys and two girls to the front of the gym and tells them to perform the ritual for the rest of the class. One of the boys yells out a command and the group forms a straight line, bows, and calls out "*onegai shimasu*" in unison. After a short pause, everyone turns to the right, creates a new line, and crisply repeats the set of steps. The audience applauds.

Mr. Hori calls a second group, all boys, to the front of the gym. This foursome is not nearly as impressive as the first. It follows the correct procedure, but with little enthusiasm. Mr. Hori announces that their posture was poor, and makes them repeat the act. The second performance does not look noticeably better than the first, but Mr. Hori offers no additional criticism before allowing the students to return to their spots on the floor. The next group, all girls, is even sloppier. Two of the performers giggle throughout, and the other two do not even attempt to bow. Mr. Hori, looking increasingly irritated, releases the four girls. The members of the audience who are chatting among themselves now outnumber those who are paying attention.

When only five minutes of the period remain, Mr. Hori returns to the front of the room and calls the class to attention. He instructs everyone to check if the person sitting next to them is sitting straight. Upon hearing this, most of the third-year students sit up; a few do not respond.

Mrs. Sakamoto walks over to four girls who are lying on the floor and tells them to pull their legs up against their chests. Two of the girls follow this direction; the other two ignore it.

Mr. Hori informs the students that he thinks they did a really good job and thanks them for their effort. After pausing briefly, he adds, "But you can do better. I would give you a score of twenty out of one hundred." He then demonstrates improvements they could make, such as holding their hands straight at their sides when they bow. Mr. Hori informs the group that it will continue to practice bowing and stretching the next time they meet.

This third-year P.E. lesson captures the tensions that many middle school teachers experienced as they attempted to adapt to changes in both their students and to the current approaches to guidance advocated by MEXT. In all three middle schools in my sample, instructors struggled to provide the appropriate balance of discipline and support to pupils whose needs, they believed, were more extensive than was common only a few years earlier. School employees could no longer depend on adolescents to compliantly adhere to the expectations of adults. Responding to long-standing criticism about excessive rigidity in the secondary schools, teachers were applying the concept of relaxed education to student supervision as well. As the third-grade P.E. lesson illustrates, most found it quite difficult to loosen up and maintain order at the same time.

Mr. Hori endeavored to straddle traditional approaches to class management and the more flexible, student-centered practices advocated in conjunction with *yutori kyoiku*. Following a ritual used in secondary schools for decades, he sought to establish a dependable routine that would create order in his class, and to instill in students a sense of seriousness that they would display throughout the year. As LeTendre (2000) has observed, Japanese teachers tend to believe that "given proper routines, young adolescents [can] control their behavior and organize themselves quite effectively in groups" (119). Yet the power of such routines has always depended on a delicate balance of clearly communicated behavioral expectations, student obedience, an established system of peer monitoring, as well as the presence of a teacher willing to assert his authority when necessary. In Mr. Hori's class, however, students seemed to understand that misbehavior would not generate any serious consequences. That reality undermined teacher authority. In the relaxed environment of his gym, Mr. Hori lacked an effective response to displays of misbehavior.

The third-year students realized that they had a choice whether or not to follow their teachers' instructions. The third graders capitalized on the freedom provided to them: about half of the group performed according to Mr. Hori's specifications; the other half displayed some form of resistance to authority. The most obvious sign of nonconformity was communicated visually. In the past, students who did not follow their school's dress code could face serious disciplinary consequences. That was not the case at Hama, or any of the other middle schools I visited. These institutions no longer "demand tremendous conformity in external presentation" (LeTendre 2000, 55). Not only did Mr. Hori's pupils come to class without some of the standard pieces of the physical education uniform, but many of them went to great lengths to alter the items that they did wear. One could argue that slicing a pair of gym pants from ankle to knee in four places constituted defacement of the school uniform. Yet neither Mr. Hori nor Mrs. Sakamoto commented on such infractions. They did not express criticism to students with long or dyed hair, makeup, or pierced body parts. It was difficult for me to identify the lines that divided acceptable and unacceptable dress.

Also notable was the lackadaisical attitude displayed by a large percentage of the students. As I state above, several of the third-year students did take the activity seriously, using the independent practice period to hone their bowing skills. They were outnumbered, however, by pupils who invested minimal effort in the activity. Some followed Mr. Hori's directions at a surface level but socialized with their friends when not being observed by a teacher. Others made no attempt to disguise their disinterest in the proceedings. Through silence, refusal to follow directions, and verbal comments, they expressed a critique of the lesson.

The two teachers—both veteran teachers who were well liked by students—appeared unsure about how to respond to student resistance. It is quite possible that in a pre–relaxed-education environment, the instructors would not have tolerated such displays of disrespect; students who refused to follow instructions would have been sternly reprimanded or punished. But Mr. Hori and Mrs. Sakamoto avoided exercising their authority in a heavy-handed manner. The teachers did not raise their voices or scold individuals who chose not to take the activity seriously. Instead, they encouraged and cajoled misbehaving pupils, to little effect. The difficulties that Mr. Hori and Mrs. Sakamoto experienced during this lesson are illustrative of the challenges faced by teachers in all the middle schools I studied, regardless of their subject-area specialty. Instructors understood the rationale that was driving the shift to more student-friendly mentoring approaches, but very few had figured out how to follow such advice and maintain order in their classrooms at the same time.

Social Foundation for Relaxed Student Guidance

The trend toward more permissive approaches to student guidance is consistent with the great value attached to maintaining harmony at the interpersonal level in Japanese society (Krauss, Rohlen, and Steinhoff 1984). Lebra (1984) identifies specific strategies that are commonly used to reduce the chances that disagreements among individuals will produce overt tension among the members of a social collective: anticipatory management, negative communication, situational code switching, triadic management, displacement, self-aggression, and conflict acceptance (55–56). In the past, the power asymmetries that characterized teacher-student relationships reduced the pressure placed on instructors to prevent conflict from bubbling to the surface in their classrooms. As the central authority figures in schools, they were given license to confront misbehaving students (Miller 2010). Awareness of the extensive authority wielded by adults reduced the frequency of student resistance. Another interpretation of this situation would be that in forcefully exerting their authority, teachers initiated short bursts of conflict so as to achieve enduring group harmony. Severe responses from faculty to what might be considered even minor infractions of school rules (such as wearing skirts that were too short or bringing candy to school) served to warn the school community that such behavior would not be tolerated.

The teachers I observed for this study went to great lengths to avoid such eruptions from occurring. The approach they most frequently employed in attempt to avoid conflict was anticipatory management, to use Lebra's term. For example, they devised seating charts that separated students prone to misbehavior, or alternated rows of boys and girls. Another common practice was to facilitate class discussions about the importance of following school rules, and the consequences of failing to do so. In these talks, teachers tried to instill in students a sense of personal responsibility that would help them make wise choices. During a second-grade homeroom meeting I observed at the beginning of the academic year, Mr. Aosaki delivered the following speech to his class, in a very calm and supportive manner:

> The principal told me that Hama students usually score slightly below 50% on the prefectural achievement tests. At the last school where I worked, kids also scored below average, but they gradually improved and many more students went to high school after graduation. It doesn't take a lot to improve—

> just high expectations and concentration. I heard that the school has a good baseball team. If kids can do well at baseball, they can also do well at other things. If you concentrate on other things like you do in sports, you will gradually improve in those areas too. You all have to come to middle school, but after you graduate, things will become much more free—you will get to make many choices, about school as well as other things. It is important for you to start focusing and thinking about what you want to do with your future. Even little choices matter. For example, I noticed that most students are wearing skirts that are the proper length. They will probably make them a bit shorter in the future, and then continue trimming them until they are really short. Think about decisions like that and how they reflect on you.

Anticipatory management, such as the lecture given by this homeroom teacher, depends on student follow-through to yield its desired outcomes. Consistent with the framing of the middle school as a site of transition from childhood to adulthood, Mr. Aosaki shared his thoughts with his students but emphasized that they ultimately needed to take responsibility for their own actions—that they determined their own fate. This message did not represent a departure from the ideas that have traditionally anchored student guidance in Japanese middle schools; but in the contemporary setting, students have greater leeway to apply that advice as they see fit or are capable. In the past, the systems of social control used in the middle schools prevented most students who struggled academically from overtly challenging authority. That is no longer the case.

Lebra's list of strategies for avoiding confrontation does not include a common practice I observed in Japanese schools. When faced with students who did not follow approved scripts, teachers often attempted to modify their behavior through gentle *prodding*. Rather than directly state their displeasure with the pupil, they used indirect physical or verbal cues in attempt to induce a change in behavior. They often resorted to this approach when more subtle methods—such as Mr. Aosaki's lecture about ignoring rules—failed to produce the desired response. The force of the prodding was adjusted to fit the severity of the issue, the attitude of the target student, and the setting. Responding to undesirable behavior in this manner allowed teachers to communicate their displeasure to pupils without delivering ultimatums or punishments.

School employees also used prodding in public situations—such as school assemblies or special events—where holding extended conversations with students might be awkward. In these settings, adults gently encouraging pupils to modify their appearance or behavior. At one schoolwide assembly I attended, for example, teachers lined the perimeter of the gym while a series of speakers delivered speeches about the need for everyone to do a better job of keeping the campus clean. Throughout the meeting, first- and second-year students remained seated in straight lines, listening quietly. Many third graders, in contrast, shifted from their original positions and began chatting with their neighbors. Spotting these breaches of etiquette, several of the third-grade homeroom teachers intervened. Careful not to interrupt the proceedings, they walked through the gym and moved the bodies of pupils into the appropriate positions: pressing their arms against the smalls of students' backs to get them to sit up straight, repositioning their legs, and pulling their arms to the front of their bodies. The vice principal approached a boy who had removed the jacket of his uniform, untucked his white shirt, and pulled his pants below his hips. Without saying anything, the administrator attempted to push the boy's shirt into his pants, but the student pushed him away. After several unsuccessful attempts, the vice principal gave up and left. About two minutes after the vice principal departed, the boy tucked in his pants and put on his uniform jacket. The teachers and vice principal did manage to effect some change in the appearance of the third graders at this assembly, but the methods they employed were time and labor intensive. Furthermore, although harmony was maintained, even after teachers prodded the students, their behavior and appearance was less than stellar.

Teachers also used the prodding technique in the classroom. The combination of nudges, carefully worded requests, repositioning of students, and hand gestures they utilized often resembled a choreographed dance. Following the moves of the dance and lecturing at the same time was quite challenging. Rarely did I observe an educator give in and respond harshly to students who continued to act out, even after repeated attempts to manage the behavior of pupils through prodding proved unsuccessful. Novice as well as veteran educators were more likely to encourage changes in pupil conduct than to exert their authority directly. This often exacerbated the stress experienced by instructors and emboldened students to challenge teachers, both directly and indirectly.

Clearly, shifts in the approved approaches to managing student behavior have produced changes in institutional culture, authority hierarchies, and student attachment to middle schools. In the next section, I examine students' responses to the more *yutori* guidance practices used in the middle schools.

Student Responses to Increased Autonomy

Adolescents in Japan have always challenged authority, but in the past they usually conveyed their dissatisfaction subtly or in locations removed from campus (White 1987). Middle school students have learned that they no longer have to be so discreet. In the schools I visited, second-and third-year students unapologetically adjusted their bodies and possessions to assert their individuality. As I mention above, boys as well as girls grew their hair longer than was officially permitted; they also dyed it a variety shades. Boys' sideburns sometimes extended below their cheeks. Girls wore makeup and jewelry that could be quite flashy. Individuals of both genders pierced their ears, lips, and eyebrows. Students shortened the hems of their uniforms, removed the cuffs, added additional layers, and left pieces (such as neckties) at home. They also modified accessories and physical spaces to fit their personalities. Backpacks were often covered with stickers, ornaments, and decorative patches. Rarely did I sit at a desk that was free of graffiti. Pupils used a variety of instruments to make their mark: pens, stickers, knives, and the like. (One day I sat at a desk that had been inscribed with the phrase "sex pencils," which brought a smile to my face). They also placed a variety of objects (tape dispensers, stuffed animals, plastic and metal figurines) on top of their desks to create a sort of portable office space.

Some might consider these examples of resistance trivial or insignificant. Teachers in other parts of the world face challenges to authority far more serious than dyed hair or graffiti-covered desks. In the Japanese context, however, acceptance of these acts represented a sharp detour from previous practice. Only a few years ago, schools cracked down on even minor infractions of rules. On the campuses I studied, such actions were generally accepted without protest. When I asked teachers about this, they expressed frustration with the situation but did not feel that they had any recourse. As one instructor at Hama Middle School told me, "Piercing is not permitted, but there is nothing we can do about it. We have talked with the parents, but nothing happened. It bothers me, but I don't know what else I can do."

Relaxed enforcement of school rules enhanced the autonomy enjoyed by students, who in the past were required to adhere to those policies or face serious consequences. Many treated school rituals designed to serve an integrative function as "empty formalities" (Geertz 1960) that had little connection to their immediate needs. Capitalizing on the mismatch between official school policies and their implementation on campus, adolescents questioned, criticized, and resisted behavioral directives with increasing boldness. Teachers may have been inclined to avoid conflict, but not all students place a high priority on preserving group harmony.

I do not mean to imply that middle school classrooms in Japan are the anarchic sites of youth rebellion that media reports on classroom collapse (*gakkyu hokkai*) sometimes suggest. I did not witness any secondary teachers who had completely lost control of a group of pupils. In most rooms I visited, the majority of students sat quietly at their desks, followed the rules, and performed the assigned tasks. For a variety of reasons, the absence of negative consequences for misbehavior did not tempt such students to challenge authority. Those with promising academic futures tended to focus on lessons regardless of the instructor's approach to class management. The pressures of the entrance examination system supplied them with the motivation to invest in academic activities. Another carrot that good students chased was the possibility of receiving one of the recommendation letters (*suisen*) given by the faculty to reward select individuals for their academic accomplishments. Third graders who were awarded *suisen* received priority in the admissions process—and were not required to take written entrance examinations. As one would expect, students who invested in learning activities tended to come from families firmly committed to education.

Displaying an oppositional stance toward the school and its employees could jeopardize the opportunities available to individuals whose futures were predicated on scholastic success. But the middle school students who were most likely to "subvert or sabotage the normative codes of the dominant school order" (McLaren 1985, 87) were rarely those who had been identified as having promising academic futures. This tended to desensitize them to threats about the long-term consequences of their misbehavior. A reduction in educational options was not likely to concern adolescents who were not actively participating in the academic competition. Instead, they tended to make decisions based on their most immediate needs.

Forms of resistance displayed by disaffected middle school students varied substantially. Most of the classes I observed included both pupils who compliantly sat through the lectures delivered by their teachers, and others who expressed their disinterest in the proceedings. It was easy for instructors to overlook individuals who were tuned-out or sleeping. The presence of disengaged adolescents is nothing new to the secondary classroom. More obtrusive actions included throwing notebooks, punching other students, moving desks from their assigned positions, sitting on the floor, and leaving the room in the middle of a lesson.

The paucity of meaningful short- as well as long-term penalties for insubordination expanded the autonomy enjoyed by pupils who did not conform to the institutional social order. Teachers, in turn, felt constrained by the limits to the guidance procedures deemed acceptable in the relaxed-education era. Most of the educators I interviewed felt that it was important to earn both the trust and respect of their pupils. As one teacher posited, "Teachers should treat students with kindness—but not try too hard to be their friends. Young teachers today sometimes make this mistake. Although teachers should be friendly to students, the students must also look up to them with respect." Another middle school instructor told me that "many of my established ideas about what students should be like and what they should do have been broken. My fixed ideas have become very unstable. The border between student and teacher is shifting. There needs to be a better balance between group and individual needs."

Some of the more experienced instructors I observed were not waylaid by the changes that had occurred; finding the appropriate balance of firmness and flexibility, they earned the respect of their students and maintained order in the classroom. Those individuals were outnumbered by colleagues who engaged in an ongoing search for nonconfrontational strategies they could use to keep students focused in class. For many, speaking softly without the aid of a big stick was no simple task. The enormity of this challenge created stress and feelings of futility that could be quite debilitating.

Home-School Connections

Compounding the challenges facing teachers as they attempted to maintain order in the classroom were extensive changes in the social fabric of Japanese communities. As described above, instructors believed that many of their pupils did not display appropriate respect toward adults. In addition, teachers no longer felt that they could depend on parents to reinforce the values that anchored social interactions on campus. According to faculty and administrators I spoke with, the behavioral issues that surfaced at school were exacerbated by parents who did not adequately support their children or the school. Such tensions created both psychological and logistical difficulties for teachers.

Verifying claims about ineffective parenting would be a difficult task. Although I did interview mother and fathers about their views on relaxed education, I did not conduct formal observations of them interacting with children away from school. The volume of the concerns expressed by teachers, however, pronounced that this was an issue that deserved more attention. And evidence of parent-child and parent-school rifts did occasionally surface in the schools where I was working. The most striking example of this occurred in the Hama Middle School teacher room:

At 8:15 one morning, the day of the second-grade class trip to the mountains, two girls, Mari and Nana, engage in a long and heated conversation with Mr. Uehara and Mrs. Yano, the teachers responsible for leading the trip. Mr. Uehara states that there is a school rule prohibiting students from bringing cell phones to school, and anyone who breaks a rule cannot go on the trip. He says that if the girls agree to leave their phones behind, they can join their classmates, who are waiting at the train station. The girls, however, do not find this proposal acceptable, and state so quite emphatically. Angered by this response, Mr. Uehara tells the girls that he is really upset by their attitude and because they are not listening to him. Several minutes later, observing no sign of contrition from the girls, the head teacher intercedes: he advises them to listen to what the teachers are telling them and calls Mari's father on the phone to explain to him what has happened. By this point, Mari is sobbing heavily. After several unsuccessful attempts at speech, she finally grabs the phone and complains to her father that this is a terrible experience for her ("*Kore wa taihen da*"). She screams "*Yada!*" (roughly translated as "no way," or "terrible") into the receiver, slams it down, and walks to a table in the back of the room.

Mr. Uehara and Mrs. Yano join the girls at the back of the room to discuss the incident. From my desk I cannot follow their conversation. Just before 9:00, Mr. Uehara walks to the front of the room and informs the head teacher that Mari's mother is on her way to school and will take her daughter home because Mari refused to turn over her cell phone. While this is going on, Nana picks up her backpack and slips out of the room. Mr. Uehara calls out, "Where are you going?" but receives no response. Mr. Uehara and Mrs. Yano run after Nana. After approximately five minutes, Mr. Uehara returns and tells the head teacher that Nana has escaped from the campus and cannot be found. The other teachers in the room continue chatting and working, as if nothing unusual has occurred.

Ten minutes later, Mrs. Uehara, Mrs. Yano, Mari, Nana, and their mothers return to the faculty room and sit down at the table in the back. Both mothers are dressed in skirts and blouses, resembling businesswomen on their way to a meeting. As soon as everyone is seated, Mr. Uehara intones, "You have been disrespectful. It is important not to bring a cell phone to school, but even more important to follow school rules." When Nana begins to interrupt him, the teacher yells at her to be silent. Using informal Japanese, Nana replies, "I understand" (*Wakatte iru*). In a shaky voice,

Nana's mother adds, "It's the same with everyone—adults have to follow rules too. You need to be considerate of the people around you." The teacher orders the girls to write a statement that conveys their intention to follow school rules in the future and to sign their pledges. Mari's mother says she thinks this is a good idea, but that it would also be helpful if the teachers spoke with each girl individually, because she is worried that her daughter might not seriously reflect on what she has done (*"Honto ni hansai ni naranai"*).

Finally, after both girls have written and signed their pledges, they gather their things and prepare to leave. Nana's mother asks Mr. Uehara for directions to the field-trip site. Mari calls out something to Mr. Uehera. I don't make out her words, but her mother becomes visibly upset. "Why? Why? Why do you do this?" she asks Mari, and begins crying. The mother and daughter yell at each other for several more minutes. Finally, they pick up their belongings and prepare to leave. Mari's mother apologizes to the teachers for the intrusion, and the parents and children exit the room. I hear Mari and her mother continue to scream at each other in the hallway. Mr. Uehara closes the door to the room, leans against the door, and sighs.

The next day I asked Uehara-sensei to explain to me what happened before and after the explosion in the faculty room:

CB: Can you explain to me the problem that occurred with the girls on the day of the field trip?

US: There were two problems: (1) cell phones; (2) uniforms. The girls refused to give in with either. I think the parents understand what we want the students to do, but they can't control their children. We wanted them to do certain things, but they refused. Finally, the children understood what I meant and they were allowed to go on the field trip. In the mountains they did very well. They didn't cause any problems at all. . . . Some of the parents are okay. But the problem is Mari. Her parents are very difficult parents. This is a very big problem. They don't understand what to do. They are very weak. Sometimes Mari ignores her parents. That makes the problems at school more difficult.

CB: What do you think can be done to help these children?

US: I think we need to be more strict. But it might take time—a couple of years—before things really change. It is mostly a family problem, I think. Maybe 90 percent a family problem. They are nice kids as friends, but it is very difficult to work with them as students. Some teachers have given up on them.

CB: Why haven't you given up on them?

US: Because I am waiting for them to change.

CB: Did the students bring their mobile phones on the field trip?

US: No. We won!

This incident underscores the complex relationship between families and schools in contemporary Japan. Teachers no longer feel that they can assume parents will provide the support their sons and daughters need to succeed in school. In the middle schools I studied, teachers frequently talked about the difficulties students experienced in school as a result of problems in their homes. Although most adolescents came to school academically and emotionally prepared to learn, teachers believed that the number of students who did not receive the parental support they needed was growing steadily. In response to this trend, schools felt compelled to educate parents as well as children.

When discussing issues such as teacher authority, student-teacher relationships, and school culture, educators frequently referred to changes in the families they served. Student and parent behavior were often difficult to disentangle. At almost every middle school I visited, educators described how the expanding gap between home and school was complicating their work:

MR. HOTTA (MIDDLE SCHOOL VICE PRINCIPAL): In the past, parents clearly communicated to children what was expected of them, as students and as members of society. They made sure that their children did what was expected of them. That is no longer the case. Now there are many parents who aren't sure how to raise their children. They have trouble carrying out their responsibilities as parents.

MRS. NAKAGAWA (MIDDLE SCHOOL COUNSELOR): These days, it's easy to do many things merely by pushing a button—in daily life, at work. But it's not that easy with children. They require more attention. For example, before it was hard to imagine parents sending their children to school without making them breakfast, but there are many families like that now. Adults want to solve problems simply by pushing a button. That isn't possible when it comes to raising children.

MR. TOMITA (MIDDLE SCHOOL SOCIAL STUDIES TEACHER): The number of "unbelievable" parents is increasing, families who do not pay school fees, do not spend time with their children, who do not prepare meals for their children but just give them money to buy something at a convenience store—that kind of families is increasing. So we have to teach not only the students, but also the parents. Even then we can't depend on parents to support education. We have to provide parent education.

MRS. TERAKAWA (MIDDLE SCHOOL JAPANESE TEACHER): Before, parents were very strict, but now they indulge (*amaeru*) their children. Also, gaps between high- and low-achieving students have increased a great deal. Kids whose parents have strong educational backgrounds excel in school, while those whose parents did not, struggle. I think most of the problems kids experience today are tied to their parents.

As teachers attempted to implement *yutori kyoiku* policies, they were also responding to extensive changes in children and in families. The "intensive program of social control" (Fukuzawa 1994, 83) that previously produced a dependable sense of order in most schools, was beginning to unravel. Students like Mari and Nana did not hesitate to resist school authority or disregard rules that undermined their personal freedom. In the past, teachers could forcefully respond to such transgressions, confident that parents would support their actions. That is no longer the case. As Mrs. Terakawa notes, not all guardians reinforce the norms or behavioral expectations designed to create order in middle schools. This development created ongoing challenges for teachers as they attempted to maintain order on campus and in the classroom.

Coping Strategies

When their attempts to guide students using nonconfrontational strategies such as anticipatory management and prodding did not produce their desired outcomes, teachers often resorted to two other management techniques described by Lebra (1984): self-aggression and conflict acceptance. Lebra includes a range of behaviors under the term self-aggression, from remonstrative compliance to guilt to suicide (47–53). Common to all types of self-aggression is acceptance of responsibility for the actions of others as a mechanism for reducing stress. This was often true of teachers who failed to establish productive connections with students. Instructors who experimented with multiple management strategies and still faced resistance in the classroom frequently began to question their own abilities.

The middle school educators I observed devoted innumerable hours to their work as teachers and mentors. Their ongoing inability to engage unruly students generated feelings of guilt, self-recrimination, and helplessness. Younger teachers in particular often lacked a history of positive accomplishments to offset the frustrations they experienced. The most severe example of self-aggression I witnessed occurred when a combination of difficulties managing students and keeping up with her work proved overwhelming to a math teacher. The woman lost her appetite, had trouble sleeping, experienced a shortness of breath, and her fingertips became numb. After a short hospital stay failed to improve her condition, the woman was put on leave for the remainder of the semester.

Another common response to recurring student resistance was resigned acceptance of less than ideal conditions in the schools. Acknowledging the limits of their influence over students, teachers sometimes acceded to changes that were too diffuse and unwieldy for them to control. In the classroom, they ignored students who tuned out or displayed resistance, and directed their lectures to those who were paying attention. If students chatted in the back of the room, the teacher simply increased the volume of her voice. For many, acceptance represented a form of self-preservation. Attempting to reform rebellious adolescents was too exhausting, given the multiple responsibilities assigned to school employees. In another era—when acts of resistance were less frequent, respect for teachers greater, and families dependably lined up in support of schools—the teachers I interviewed might have taken a more proactive stance; in the contemporary context, many opted to follow the path of least resistance.

Implications of Findings Related to Student Guidance in Japan

This analysis of the effects of Japan's relaxed-education policies on student-teacher interactions underscores the depth of change associated with any fundamental school reform effort. Although reports on *yutori kyoiku* tend to focus on the effects of those policies on academic achievement, attempts to reduce pressure in schools were more pervasive than has been acknowledged. As this chapter illustrates, the shift to more relaxed learning environments influenced student-teacher interactions in unanticipated ways. Those changes transformed the learning environment in many middle school classrooms I observed, and created widespread uncertainty for the individuals charged with implementing the new curriculum. The destabilization associated with revised guidance procedures and configurations of authority created an environment, I would argue, that proved as taxing for teachers as did modifications to the curriculum. In many cases, the interplay between changes in guidance practices, curricula, and student attitudes about school created formidable challenges for middle school instructors.

Ideally, I would end this discussion with descriptions of institutions or individuals that managed to balance academic rigor and students' emotional well-being. The last section of the chapter would include examples of guidance strategies employed by Japanese teachers that could be borrowed by educators in other schools in Japan and abroad to create orderly and supportive learning environments. The observation and interview data I collected, however, yield no such facile solutions. Instead, they accentuate the daunting complexity of inspiring adolescents and maintaining high academic standards at the same time. In place of such a class management toolbox, I offer a set of observations about the complex relationship between school guidance and academic accountability:

Japanese adolescents are sensitive to their status within a school hierarchy. They are keenly aware of—and concerned about—the perceptions of others regarding their abilities, personalities, appearances, skills, and power. Middle school students actively seek to improve their social standing, and shape their behavior to conform to locally, nationally, and globally constructed cultural norms. Individuals who fail to achieve an acceptable level of peer respect frequently remove themselves from the dominant school culture. Some disaffected students withdraw in the classroom, remaining physically present but emotionally isolated; others brazenly challenge authority.

Although oppositional relationships between adolescents and schools are common in many other countries, the powerful influence of high-stakes tests in Japan exacerbates the intensity of school life and feeds the social sorting that takes place. In the middle schools I visited, status hierarchies became apparent precisely when students started to prepare for high school examinations. At that point, the democratic social environment that characterized their previous years in school was replaced by a vertically organized hierarchy heavily influenced by one's academic standing. Pupils who received low marks on examinations were more likely to develop on oppositional stance to school than those with bright academic futures.

Relaxed-education courses did provide some respite to students who received low grades in core academic subjects. Those individuals often displayed interest in learning and extracurricular activities that did not measure their success or failure based on test scores. In the schools I studied, students who struggled in core academic subjects often showed increased enthusiasm for hands-on, activity-based activities than for lecture-driven lessons.

Teachers frequently had trouble following MEXT directives related to student guidance. Many found that broad proclamations about more "friendly" approaches to class management were difficult to apply in their classrooms. The absence of a detailed set of procedures that could be used in a relaxed school environment left many instructors feeling unmoored. Lacking such information, teachers tended to use pieces of a school guidance system that had been effective in previous decades. Yet partial implementation what had been considered an effective web of practices no longer produced the expected outcomes. Challenges associated with unpredictable guidance practices exacerbated the uncertainties experienced by teachers as they attempted to implement the relaxed-education curriculum.

One clear and unequivocal conclusion that can be derived from this picture of uncertainty is that decisions related to school guidance have a direct and cogent influence on the outcomes of education reform initiatives. Encouraging teachers to act as allies in the classroom and avoid confrontations with their students may reduce the pressure experienced by adolescents, especially those with poor academic track records—but also provide the freedom to challenge authority with greater confidence. Applying more rigid methods and holding students more accountable—academically and socially—in contrast, may reduce the motivation of students who do not perform well in core academic subject classes. The importance attached to high-stakes tests appears to heighten their feelings of inadequacy. Skillful teachers may find ways to act as supportive ally within a test-driven learning environment, but evidence from Japan suggests this is no easy task. Even the most experienced educators I observed had difficulty performing as both student ally and class manager in the relaxed-education era. Although the context for teaching and learning in the United States differs from that in Japan, the findings of this study underscore the importance of carefully considering student-teacher interactions—in addition to test scores—when analyzing the impact of education reform policies.

NINE

Broadening the Discussion

The evidence presented thus far indicates that *yutori kyoiku* policies had minimal impact on the instructional program in Japanese schools. As I note, teachers were generally hesitant to follow reform guidelines that did not quickly produce the outcomes predicted by MEXT, or when they perceived of the new curriculum as competing with established practices in their schools. Parents, teachers, and administrators all expressed concern that introduction of the relaxed curriculum would reduce the amount of instructional time that would otherwise be used to cover material likely to appear on entrance examinations. When confronted with that possibility, even individuals who agreed with the goals of relaxed education resisted change. The demands of an examination-driven system created a barrier that was too formidable to overcome.

In this chapter, I expand the scope of my vision and consider the effects of education-reform policies recently enacted in Asian countries that regularly appear alongside Japan near the top of international league tables. What lessons can be learned from the highly regarded education systems in South Korea, China, and Singapore? How are they organized to produce excellence? Is Japan an outlier, or one of many nations that have attempted—and struggled—to reduce the influence of testing in schools? Have any of those countries managed to raise academic achievement without generating excessive pressure on their students? If so, what strategies have they used that might be implemented in other nations eager to join them at the top of the international achievement rankings?

Next, I examine the trajectory of educational reform in another country that has also received considerable attention as a result of its impressive performance on TIMSS and PISA: Finland. Although Finnish students appear alongside their peers from China, South Korea, and Singapore near the top of international league tables, government leaders in Finland charted a unique pathway to success. The process of formulating policy as well as the specific tactics employed by Finnish education differ from those commonly relied on in Asia. Education planners in Finland, for example, decided that test-based accountability was not a prudent way to leverage change in schools. Descriptions of the approaches and effects of education policies implemented in Finland add a layer to the topic of relaxed education that should not be overlooked.

Finally, I redirect my gaze to the United States. Delving below the rhetorical claims anchoring policies such as the No Child Left Behind Act, I examine research that assesses the impact of new accountability mandates on student learning. More than a decade has passed since NCLB was enacted. Has the legislation produced the results its authors predicted? Do analyses of the effects of the reform confirm that tightly prescribing and monitoring teacher behavior is a more effective reform strategy than the more flexible method employed in Japan? Have there been any unexpected consequences of expanding the influence of examinations in public schools? Scholarship that addresses these questions provides a strong evidentiary base that was not available when NCLB and the relaxed-education policies were introduced. Studying that literature can provide valuable insights into the process of reforming schools with the goal of balancing academic rigor and student engagement.

Perspectives from Other Locations

Looking east for ideas and lessons related to educational reform seems to make a great deal of sense, given the notable performance of schools in China, Singapore, and South Korea. These three education systems are frequently held up as models worthy of emulation. Reporters, politicians, and education officials have all studied practices in Asian schools and attempted to identify specific practices that promote academic success, and might be used by teachers in other contexts to produce similar results.

The excellent reputation of these education systems is particularly impressive if we consider the speed and scope of their development. Governments in all three nations facilitated major restructuring of their education systems in less than fifty years. This suggests that effective policy planning can leverage significant changes in teaching and learning. Regarding the schools as vital components of nation building, politicians treated education as a critical component of national integration and economic survival. Rather than search for quick fixes, they developed a set of overarching goals, and tailored supporting policies to match those goals. Capitalizing on the insights they acquired from studying school systems in other locations, bureaucrats outlined long-term reform plans that were implemented in a series of stages.

Initially, education planners focused on expanding access to schools and providing citizens with basic literacy and numeracy skills. They accomplished this task quite with remarkable efficiency. The Cultural Revolution "resulted in a massive disruption of education in China" (Deng and Treiman 1997, 400). During this period, the government shut down all secondary and tertiary institutions, and the purging of citizens labeled "class enemies" decimated the teaching force. In 1980, the Chinese government set a goal of achieving universal primary education, and by 2000 the enrollment rate of all school-age children reached 99%. Between 1990 and 2005, the transition rate to tertiary schools in China leapt from 27.3% to 76.3% (Wu 2007). The Singaporean government also regarded education as a critical aspect of national integration. In 1959, when the former British colony became self-governing, a majority of its citizens was illiterate and unskilled; education was available only to the affluent. By the mid-1960s, all Singaporean children had access to primary education, and a decade later the same was true of lower secondary education (Stewart 2011). And South Korea made the transition from "a nation where a majority of the adult population to one of the world's most schooled societies" (Seth 2012, 17) in less than fifty years. At the end of the twentieth century, enrollment rates at all levels of schooling in China, Singapore, and South Korea were comparable to those in most Western European countries (Seth 2012; Stewart 2011; Wu 2007).

Another facet of educational development in Asia that generated widespread attention was evidence indicating that not only had the percentages of children who attended school increased, those students were entering the workforce with solid academic foundations. As table 9.1 illustrates, South Korean, Chinese, and Singaporean children performed admirably on assessments of basic academic skills.[1] They demonstrated their intellectual prowess at the elementary and secondary level, in math as well as science. These education systems appeared to be producing a steady supply of citizens well prepared to fuel economic growth.

The heavy representation of Asian nations at the top of international achievement rankings drew attention to the great promise of educational reform—but also to highlight ineffective policies. Journalists around the world used the results of TIMSS and PISA to accentuate the shortcomings of countries that trailed Japan, China, Singapore and South Korea in the

Table 9.1. PISA results: Top 10 performers over time

	READING					
	2003		2006		2009*	
1.	Finland	543	Korea	556	Shanghai	556
2.	Korean	534	Finland	547	Korea	539
3.	Canada	528	Hong Kong	536	Finland	536
4.	Australia	525	Canada	527	Hong Kong	533
5.	Liechtenstein	525	New Zealand	521	Singapore	526
6.	New Zealand	522	Ireland	517	Canada	524
7.	Ireland	515	Australia	513	New Zealand	521
8.	Sweden	514	Liechtenstein	510	Japan	520
9.	Netherlands	513	Poland	508	Australia	515
10.	Hong Kong	510	Sweden	507	Netherlands	508
	MATH					
	2003		2006		2009*	
1.	Hong Kong	550	Finland	548	Shanghai	600
2.	Finland	544	Korea	547	Singapore	562
3.	Korea	542	Netherlands	541	Hong Kong	555
4.	Netherlands	538	Switzerland	530	Korea	546
5.	Liechtenstein	536	Canada	527	Taiwan	543
6.	Japan	534	Japan	523	Finland	541
7.	Canada	532	New Zealand	522	Liechtenstein	536
8.	Belgium	529	Belgium	520	Switzerland	534
9.	Macao	527	Australia	520	Japan	529
10.	Switzerland	527	Denmark	513	Canada	526
	SCIENCE					
	2003		2006		2009*	
1.	Finland	548	Finland	536	Shanghai	575
2.	Japan	548	Canada	534	Finland	554
3.	Hong Kong	539	Japan	531	Hong Kong	549
4.	Korea	538	New Zealand	530	Singapore	542
5.	Liechtenstein	525	Australia	527	Japan	539
6.	Australia	525	Netherlands	525	Korea	538
7.	Macao	525	Korea	522	New Zealand	532
8.	Netherlands	524	Germany	516	Canada	529
9.	Czech Republic	523	United Kingdom	525	Estonia	528
10.	New Zealand	521	Czech Republic	513	Australia	527

*Singapore and Shanghai participated in PISA for the first time in 2009.

Source: OECD (Organization for Economic Cooperation and Development) PISA results for 2003, 2006, and 2009

Table 9.2. TIMSS results: Top 10 performers over time

	2003							
	Math				Science			
	Fourth grade		Eighth grade		Fourth grade		Eighth grade	
1.	Singapore	594	Singapore	605	Singapore	565	Singapore	578
2.	Hong Kong	575	Korea	589	Taipei	551	Taipei	571
3.	Japan	565	Hong Kong	586	Japan	543	Korea	558
4.	Taipei	564	Taipei	585	Hong Kong	542	Hong Kong	556
5.	Belgium	551	Japan	570	United Kingdom	540	Estonia	552
6.	Netherlands	540	Belgium	537	United States	536	Japan	552
7.	Latvia	536	Netherlands	536	Latvia	532	Hungary	543
8.	Lithuania	534	Estonia	531	Hungary	530	Netherlands	536
9.	Russian Federation	532	Hungary	529	Russian Federation	526	United States	527
10.	United Kingdom	531	Malaysia	508	Netherlands	525	Australia	527

	2007							
	Math				Science			
	Fourth grade		Eighth grade		Fourth grade		Eighth grade	
1.	Hong Kong	607	Taipei	598	Singapore	587	Singapore	567
2.	Singapore	599	Korea	597	Taipei	557	Taipei	561
3.	Taipei	576	Singapore	593	Hong Kong	554	Japan	554
4.	Japan	568	Hong Kong	572	Japan	548	Korea	553
5.	Kazakhstan	549	Japan	570	Russian Federation	546	England	542
6.	Russian Federation	544	Hungary	517	Latvia	542	Hungary	539
7.	England	541	England	513	England	542	Czech Republic	539
8.	Latvia	537	Russian Federation	512	United States	539	Slovenia	538
9.	Netherlands	535	United States	508	Hungary	537	Hong Kong	530
10.	Lithuania	530	Lithuania	506	Italy	535	Russian Federation	530

Note: Finland and Mainland China did not participate in either version of TIMSS.

Source: USDOE, National Center for Education Statistics

education race. Headlines such as "Worldwide Survey Finds US Students Are Not Keeping Up" (Schemo 2000) and "Across Globe, We Have a Lot to Learn" (Zakaria 2006) rubbed salt into the wounds of teachers in underachieving nations. This situation was used as a call to rally the troops into action. An article in the *Australian Financial Review* posited that "when looking at the results of the TIMSS study the most obvious thing to note is that the Asian tigers consistently outperform their Western counterparts. . . . This, however, should not stop us from learning from their experience and identifying what can help us be the world's best" (Donnelly 1998). According to an article published in the *Los Angeles Times*, upon learning of America's poor showing on the test, President Bill Clinton "challenged his country's schools—which do only so-so internationally—to match the scores of Singapore" (Colvin 1997).

From the outside, it appeared that solutions to the problems plaguing American schools could be found in the East. Inspired by the performance of Asian students on international achievement tests, school districts in the United States, Australia, and the UK all adopted curricular materials that had proven effective in Asia (Gowen 2001; Garelick 2006). By the spring of 2001, for example, Singapore Math was "being used in more than 140 schools, 8 of them public, with major pilot programs in Baltimore; Paterson, N.J.; Chicago; Marshall, Wis.; Murrysville, Pa., and the North Middlesex Regional School District in Massachusetts" (Gowen 2001). Seduced by the impressive accomplishments of their Asian neighbors, education officials hoped that exposing the students in their schools to textbooks published abroad would propel them up the achievement rankings.

Widespread support for learning in Asian societies, rapid modernization of school systems, and strong performance on examinations may have elicited envy from observers abroad; inside these countries, though, rising test scores generated widespread concerns about the goals and direction of their education systems. At the same time that foreign observers were flocking to Asia in search of the secrets of academic success, contentious debates were raging throughout the region. Government officials in China, Singapore, and South Korea were all challenged to respond to cogent criticism of their schools. In these settings, education stakeholders expressed similar concerns: Children may have earned impressive test scores, but at what cost? Did products of these systems develop the creativity and critical thinking skills necessary for success in the twenty-first century? Was excessive academic competition responsible for growing social maladies among the nations' youth?

Concerns about the negative consequences of testing and competition led to the introduction of an array of reform initiatives throughout Asia. The similarities among those policies, which were formulated separately, were striking. As with *yutori kyoiku*, the initiatives were framed broadly, seeking to transform both curriculum and pedagogy at all levels of schooling. According to a series of reports published by the Chinese government, although the nation's teachers efficiently transmit factual information, students were not developing the social skills, creativity, or practical capabilities they needed to live fulfilling lives (Strauss 2013). Critics pointed to the interplay of a number of factors that created to this troubling situation: the prevalence of lecture-based instruction and rote learning, unnecessary homework assignments, neglect of students with learning difficulties, and a mismatch between school curricula and the demands of daily life (An, Hannum, and Sargent 2008; Pepper 1996). The most vociferous calls for change, however, focused on the detrimental effects of examination-driven education.

In response to these concerns, the Chinese government promulgated a group of reforms that aimed reduce the emphasis on examinations. The most ambitious of these was referred to as *suzhi jiaoyu* (or "education for quality"). *Suzhi jiaoyu* encouraged schools to revise both the content and delivery of the curriculum. Emphasis was placed on tailoring course offerings to better align with student interest and local conditions. In addition, textbooks were revised to include more activities explicitly designed to develop children's independent thinking and problem-solving skills, ability to work collaboratively, and capacity to think critically. In tandem with these modifications to the curriculum, the Ministry of Education encouraged teachers to make their pupils more active participants in the learning process (Dello-Iacovo 2009; Pepper 1996). Education officials instructed schools to reduce the amount of homework assigned to students, limit the number of instructional hours, and de-emphasize testing (Kipnis 2001). Recommendations designed to support *Suzhi jiaoyu* were written into a series of legislative acts, including the 2001 Tenth Five Year Plan and the 2003–2007 Action Plan for Invigorating Education, that were phased in gradually; by 2005, almost every region of China was supposed to follow the new curriculum as stated in MOE policy (Dello-Iacovo 2009). Later, the Ministry added a requirement that schools incorporate local topics into the curriculum.

Education officials in South Korea were forced to respond to similar issues. Abelmann, Choi, and Park (2012) observe that in Korean society has adapted rapidly to changes in technology, media, and commerce, but "mainstream schooling has been burdened by its fixed and homogenous curriculum, allowing for only limited creative expression" (2). Beginning in the 1970s, critics lamented the deleterious effects of the nation's "entrance examination hell." Targets of their reproach included excessive amounts of homework, emotional anxiety associated with entrance tests, competition among students, and the tendency to evaluate individuals based on the prestige of the schools they attend (Sorensen 1994). Instructors frequently focused lessons on test preparation and expected pupils to memorize large sections of textbooks. Education stakeholders often felt they had no choice but to shape their behavior to fit the demands of entrance examinations. Many parents hired tutors or sent their children to cram schools to increase their chances of passing entrance examinations. Members of the Korean Teachers' and Educators' Union asserted that high-stakes testing generated excessive competition in schools and undermined children's academic development (Kang 2012). Their apprehensions were validated in a report published by the UN Committee on the Rights of Children, which stated that the stress associated with examination-oriented education in South Korea constituted a human rights violation (Park 2011).

These concerns led to widespread claims that the Korean education system was in a state of crisis. In response, the government created a Presidential Commission on Education Reform (PCER) in 1994. After studying conditions in public schools, the PCER issued a series of reform recommendations. These included revising the curriculum so as to place greater emphasis on humanities and creativity, modifying college admissions procedures, and introducing more authentic assessment procedures (Lee 2001). A number of ambitious policies were enacted in succeeding years. Those reforms encouraged schools to institute "open education" approaches that focused on "the whole learning process" (Kim 2004, 128). In support of that goal, a broader and more balanced curriculum was introduced. Teachers were delegated greater decision making authority and encouraged to tailor the curriculum to fit the unique needs of their students. The reforms approved during that period have been called the most radical and comprehensive educational reforms ever embraced by the Korean government (Abelmann, Choi, and Park 2011, 2).

In 1995—only thirty-six years after Singapore became an independent nation—its fourth graders earned the highest scores in the world on the mathematics section of TIMSS. Those results made Singapore the envy of education planners around the globe—but masked domestic concerns about the state of the nation's schools. Conscious that "the price of high academic performance can be staggering" (Tan 2010, 53), the Singaporean government pursued an aggressive educational reform agenda. The Ministry of Education launched a series of campaigns designed to blunt criticism that Singaporean schools were too rigid and narrowly focused on core academic subjects. Instead, they needed to be more "flexible, to cope with pupils who mature mentally, physically, emotionally and socially at different rates" (Singapore Ministry of Education 2014).

The "Thinking Schools, Learning Nation" initiative, introduced in 1997, was designed to address such concerns. The ministry directed schools to reduce the prevalence of rote learning, standardized tests, and facilitate more "holistic learning" in the classroom (Ng 2008). In addition, the curriculum was expanded to include a more diverse array of offerings, and teachers were advised to use portfolios to assess student learning. The Master Plan for Information Technology in Education, enacted in the same year, integrated information technology into all areas of the curriculum (Tan and Gopinathan 2000). And the 2006 "Teach Less, Learn More" stressed that education should prepare students for life, rather to pass tests (Ng 2008; Tan 2010). The ultimate goal of this campaign was to "touch the hearts and engage the minds of learners by promoting a different learning paradigm in which there is less dependence on rote learning, repetitive tests, and instruction, and more on engaged learning" (Stewart 2011, 120).

Underlying all the reforms was concern that graduates of Singaporean schools often lacked the creativity and critical thinking skills required of leaders. According to this line of thought, the nation's schools produced a steady stream of dependable white-collar workers but few individuals who excel in their fields on an international scale; the rigid curriculum and emphasis on testing encouraged a follower's mentality, rather than a leader's (Tan 2010). As has been the case since Singapore achieved independence, education planners were intent on reshaping the school system to better meet the needs of its citizens. Studying best practices in their own schools and abroad, they sought to make learning more meaningful and less stressful for children.

Common Threads

How did educators respond to the above policies? Have researchers observed any changes in instructional practice since the initiatives were enacted? Does the evidence they collected reveal that Chinese, Korean, or Singaporean teachers have followed reform directives more faithfully than their peers in Japan? When I began writing this chapter, I originally planned to describe the effects of each reform separately. But I revised my approach due to the extensive overlap in policy outcomes that scholars have documented. Included extended analyses of each initiative, I realized, would become repetitive. Therefore, I will synthesize the research on efforts to reduce pressure on students studying in Asian schools.

In all three countries, firmly established educational traditions and values have proven remarkably resilient. Proposals crafted to reduce the intensity of K–12 initially generated positive response from parents and educators, but teachers struggled to implement reforms according to plan. As was the case in Japan, rhetorical commitment to change did not leverage significant shifts in instructional practice. As a result, plans to lessen the intensity of schooling in China, Korea, and Singapore all fell short of their predicted outcomes. The following created obstacles to change at the school level:

- Traditional reliance on transmission-oriented instruction;
- Teacher skepticism about the advisability of the changes advocated;
- Additional demands placed on school employees;
- The influence of entrance examinations; and,
- Concerns that reducing pressure on students will result in less rigorous academic preparation.

These factors stalled or led to partial implementation of policies enacted in all three countries. China's *suzhi jiaoyu* policies were introduced nation-wide, using a single set of reform guidelines, but researchers have discerned significant inconsistencies in their implementation. Although some individual schools (mostly elite and private institutions) managed to meet the goals for reform, they were outnumbered by institutions whose teachers hesitated to shift to the student-centered instructional methods advocated by the Ministry of Education. On a survey of 246 Chinese county education bureau heads, "74.38% thought it was very difficult to proceed with *suzhi jiaoyu* reforms under the current examination assessment system and 19.01% thought it was impossible" (Dello-Iacovo 2009, 247). The results of the reforms introduced in Korea were also disappointing. Despite the declared objective of reducing the stress experienced by students and teachers, introduction of "Open Education" appeared to produce the opposite effect: the volume of the national curriculum actually increased as course offerings expanded to include more "nonacademic" subject matter. Additionally, teachers came to realize that using performance assessments, rather than standardized tests, to measure student progress would remain "just a dream" until college entrance examination procedures are modified (Dello-Iacovo 2009). In Singapore, uneven implementation of the "Thinking Schools, Learning Nation initiative" raised questions about whether or not teachers can be convinced to revise their pedagogical practices to fit reform plans. In many schools, instructors continued to focus on intensive drilling and repetitive practice to introduce new concepts (Tan and Gopinathan 2000). These results led Tan (2010) to assert that "considering the price for standardized curriculum and testing [in Singapore], the United States might be better served by preserving the creative elements that its education system and students seem to bring about" (56).

The common challenges that confronted educators across Asia as they attempted to make learning more relevant and appealing to students underscore the depth of change necessary to create a "relaxed" education system. In each location, entrance examination–related pressures exerted a powerful influence on decision making in the schools. Even when directed by education officials to reduce emphasis on high-stakes tests, local education stakeholders continued to make decisions based on the most immediate demands and rewards tied to those assessments. Dello-Iacovo (2009) observes, "Reform attempts have been numerous and varied but the examination-oriented 'regular system' has proven remarkably resilient, bouncing back with renewed vigour after each assault" (242). This statement, though crafted with reference to China, aptly describes conditions in all the education systems discussed in this chapter thus far. In these settings, efforts to balance academic rigor, student engagement, and attention to children's emotional well-being have fallen short of expectations again and again.

This evidence raises some thorny questions related to academic achievement and educational reform. Education planners in China, Japan, Singapore, and South Korea promulgated reform policies that expanded access to schooling and also provided students with strong literacy and numeracy skills. International achievement tests attest that students educated in these systems perform admirably, compared to their peers in other countries. But in all these settings, high-stakes tests served to motivate pupils to invest in their studies and to solidify public support for education. The information presented in this chapter details the disturbing consequences of attaching great weight to such tests. Is it possible to raise academic standards without relying on examinations to convince education stakeholders to buy-in to a reform initiative? Can the curricular and pedagogical methods common to Japanese elementary schools be used at the secondary level—or do adolescents and their instructors need to be held accountable through high-stakes tests?

In the next section, I examine the trajectory of educational reform in another part of the world. In that country, students have excelled on standardized tests—without experiencing the anxieties decried by critics of Asian schools. Research conducted there calls into question many of the arguments that are commonly used to support education-reform policies, including NCLB and RTT.

Breaking with Tradition

Over the last decade, the nation that has received perhaps the most attention for its educational accomplishments is Finland. As late as 1970, only 30 percent of adults residing in Finland completed an upper secondary education (Schwartz and Mehta 2011). In the 1980s, when reporters in search of solutions to America's educational woes were focused on Asia, Finland had yet to distinguish itself from other European education systems. According to Schwartz and Mehta (ibid.), "Finland rarely, if ever, appeared on anyone's list of the world's most outstanding education systems" (51). Many observers were taken aback by the results of the 2000 PISA tests. Of the thirty-two countries that participated in PISA, Finland scored first in reading literacy, third in science literacy, and fourth in mathematical literacy. These accomplishments are particularly noteworthy given the unique reform scheme implemented in Finland. Finnish education planners managed to raise achievement levels without using high-stakes tests to secure commitment to education, as was common in Asia. Instead, teacher professionalism and autonomy generated the energy that propelled the school system forward. Finland's unconventional blueprint for educational renewal makes it a fascinating case study.

The roots of Finland's recent educational successes were nurtured in the 1970s, when bureaucrats began to develop the philosophical and educational principles that guided policies enacted in succeeding years. These principles emphasized the need to equip students with strong critical thinking skills and a sense of independence. To support this objective, the system was converted from a hierarchically stratified collection of schools into a single comprehensive system. Underlying this shift was the belief that a single learning institution "could serve all students equally well regardless of family background" (ibid., 56). An ambitious set of policies that supported that vision was ratified in 1985. Secondary schools were reorganized to create more choice and flexibility for students, and to pay greater attention to the individual needs of students (OECD 2010). This laid the foundation for the creation of a "trust-based school culture" tethered to the idea that "teachers, together with principals, parents, and their communities, know how to provide the best possible education for their children and youth" (Sahlberg 2007, 156–57).

In many respects, Finnish education exemplifies the "relaxed" approaches that that Asian governments have been pursuing. In Finland, children do not typically begin their formal education until the age of seven. The schools they attend embrace the notion "of learning as an individual and communal process of building knowledge and skills. . . . Learning results from the pupils' active and purposeful activity, in which they process and interpret the material to be learned on the basis of their existing structure of knowledge" (FNBE 2004, 16). The national curriculum provides direction in terms of instruction in traditional academic skills but also encourages schools to promote skills and attitudes not typically measured on high-stakes tests. For example, in grades one through nine, pupils spend between four and eleven periods each week exploring art, music, carpentry, metalwork, textiles, and cooking (Abrams 2011). Upper secondary students become eligible to graduate when they satisfactorily complete a total of seventy-five courses, rather than after they pass a fixed number of years in school. And to ensure that children lead balanced lives, they are provided plenty of time to do things other than study: the Finnish school year is shorter than any other OECD country (Schwartz and Mehta 2011). The elementary school day includes seventy-five minutes of recess, compared with an average of seven minutes in the United States (Abrams 2011).

As noted above, this shift to an inclusive, flexible, and child-centered direction has not undermined Finnish children's cognitive development or academic competitiveness. Finland appeared at or near the top of the PISA rankings published in 2000, 2003, 2006, and 2009—despite spending substantially less money on education than the United States.[2] Furthermore, Finland's ascent up the international league tables did not generate the widespread criticism about the excessive costs of academic competition that plagued Asian ministries of education. One explanation for this is that Finnish education planners consciously reconstructed the system to fit a carefully developed set of core principles. Changes in curriculum and instruction were tailored to fit the educational principals formulated during the 1970s and reinforced in succeeding years. As Sahlberg (2011) observes, "Perhaps it is due to these philosophical aspects of educational change that Finland remained immune to the winds of market-driven education policy changes that arose in many other OECD countries in the 1990s" (34). Increases in achievement test scores were an unexpected by-product of effective policy design rather than the objective of that process.

Although Finland demands a great deal of its teachers, it has not used formal accountability systems to incentivize the work of educators. Instead, the system attracts well-qualified and educated individuals into the teaching profession, and encourages them to use their professional expertise to enhance the learning experiences provided to students. Instructors gauge their pupils' needs using an array of measures other than examinations. In Finland, "education authorities and especially teachers have not been convinced that frequent external census-based testing and stronger accountability would be beneficial to students and their learning" (Sahlberg 2011, 39). Students are required to take only one standardized test during their academic careers: the National Matriculation Examination, which measures their mastery of the secondary curriculum and is a prerequisite for admission to higher education.

Skeptics often use Finland's homogeneity to call into question the significance of its recent educational success. The reform policies adopted in Finland, they argue, are unlikely to produce similar outcomes in countries with greater income disparities or more ethnically diverse student populations. Although it is true that the percentage of immigrants in Finland is relatively low, that reality does not diminish the recent transformation of the Finnish education system. Finland's demographic profile is similar to that of other Scandinavian countries, yet qualitative as well as quantitative data demonstrate that Finland's reform design has produced more positive outcomes than any of its neighbors. As table 9.1 illustrates, Finland is the only Scandinavian nation that has consistently ranked among the top nations on PISA tests. No other country in the region has placed among the top ten performers in more than one subject area, and none appear at the top of the league tables for PISA 2009. It would be hypocritical of me to draw conclusions about educational effectiveness based solely on standardized test scores. However, ethnographic studies of Scandinavian schools establish that Finnish educators stand apart from their peers in terms their ability to concomitantly engage and challenge students (Arensen and Lundahl 2006; Dall 2011; Tucker 2011). This body of evidence suggests that it is possible to raise student achievement without relying on high-stakes tests to ensure compliance with reform mandates.

Reform in the United States: A Different Trajectory

The four nations discussed in this chapter—China, South Korea, Singapore, and Finland—have been moving along reform pathways leading in different directions than the US education system. Responding to widespread concerns about the negative effects of high-stakes tests, education planners in Asia attempted to minimize the influence of examinations on instruction. During the same period, Finland engineered an education turnaround by reducing testing and accountability pressures, going so far as to abolish its national school inspectorate in 1991. The USDOE, on the other hand, emphasized the positive aspects of examination-related pressure in promoting educational reform.

Proponents of high-stakes testing systems asserted that holding educators more accountable would make American students more academically competitive and narrow the achievement gap. Have those predictions proven accurate? More than a decade has passed since the No Child Left Behind Act (NCLB) was enacted, and researchers have published a wealth of studies that chart its effects on teaching and learning. That research evidence can help us answer questions a set of important questions: Has NCLB produced the achievement gains forecast by its authors? Have the gaps separating children with different ethnic and socioeconomic profiles narrowed? In what ways have new accountability procedures influenced teacher behavior? Have researchers recorded any unexpected outcomes of the legislation? One simple observation that cannot be disputed is that NCLB's ultimate goal of achieving universal literacy in mathematics and reading by 2014 has not been met. In recognition of this reality, targets and deadlines have been adjusted, waivers granted to districts that have struggled (see below for specific examples of this).

What about the objective of facilitating consistent adequate yearly progress (AYP) for all students? What headway has been made toward that goal? Scores on the tests administered and analyzed at the state level indicate gradual improvements across grade levels and subgroups since NCLB was authorized. For example, analysis of test-score trends in North Carolina registers "small accountability-induced increases for Black and poor students, larger effects for Hispanics, and effects in reading that are roughly comparable in size to effects in math (Lauen and Gaddis 2012, 202). In New York, the proportion of children who achieved proficiency appeared to increase in the years following introduction of NCLB. The percentage of fourth and eighth graders who met learning standards established under New York City Mayor Michael Bloomberg, for instance, climbed by between 16 and 30 percentage points (Medina 2010).[3]

But claims of success made by the states proved to be somewhat illusory. One reason is that the autonomy provided to states made it possible for them to adjust test content as well as the criteria for proficiency. Many simply lowered minimum passing scores on achievement tests, which allowed them to report that schools were meeting performance targets. Questions about the reliability of reported achievement test data, however, prompted several researchers to compare the results of those instruments to marks earned by students in the same states on the NAEP (National Assessment of Educational Progress), a more reliable measure of academic achievement. Those analyses revealed significant discrepancies in pupil performance. For example, the Texas Education Agency (TEA) reported that 85.1% of fourth- and eighth-grade students were proficient readers, whereas only 28.6% of test takers in Texas earned that distinction on the NAEP test. In Nebraska, those figures were 90.5% and 34.8% (Ravitch 2010). Results from a new set of exams designed to more accurately measure student mastery of concepts included in the Common Core learning standards thrust New York schools into the headlines in 2013. Education officials were challenged to explain a dramatic plunge in scores: between 2012 and 2013, the percentage of students who passed the reading portion of New York's achievement test fell from 55% in 2012 to 31%, and from 65% to 31% in math. Furthermore, large gaps continued to separate native English-speaking Caucasian children from their black, Hispanic, and ESL peers and students with learning disabilities (Hernandez and Gebeloff 2013).

Research that analyzes longitudinal data collected in multiple states—or that compares state-administered tests with NAEP scores—generally finds minimal or no gains in student achievement since NCLB was enacted. Nichols, Glass, and Berliner (2005), for instance, maintain that "there is no convincing evidence that the pressure associated with high-stakes testing leads to any important benefits for student achievement" (i). Harris and Herrington (2004), who reviewed research that measured the impact of high-stakes testing over a fifty-year period, conclude that heightened accountability has had only a moderate effect on academic achievement. According to Ritter et al. (2004), approximately half of all reforms they studied that relied on high-stakes testing to raise student achievement produced positive results, and half had mixed or negative results. Nichols, Glass, and Berliner (2005) analyzed the effects of tests administered across the country in support of NCLB. The data they collected establish that those tests: (1) did not bolster student achievement, as measured by those instruments; (2) have not made a dent in the achievement gap; and (3) have been accompanied by elevated drop-out rates (7). Another report, published by the Economic Policy Institute (EPI), looks at the influence of high-stakes testing on student achievement and teacher behavior across the country in the years NCLB after introduced. The authors conclude that existing evidence "does not provide a very promising picture of the power of test-based accountability to improve student learning (EPI 2010, 5). Furthermore, introduction of test-based accountability has done little to reduce achievement gaps. Analysis of NAEP scores over time reveals that while in some states African American students earned higher scores on the tests, "the rate of improvement was not much better in the post- than in the pre-NCLB period, and in half the available cases, it was worse" (EPI 2010, 5).

The accountability systems introduced in conjunction with NCLB have had some strong and unanticipated consequences on curriculum and instruction. One disturbing consequence has been the prevalence of cheating among students, teachers, and district administrators. Several school districts that garnered national attention as a result of dramatic increases in AYP scores were subject to equally intense scrutiny when inconsistencies in test data caused many to question the validity of those data. Rod Paige, you may recall, served as the superintendent of the Houston Independent School District (HISD) before ascending to the position of US Secretary of Education. Several key components of NCLB were modeled after reforms enacted by the HISD under Paige's leadership. Both Paige and President Bush frequently referred to the "Texas Miracle" as they promoted NCLB (Winerip 2003). Only a few years later, however, unexpected jumps in test scores and statistical irregularities in test data reported by twenty-three schools spurred the HISD to initiate an internal investigation. Six Houston teachers were subsequently fired and three administrators demoted. Later, an analysis of standardized test scores across Texas found evidence of irregularities in 609 of the state's 6,112 public schools (Stinson 2006).

As I write this chapter, evidence that gains in student achievement are more myth than reality continues to accumulate. A story published in the *New York Times* reports that an investigation into evidence of cheating in Atlanta found that 178 principals and teachers in the city participated in unethical processes associated with standardized tests (Fausset 2014). The principal of a high school located near my office was recently suspended after the scores of several students jumped by 30%-40% on the New York State Regents' Examinations. When I asked a teacher in the district if she thought the principal had done anything unethical, she replied, "Maybe, but not anything more than other administrators in the area." While this is a single anecdotal event, research implies that it has some foundation. Concerned about widespread accusations of cheating on high-stakes tests, the US Government Accountability Office administered a web-based survey of testing administrators in all fifty states and the District of Columbia. Officials in forty states documented allegations of cheating on high-stakes tests, with thirty-two reporting that the incidents were so severe that test scores had to be canceled or invalidated (USGAO 2013).

New testing mandates have also led to extensive revisions of curricula, at all levels of the system. In both NCLB and RTT, assessments of school performance are based primarily on evidence of student achievement in language arts and mathematics. Limiting the number of tested subjects does make the process of administering and evaluating achievement simpler, but it also creates a curricular hierarchy. Alert to the reality that the rewards and penalties specified in NCLB are tied to adequate yearly progress (AYP) in just two subjects, teachers adjust their schedules and instructional methods to fit new accountability measures.

Studies that specify the effects of NCLB at the classroom level show that since NCLB was enacted, instructional hours devoted to subjects such as art, music, and electives have been reduced. Even subjects usually considered part of a standard academic curriculum (such as history, science, and foreign language) are receiving less attention from teachers than was true prior to 2002 (Groen 2012; McMurrer 2007; Sunderman et al. 2004). For example, almost half of the teachers who responded to a survey administered by the Civil Rights Project at Harvard University reported that the sanctions and AYP requirements introduced in conjunction with NCLB prompted them to de-emphasize or neglect untested topics. In addition, approximately 70% of the teachers who completed the survey stated that they had increased the time they spend preparing students for standardized tests (Sunderman et al. 2004). The Center on Education Policy (CEP) polled 349 school districts across the country about the impact of NCLB on curriculum and instruction in their schools. According to figures supplied by those districts, the instructional time reserved for language arts increased by an average of 47%, and mathematics by 37%. To make room for this expansion, schools reduced time allocated to other subjects and activities (social studies, science, art, music, physical education, lunch, and recess) by an average of 32%, or thirty minutes per day. Furthermore, a study published by the US Government Accountability Office concludes that teachers working in schools with higher percentages of low-income or minority students are more likely to reduce instructional time in the arts than instructors at other schools (USGAO 2009). This body of research evidence buttresses Groen's (2012) assertion that "this curricular transformation under NCLB may prove to be as historically significant to curriculum development in the 21st century as the Committee of Ten Report was in influencing curriculum changes in K–12 schools in the 20th Century" (7).

Teachers have also adjusted the specific topics they focus on, paying greater attention to content and skills likely to appear on standardized tests. Because high-stakes assessments are composed primarily—if not entirely—of multiple-choice questions, teachers are increasingly using class time to introduce and rehearse test-taking strategies with their pupils. According to the EPI study referred to above, "an emphasis on test results for individual teachers exacerbates the well-documented incentives to focus on narrow test-taking skills, repetitive drill, and other undesirable instructional practices" (EPI 2010, 16). For instance, rather than lead a discussion of a text that challenges students to think critically and creatively about what they have read, an instructor may feel compelled to review factual information that appeared on previous versions of a high-stakes test. I observed a similar tendency in Japanese middle school classrooms, where instructors frequently skimmed through textbook chapters and concentrated on sections that included material most likely to be included on entrance examinations.

Heightened emphasis on testing has also had an impact on student-teacher relationships. Barrett (2009) notes that one of the consequences of NCLB has been that "internal beliefs and commitments are often overridden by the pressures of the external demands placed on teachers" (1024). As a result, educators may feel obligated to place a greater priority on test scores than on children's social or emotional development. Several studies report decreases in the amount of time teachers spend supporting the non-academic needs of their pupils since NCLB was enacted (Day 2002; Laskey 2005; Ng 2006; Valli and Buese 2007). This scholarship establishes that as accountability pressure expands, instructors tend to devote less attention to nurturing and maintaining positive relationships with their students; they also become stricter and more demanding in the classroom (Mausethagen 2013). These troubling by-products of high-stakes testing are rarely acknowledged in government reports on NCLB.

Learning from Experience

The United States Department of Education continues to make policy recommendations based on the assumption that accountability is the key to school improvement. Many observers expected the Obama administration to reject—or at least dilute—components of the No Child Left Behind Act (NCLB) that linked federal funding with high-stakes testing requirements. But the changing of the guard was not accompanied by a significant shift in education policy. Although Race to the Top, the most noteworthy education legislation passed under Obama to date, relies on financial incentives (through competitive grants) rather than mandates to hold schools accountable for student achievement, it has not alleviated test-related pressures. RTT does allow state governments to apply for waivers that release them from some of the mandates specified in NCLB (such as 100% proficiency by 2014). Clearly, the opportunity to opt out of NCLB was quite appealing: by October 2014, forty-five states had applied for waivers, forty-three of which were approved (USDOE 2013). In exchange for greater flexibility, however, states were required to subscribe to another set of requirements, which included linking teacher evaluations to student performance on standardized tests and instituting career-readiness standards. These additional stipulations have generated logistical as well as financial challenges for school districts. The federal government has already withdrawn the waivers previously granted to Oklahoma and Washington.[4] Many states that were initially enthusiastic about the possibility that RTT would trim educational red tape are now struggling to comply with the requirements outlined in the waivers they submitted (Klein 2012). Since the introduction of RTT, numerous states and school districts that originally entered into the competition for additional federal funds have declined to do so in the second and third rounds, preferring to devote their efforts to other programs (USDOE 2014).

High-stakes tests continue to exert a powerful influence on American schools. One could argue that RTT actually intensified test-related pressures experienced by schools, teachers, and students. Yet, as the information presented in this chapter makes clear, research conducted domestically and internationally calls into question the wisdom of relying on examinations to drive education reform. Studies that analyze the effects of accountability systems introduced in support of NCLB indicate that requiring states to test students each year and determine rewards and sanctions based on the results of those assessments has not raised student achievement or narrowed gaps between rich and poor children to any significant degree. Testing mandates have, however, reduced the breadth of curricula and undermined the autonomy and morale of teachers. These realities provide an ironic twist to a reform agenda that champions the benefits of evidence-based decision making.

One might expect—or hope—that education legislation in the United States would be informed by the practices and experiences of other developed nations, but that has not been the case. Throughout Asia, education planners continue to search for procedures that can be institutionalized to reduce the emphasis on testing. Japan, China, Singapore, South Korea, and many other countries have set in motion policies that seek to shift the emphasis in schools from rote learning and test preparation to the deeper investigation of ideas. The policies they have enacted in support of that goal are remarkably similar. They all include reductions in instructional hours, curricular revisions that aim to make learning more meaningful to students, and the promotion of more-active pedagogical techniques. These efforts are notable for their ambitious goals—and disappointing results. Like Japan's relaxed-education reforms, policies approved in China, Singapore, and South Korea have failed to shake the philosophical foundations of their schools. Students, parents, teachers, and policy makers all recognize the detrimental aspects of their education systems, but entrenched practices limit their ability to alter the status quo. Pervasive and cogent criticism across Asia of examination-driven education suggests that schools should use other incentives to motivate students and teachers.

Expanding the influence of assessments can undermine a teacher's ability to facilitate the intellectual growth of her pupils. Even educators who display great commitment to their work often find it difficult to resist the power of high-stakes tests. Cognizant of the powerful influence those assessments have on the educational and employment opportunities provided to students, teachers often feel they no choice but to emphasize test preparation over student engagement or the development of "twenty-first-century skills." In this way, linking rewards and sanctions to test scores can constrain pedagogical innovation. Once practices and expectations designed to hold schools accountable for student performance on achievement tests take root, reducing the influence of those examinations becomes arduous.

Other approaches to educational reform warrant our attention. Comparative education research underscores the benefits of depending on human resources—rather than tests—to generate change in schools. Attracting talented individuals into the teaching profession, supporting their development as educators—and providing them with the autonomy to apply their professional expertise—is an effective means of raising student achievement. Furthermore, as the Finnish case demonstrates, it is possible to accomplish this feat without instituting rigid accountability systems to secure instructors' commitment to their work. Education stakeholders in the United States should consider this evidence carefully and resist pressure to accept federal mandates before high-stakes testing becomes an entrenched feature of American society. As research conducted in Asia makes clear, it is incredibly difficult diminish the influence of examinations after they take root.

TEN

US Teachers Reflect on Japanese Elementary School Instruction

In chapter 5, I assert that Japanese elementary school teachers consistently implement lessons that both challenge and engage their students. In all the elementary schools I visited, learning activities created in conjunction with the new integrated studies lesson—as well as lessons in more traditional subject areas—brought the curriculum to life for children. Guided by succinct curricular guidelines, instructors capitalized on the autonomy provided to them to create stimulating learning environments. They set high academic expectations for all pupils and organized the school day so that children were constantly moving, thinking, working with their peers, and coming up with original ideas. The data I collected indicate that Japanese elementary schools contain many of the features that educational planners in the United States are trying to institutionalize in American schools. In the classrooms I observed, teachers consistently held their students to high standards in all subject areas and also managed to spark their interest in learning.

Is it possible that some features of Japanese elementary schools could be adapted to strengthen the quality of instruction provided to children enrolled in schools located outside of Asia? In this chapter I explore that question. Drawing from a cross-national study of educators' views about teaching effectiveness I participated in, I compare the opinions expressed by teachers working in Asian and American elementary schools. Comments expressed by participants in that study suggest that educators encircled by systems whose differences are often amplified in the press may be more philosophically aligned than is commonly acknowledged. However, teachers who share common views about instructional effectiveness employ distinct pedagogical approaches as a result of school cultures and reform trends.

The cross-national study referred to above was inspired by *Preschool in Three Cultures*, the seminal work authored by Joseph Tobin, David Wu, and Dana Davidson (1991). Using the methodological approach from that work as a model, a team of researchers interviewed teachers in Japan, China, Singapore, and the United States about the abilities that contemporary schools focus on, and the instructional approaches most likely to promote those abilities. Coordinated by scholars at the University of Tokyo Graduate School of Education, we produced a collection of videos filmed in elementary schools in the four countries. Employing an approach similar to that used in *Preschool in Three Cultures*, we screened those videos to groups of teachers in all the participating countries.[1] In the focus group discussions that followed, we asked viewers to comment on the pedagogical methods employed by the instructors in the videos, and to analyze the strengths and weaknesses of the lessons. All the researchers involved in the project worked together to develop an interview protocol, create coding systems, and discuss the findings. For the American component of the video study, teachers in California and New York were interviewed. I facilitated the discussions in the New York, and also reviewed and analyzed the transcripts of all interviews held in the United States and abroad.

The learning activities captured in videos were not selected as representative examples of instructional approaches common in a particular country. Instead, we included lessons that we thought would highlight distinctive pedagogical practices and provoke lively discussions about "the core beliefs, goals and concerns about early childhood education in each culture" (Tobin et al. 2009, 9). We deliberately included a balance of learning activities that were considered more traditional and those that aimed to cultivate "new" abilities (critical thinking, creativity, oral communication, collaboration, self-evaluation, and so forth). In the focus group discussions that we conducted, participants were asked to comment on the effectiveness of the lessons they observed, the skills the various lessons supported, and the relevance of the lessons to their own schools and classrooms. Each focus group included four to eight teachers from a single school. Reflecting demographic patterns in US elementary schools, the vast majority of participants were female. The sample included first- through sixth-grade teachers who had between four and thirty years of classroom experience. Although the project coordinated by the University of Tokyo was not explicitly connected to my independent research, the interview data generated by the video study afforded additional perspectives on the issues that anchored my study of *yutori kyoiku*.

In this chapter, I report on the focus group discussions with American teachers. Although it would be interesting to compare data collected in all four countries, the comments shared by American educators most directly highlight the themes I am investigating in this book. First, I summarize general patterns in the observations shared by American teachers. Next, I examine their reactions to two of the Japanese lessons that were included in the sample.[2] One of the lessons was a math activity that required Japanese sixth graders to scatter a handful of colored stickers on a page and then devise methods for calculating the area of the figure formed by the stickers. Another captured an Integrated Studies activity in which third graders ventured into the community and interviewed independent shopkeepers about their work.

As they evaluated the two lessons, participants spoke at great length about the techniques employed by the instructors in the videos. The activities filmed in Japan also stimulated participants to contemplate deeper questions about the goals and direction of the American education system. As they discussed the videos, interviewees frequently referred to tensions between their understandings of what was best for their students and the instructional methods that were favored by their employers. Many felt conflicted about the multiple, often competing demands placed upon them as a result of accountability systems that had been installed in conjunction with NCLB. Veteran teachers were particularly troubled by that reality and reminisced about the professional autonomy they enjoyed before standardized testing became such a central focus in the schools. Interview data from the video study indicate that teachers working in a variety of settings are struggling to meet the goals of relaxed education in environments that encourage competition and the ranking of students.

Unanticipated Consensus

Given the intensity of recent debates about high-stakes testing and student achievement in the United States, one might expect discord to pervade the focus group discussion transcripts. It would seem logical that classroom teachers, like education pundits and journalists, would express conflicting views about how schools should respond to current educational challenges. Surprisingly, this was not the case. Teachers' comments about the videotaped lessons were marked by a surprising degree of cohesion. Although the interviewees who participated in this study were working in several different districts, the opinions they articulated were consistent. The teachers offered valuable insights into the topic of educational reform and the challenges associated with raising learning standards in public schools.

Their perspectives on the challenge of raising student achievement contrasted starkly with the ideas driving policies such as NCLB and RTT.

The teachers we interviewed spoke at great length about their professional goals and responsibilities. Their opinions about the mission of contemporary schools echoed those articulated in USDOE publications in several respects. For instance, when asked to describe the skills and abilities that contemporary schools should cultivate in their students, educators interviewed in California and New York underscored the importance of cultivating what I would call deep and flexible intelligence. They noted that while it is important for children to master content knowledge, memorizing facts and procedures is not enough. To succeed in contemporary society, citizens must apply what they know to an array of situations.

That view came across most clearly in response to a videotaped lesson filmed in the United States that focused on teaching an algorithm for long division. During the activity, children were instructed to follow a set of steps to divide a three-digit number by a single-digit number. The rather traditional pedagogical approach did not elicit positive reviews from viewers. A common theme of teacher criticism was that the lesson encouraged children to follow a procedure for solving division equations without thinking about what they were doing. One person offered, "I had a hard time following it from the beginning, from the get-go. It was definitely formula-based, and you would have to know the formula or if you didn't understand it, the whole lesson is meaningless." Another explained that "I do the same thing in my class. I model [a procedure], but then I have to explain it to the class. They get excited. They think more and learn more . . . If they explain it to someone, then it sinks in a lot more. That means they can do it." Teachers emphasized the importance of challenging students to move beyond what Ma (1999) has termed the "surface aspects of the algorithm" (27) to develop more thorough conceptual understanding of mathematical ideas.

The videos of language arts and social studies lessons also sparked participants to consider how teachers can best prepare children to respond to the challenges they are likely to face in the future. As was true of responses to the math lessons, teachers were not impressed by activities that transmitted information efficiently but did not require students to use higher-order thinking skills. According to most of the interviewees, simply learning a body of facts about a piece of literature or an historical event is not sufficient; educators need to develop a wider range of aptitudes in their students. After watching an American fourth-grade teacher lead a discussion about the life of Walt Disney, one participant stated that "when these children grow up, they're not going to be calling and responding to their boss. They're going to need to be creative, they're going to need to use what they learn, they're going to need to talk with others and work together, and share." Another noted, "There was a lot of higher-level thinking. Even in the way the room was arranged, there's like community building and things like that, which is a life skill they are going to need in everyday life."

Educators located in different schools and states expressed a cohesive vision of the primary responsibilities of contemporary schools. In reflecting on the lessons captured in the videos, they commended teachers who encouraged their students to think deeply about the curriculum and to use their creativity to solve problems.

Interestingly, teachers' descriptions of the skills and capabilities that schools should emphasize echoed those promoted in USDOE policy documents. The individuals who participated in the video study, like recent Secretaries of Education, expressed a commitment to raising the quality of instruction provided in public schools. Another common theme was the importance of meeting the needs of all learners, regardless of their perceived abilities. I would be surprised if many of the teachers we interviewed would disagree with the notion that contemporary schools should facilitate "the access of children to effective, scientifically based instructional strategies and challenging academic content" (Elementary and Secondary Education Act, Title I, Section 1001). Both Rod Paige and Arnie Duncan have repeatedly endorsed instruction that equips children with skills they can apply beyond the classroom. In the *Guide to Education and No Child Left Behind* (USDOE 2004), for example, Paige expresses his commitment to raising "all schools to the highest levels of scholarship and motivation" (24). Teachers also stressed the value of carefully analyzing the effects of various pedagogical approaches, and using the insights gained to elevate teaching effectiveness.

Realities in Schools and Classrooms

Interview transcripts, however, revealed that surface agreement about the broad goals of education obscured some critical differences about how schools should achieve those goals. Participants in the video study voiced more complex conceptions of academic excellence than are usually conveyed in USDOE reports. The information they used to evaluate the lessons depicted in the videos was not limited to scores on standardized tests. In analyzing the videotaped lessons, teachers paid a great deal of attention to the depth of knowledge that students acquired; they also focused on the instructors' ability to engage and motivate students. Clearly, the criteria participants used to determine "highly qualified teachers" (to borrow language from the NCLB) encompassed much more than the ability to develop basic academic skills.

Interview data from focus group discussions of two of the lessons filmed in Japanese classrooms highlighted contrasts between the USDOE's strategy for school improvement and the practices that classroom teachers considered most effective. Analysis of American teachers' reactions to those lessons accentuated some critical differences in the views of policy makers and practitioners about the strategies that should be used to raise learning standards in the schools. Interviewees noted that recent policies promoted by the USDOE have made it more difficult to teach like the individuals in the videos whom they considered most effective. A common lament expressed by participants was that although they were impressed by the pedagogical approaches displayed by some of the Japanese elementary school teachers, they didn't feel that it would be feasible to implement similar lessons in their own classrooms on a regular basis.

American educators were especially intrigued by the Integrated Studies lesson they viewed. In the video, a class of Japanese third-grade children meets in the entry hall of their school to discuss the activity that will follow. The teacher appears only at the beginning of the clip, standing before his class and stating, "Let's explore the ideas shopkeepers devise so that they can do their jobs better." Next, in small groups, the children venture into the community and interview business owners about their work. Armed with clipboards, they ask questions, take notes, and draw pictures of what they see. The lesson appears quite open ended and student centered. Children conduct their research in the shops without any adult supervision. As they walk through the urban business district, cars and trucks drive past them.

Several of the American teachers who watched the video found the teacher's hands-off approach to the field trip problematic. One stated, "I wouldn't want them running around by themselves. . . . [I would want] more control, more organization." Another volunteered that the minimal supervision "made me nervous. And the screaming bothered me. And then they all just kind of charged into the street. There was no kind of structure. But again, maybe in Japan that's safe and acceptable. But it's not safe and acceptable in America." That criticism of the hands-off managerial approach is reminiscent of comments shared by American teachers in *Preschool in Three Cultures* (Tobin, Wu, and Davidson 1991).

Although many American teachers were uncomfortable with what they considered excessive freedom provided to young children on the field trip, those concerns were outweighed by almost unanimous praise for the lesson itself. They were particularly impressed by the excitement generated by the activity and its relevance to children's lives outside the classroom, as the following comments reveal:

> I loved the idea of it. I loved what it promoted—the "I wonder" thinking and then going out and researching the community. And I loved bringing it back. I think the lesson is a great idea.

> If they're asking their own questions about some aspect of the world around them and exploring their own self to find answers to those questions, I think that's beneficial because that's something they're going to need to know—different tools and different resources that they can use to answer their own questions.

> They found out the answers, they come back, they work in a small group, and they come up with a final project for the audience. All of those things are life skills. All of those things you need in a job, in a career as an adult. So I thought the lesson was an outstanding lesson.

> I like this lesson because it puts them out in the real world and then asks them to look at critical things that are real-life skills.

> I'd love my child to be in that class because of the lesson. It's like integrating field trips with lessons. And they come back really excited.

The general consensus among American teachers was that the Integrated Studies lesson developed a number of important skills in students through an activity that augmented their excitement about learning. In teams, children brainstormed questions about a topic of interest to them and then searched for answers to those questions on their own. After completing those investigations, they delivered oral reports that synthesized their findings. The lesson also served to forge connections between elementary school students and members of the surrounding community.

American teachers shared extremely positive assessments of the lesson, but several interviewees also recognized that it would be difficult to implement the activity in their own schools. Logistical as well as financial constraints would make such an undertaking unrealistic. One interviewee related, "Unfortunately, in a real-life situation, we can't do this. We need permission. Also, generally, in a suburban area, we can't take this type of field trip. And ordering a bus is a pain in the neck. Plus they only allow you to do field trips on certain days, and you have to be back at a certain time. So there are a lot of logistics to worry about." Others noted that their field-trip budgets have been cut, which limits the number of trips they can organize each year. Despite the numerous benefits of the lesson that teachers identified, few were confident that they could organize similar excursions with their own students.

A sixth-grade mathematics lesson filmed in Japan also elicited extensive comments from American teachers. In the activity, the thirty-eight students in the room are told that the day's activity will be a math game. The teacher explains that they will each receive five small wooden blocks. He instructs them to throw the blocks onto their papers and use colored stickers to mark where the blocks land. The student whose blocks scatter the farthest will be declared the winner. In the ensuing discussion, students describe strategies they might use to calculate the dispersion of their blocks: (1) draw a line connecting the five stickers and calculate the area of the figure; (2) draw a line connecting the stickers and calculate the length of the perimeter; or (3) from the corner of the paper, measure the distance to each sticker, and determine the sum of the five lengths. After each student shares a strategy, other children in the room evaluate its strengths and weaknesses.

Responses to this video were overwhelmingly positive. The informal environment in the room surprised several participants, who had assumed that Japanese classrooms were more ascetic settings for learning. According to one interviewee, "There was this ability to kind of connect with work in a very enthusiastic, playful way of thinking." The relaxed environment was conducive to risk taking and the free sharing of ideas. Another educator commented, "I liked how he seemed very energetic, and the students seemed to be energetic too. They were quick to jump up. They felt comfortable speaking in front of their classmates, taking the risk that if [their idea] wasn't quite right or if they had a suggestion from someone of how to make it better. People were bounding up to the board."

Teachers also underscored the deep thinking that the activity demanded of the children who played the game. Instead of following a procedure outlined by the teacher or in a book, they had to come up with their own problem-solving strategies. Most of the American viewers felt that such thinking would result in more thorough understanding of the concepts involved, as the statements below indicate:

> I liked the fact that there wasn't like a clear-cut answer being presented. I think so many of the problems we offer our students [assume that] there is this answer that we want to arrive at. Here it wasn't so much the answer; it was the way you try to explain it . . . it would encourage them to keep thinking.

> I thought it was kind of fun. The children really enjoyed it. They seemed to be very responsive to interacting with each other and with the teacher also. There was a lot of deductive and critical thinking.

> What jumped out for me about the lesson was that it was like what mathematicians do. They find a really interesting problem and they think about the different ways they could solve it, and what's the most efficient or accurate way that you could then generalize to other kinds of problems. So for me it was the closest to pure mathematics.

> The lesson fostered an enthusiasm and excitement about math. Those students would be inclined to study math in the future.

Another aspect of the activity that participants noted was the instructor's careful planning. Although he never used a textbook, the teacher appeared to have a clear sense of the structure of the lesson and what he hoped to accomplish. Furthermore, the instructor followed a detailed roadmap to guide instruction, yet he also responded supportively to students who went on detours. As one American teacher observed, "It was very open ended. He was letting the kids come up with a lot of ideas. He wasn't up there saying, 'This is how everyone should find area and this is what we do.'" The teacher acted more of a facilitator than a pedagogue, guiding the discussion and challenging students to solidify the lines of reasoning they shared.

Relevance of the Findings

One theme that emerged from the interview I analyzed was the cogent support for innovative teaching articulated by American participants. In comparing instructors who relied more on traditional approaches (transmission of information, memorization of facts and problem-solving strategies, review of information in a textbook) and those who employed more constructivist pedagogical approaches (cooperative learning, discussion and debate, inquiry-based learning), interviewees expressed a strong preference for the latter. The lessons that elicited the most positive comments were those that encouraged students to seek out information, draw their own conclusions, and think critically about ideas they were investigating. American teachers expressed their support for activities that challenged children to delve deeply into subject matter that was significant to their own lives. They were also attentive to both the cognitive and affective dimensions of the lessons they observed. A common view expressed by the teachers was that students were more likely to retain and apply knowledge they acquired through activities that demanded their active engagement.

The energy displayed by the children in those videos seemed to transfer to the interviewees who watched them. Activities that generated excitement among students tended to provoke lengthy comments from observers. After watching more traditional lessons, teachers offered thoughtful but more clinical analyses of what they had witnessed. They provided detailed feedback but did not often express a sense of connection with the instructors in the video. The student-centered activities, in contrast, tended to induce more detailed and enthusiastic responses. In their comments, focus group discussion members frequently placed themselves or their students in the activities captured in the videos, envisaging what it would feel like to participate in the lesson. After watching the IS and sticker math lessons, several of the participants also identified components of those activities that they might incorporate into their own classrooms.

Many American teachers identified techniques used by Japanese educators that they would like to use with their own students. In establishing those links, however, interviewees described in detail the factors that would make it difficult for them to implement lessons similar to the videotaped lessons they found most inspiring. Teacher enthusiasm for the innovative lessons was tempered by recognition that the systems in which they worked were not organized to support such instruction. The pressure placed on American teachers to transmit a large body of factual information presented one obstacle to innovation:

> I think the Japanese curriculum is structured very differently from ours. They spend much more time on one topic. I had two days to cover metric conversions. My kids, I've got to tell you, even the smart kids were clueless about it. . . . We don't have enough time.

> We know the district has tests in June, and they have to know area and perimeter, and "Boys and girls, this is how you do it." So the luxury of time, again, I think we would all like more of that. And I think we did do more of that years ago, before we had—we had a lot more time for creativity, for

> group work, and for doing little group projects with area and make them go around the whole classroom and measure things and find the area. Now we're on a tight, tight schedule. You know, you've got three days to cover it and—boom—you're on to the next thing. So, in a lot of ways, we don't have control of the curriculum.
>
> I'd like to know how many days the Japanese children are in school, how many hours a week compared to us, because obviously they had time to do this and they, don't they always outscore us on math tests? So, I mean, they are doing something right.
>
> The curriculum is aligned a lot differently there too, from what I understand. . . . They will take problems such as these and apply them to a much more narrow concept, but they'll do more problems and integration with that concept and then they'll go on to the next, whereas we have two days for this and two days for that.

Teachers also felt constrained by a curriculum that has become increasingly prescriptive and examination driven. Their comments provided confirmation of research described in the previous chapter establishing that adoption of NCLB has led to narrowing of the curriculum offered in American schools. As the following remarks indicate, many teachers feel compelled to focus on subject matter included on standardized tests, even when doing so is not in the best interests of their students:

> We received a directive from our [district office] day by day, how many days you spend on a lesson. And to me it's just not—there's no good thinking involved. And New York State imposes this very broad curriculum, and our district narrows it down a little bit more, and says, "You do this lesson, this lesson, and this lesson." There's just no teaching to understanding, no time frame. And it's very frustrating to all of us as math teachers, good teachers in this room, and it's very frustrating to all of us to be pushed like this and herded, and not really get to any level of understanding with our kids.
>
> I feel like I teach a new concept every day, and just have the time to fit in all of the other subjects. I'm lucky if I get a forty-minute block for math.
>
> There's a real ownership—that kids have that information, and that they can launch from it, they can build from it. Whereas even our brightest kids who

> take those AP math courses, I mean they have good rote learning skills, and probably pretty good problem-solving skills, but that doesn't guarantee that they can really think out of the box. And I think that's the way our whole education system is set up.

> The first thing that goes through my mind is, "How in the world would I take any of the lessons in any country?" Because I think we've all seen good teaching, and different concepts each time being taught in a very interesting way, but not ways that lend themselves well to what we are expected to report to a larger community.

The above quotations reveal a troubling tension between the goal of encouraging students to explore subject matter in great depth and a system that encourages surface coverage of a voluminous curriculum. One issue that was raised in all the focus group discussions was discord between what pedagogical practices that teachers believed were most effective and the institutional structures in which they worked. Watching the videotapes prompted numerous observers to talk about ways that the accountability systems Rod Paige and others believe would force them to work harder actually stifled innovation in their schools.

The views expressed by the teachers who participated in this study should not be generalized to represent the entire population of American teachers. The sample of teachers who participated in the video study was not random or scientific. It was composed of individuals who worked in close proximity to members of the research team. Participation was voluntary. It is possible that the views of the teachers who agreed to participate differ from those of their peers working in other settings. That should not, however, diminish the significance of their observations. Participants expressed frustration with accountability systems that undercut their professional autonomy. Pressure to prepare students to take standardized tests has increased steadily in recent years. Given the significant weight attached to those scores, the decision to reorganize the curriculum to fit the demands associated with high-stakes tests makes sense. Doing otherwise would be risky. As a result, many instructors feel obligated to teach in ways that they do not believe are in the best interests of their students. Their observations suggest that American elementary schools—like Japanese middle schools—have become intense and examination focused. In both contexts, it can be quite difficult to replicate the inspiring instruction found in Japanese elementary schools.

Common Ideals

Interview data from the video study of instructional practices in Japan, China, Singapore, and the United States offer glimpses of the great potential of public education. Teachers in the videos demonstrated that it is possible to achieve goals common to education officials in both the United States and Japan. Those educators implemented lessons that concomitantly challenged and engaged children. In the videos that elicited the most positive responses from study participants, teachers created relaxed learning environments that encouraged students to take risks and to work collaboratively to explore meaningful questions that lacked clear or simple solutions. In response to their teachers' skillful facilitation of those activities, students expanded their thinking about concepts such as effective business practices, the meaning of long division, and measurement of geometrical figures. According to members of the focus group discussions, children who participated in those lessons were more likely to retain the knowledge they acquired than were children who took part in more traditional textbook- or teacher-driven activities.

These perspectives are relevant to the current contexts for educational reform in both Japan and the United States. Critics of *yutori kyoiku* often assert that policies designed to reduce the intensity of Japanese education lowered academic standards in the schools. But the videotaped lessons that provoked the most positive responses were cognitively challenging as well as inspiring. Children who participated in those activities developed the "twenty-first-century skills" that both progressive educators and business leaders endorse: critical thinking, problem solving, creativity, and the ability to think outside of the box.

Interview data from the video study signal that when it comes to ideals about instruction, educators in the two countries are more unified than has been generally acknowledged. Japanese and American teachers who viewed the videos tended to be impressed by the same lessons and instructional techniques. Their ideals about how to best motivate and challenge students overlapped in many respects. Yet, the institutional contexts in which they operated pushed teachers in different pedagogical directions. In Japan, elementary educators are required to follow a national curriculum, but the contents are comparatively sparse. The combination of professional autonomy and a slim curriculum allowed elementary school teachers to design lessons that complemented their professional goals and expertise. Although American participants in the video study aspired to teach like the individuals in the videos they found most impressive, conditions in their schools made that difficult. Recently adopted accountability mandates undercut their sense of independence. Rather than devise original lessons they were encouraged to follow "scripts" with more predictable outcomes.

Comments shared by American elementary school teachers confirmed that the growing influence of high-stakes tests had undermined their professional autonomy. Like the Japanese middle school teachers profiled in this book, they felt pressure to cover the curriculum as efficiently as possible, even when they did not believe that doing so benefitted their students. I realize that emulating the outstanding teaching documented in the videos would be challenging. Reducing the constraints placed on educators will not guarantee positive results. But it is possible, especially when teachers are encouraged to draw from their knowledge and experience to craft original lessons and tailor instruction to the unique needs of their students. Instituting accountability systems that rely exclusively on numbers to measure success have the opposite effect. When that occurs, educators are likely to play it safe—to narrow the focus of the curriculum and focus on test preparation. It is extremely difficult for students or teachers to achieve their potential under such conditions.

ELEVEN

Looking Forward

Introduction of the relaxed-education policies in 2002 provoked intense debates about the direction of the education system. From the outside, the sense of crisis about education in Japan may have seemed puzzling. Japanese students, after all, consistently outperformed their peers from most other developed countries. High school and university graduation rates were among the highest in the world. This information often impressed observers from other countries. But inside the country, pervasive unease about the state of the nation's youth fueled calls for reform. Individuals positioned across the political spectrum used the relaxed-education reforms as a launching pad to share their views—often quite fervently—about what was wrong with the schools and what should be done to remedy their deficiencies. It was difficult to find someone who hadn't formed an opinion about relaxed education. Depending on whom you spoke to, *yutori kyoiku* might be viewed as a much-needed antidote to the nation's obsession with examinations or a dangerous threat to an education system teetering on the brink of self-destruction.

The ferocity of the debates provoked by the Ministry of Education's attempts to alleviate academic pressure revealed sharp divisions in opinion about the purpose of education in contemporary society. In the aftermath of Japan's economic "miracle," the core mission of the public school no longer seemed as clear as was true in the 1950s and 1960s. MEXT promotion of *yutori kyoiku* pushed to the surface tensions about the direction of the schools that had been simmering for years. Those tensions were linked to broader disagreements between national and local education stakeholders, progressives and conservatives, businesspeople and educators. The intensity of the disputes was striking, given Japan's reputation as a cohesive society that favored peaceful resolution of conflict (Krauss, Rohlen, and

Steinhoff 1984). Even before the relaxed-education policies were enacted, critics were calling for their repeal.

The combination of rhetorical support for goals of *yutori kyoiku* and questions about the practical implications of the reforms resulted in widespread resistance to change in the schools I studied. As their familiarity with the new curriculum increased, even individuals who initially voiced strong support for relaxed education developed doubts about the MEXT reform agenda. Ambivalent responses to what was sometimes referred to as Japan's "Third Major Education Initiative" provide fresh insights into an education system—and society—undergoing pervasive changes. The evidence I collected indicates that educators accepted the increased authority delegated to them by MEXT—but that they used that autonomy to impede many of the recommendations disseminated by the ministry. Teachers, administrators, and parents all struggled to reconcile changes in the curriculum designed to reduce academic intensity with the persistent demands of entrance examinations. Although I conducted the majority of my fieldwork in Japanese elementary and middle schools, the findings are relevant to other education systems attempting to negotiate an appropriate balance between academic rigor and student engagement.

Implementing Reform Policies in Schools

One clear finding from my research is the critical role that school-based actors play in the process of education reform. Even within a vertically organized bureaucracy, Japanese teachers enjoyed a significant amount of freedom as they responded to policy changes. Although education officials in Tokyo promulgated the relaxed-education policies, realization of those plans depended on the efforts of classroom teachers. MEXT disseminated a set of guidelines schools to follow, but entrusted teachers to mold the curriculum to fit the students and communities they served. This approach to reform had the potential to pay both political and educational dividends. MEXT bureaucrats believed that giving teachers the authority to determine the content and delivery of a portion of the new Course of Study would augment their commitment to reform; having participated in the development of the curriculum, instructors would go to great lengths to ensure *yutori kyoiku* produced positive outcomes in their schools. Another assumption driving relaxed education was the idea that reducing the contents of the Course of Study would create spaces for innovation. With fewer topics to cover, teachers could design learning activities that encouraged students to participate actively in the discovery and application of knowledge.

MEXT asserted that this shift to student-centered learning would make school more exciting and meaningful for children.

These goals sound laudable on paper, but the data I have presented in this book indicate that teachers largely resisted pressure to follow reform guidelines. The notion of redesigning the curriculum so as to attract and maintain the interest of students appealed to most of the educators I interviewed, who tended to agree with the goals of *yutori kyoiku*. During an informal lunchtime conversation, a middle school social studies instructor explained to me that she was "worried about many aspects of contemporary education, but not sure about what should be done." This observation prompted nods from her colleagues at the table. Most of the educators I interviewed felt that the system needed to be revised, but were conflicted about what changes should be made. As they developed experience with the new curriculum, teachers' enthusiasm for reform faded. Philosophical as well as practical concerns undercut their commitment to MEXT's vision for school renewal.

At first glance, it appeared that elementary school teachers were adhering to reform guidelines: the lessons they implemented were consistently inquiry based and relevant to children's lives beyond the classroom. But the prevalence of constructivist learning was not the result of a government decree. Japanese elementary school teachers have taught in this way for decades (Lewis 1995; Shimahara and Sakai 1995; White 1987). Middle school instructors, in contrast, struggled to adjust their instructional methods to fit MEXT prescriptions. The reports schools submitted to the ministry may have documented compliance with relaxed-education guidelines, but most of the middle school teachers I observed continued to rely on the transmission-oriented pedagogies they believed would best prepare their pupils for high-stakes examinations.

The autonomy MEXT offered to middle school instructors was undercut by locally constructed expectations and norms related to teaching. Tailoring pedagogy to fit the unique needs of students sounded interesting hypothetically, but this goal often proved difficult to realize in the classroom. The teachers I interviewed did not obediently follow reform guidelines. Instead, they studied the changes proposed by MEXT, and considered how those recommendations would affect their own work and the educational trajectories of their students.

In reflecting on *yutori kyoiku*, most informants expressed uncertainty about the policies they were attempting to implement. Their concerns related to the wisdom of what MEXT was asking them to do, the depth of the government's commitment to relaxed education, and public opinion about relaxed education. Teachers were quite cognizant of the controversies surrounding *yutori kyoiku*. The steady stream of dissonant messages about how the schools should respond to changes in society created stress and uncertainty for educators. Sensitive to potential backlash from the families they served, instructors hesitated to fully invest in policies that had already provoked widespread criticism. Cognizant of this reality, teachers continued to focus on preparing their students for assessments; other goals, such as strengthening pupils' motivation to learn or their zest for living, received far less attention.

Skepticism about the merits of relaxed education was exacerbated by middle school instructors' limited experience with the pedagogical approaches advocated by MEXT. Teachers often discovered that designing and implementing learning activities that supported the goals of the reforms was more difficult and time consuming than policy guidelines suggested. Delivering lectures and assigning structured problem-solving exercises produced more dependable outcomes than did the independent investigations the ministry was encouraging them to use. Another factor that undermined teacher commitment to relaxed education was the challenge of assessing student learning in courses that were not accompanied by a standard curriculum or textbook. Evaluating creativity, critical thinking, and enthusiasm for learning proved much more difficult than checking their recall of factual information. These discoveries not only created logistical difficulties for middle school teachers—they prompted many to question their instructional abilities and their relationships with students.

Research conducted in other locations draws attention to the challenges associated with changing the way people teach (Cuban 1990; Desimone 2002; Evers, Brouwers, and Tomic 2002; Goldenberg and Gallimore 1991). Convincing teachers to adopt new instructional practices requires the convergence of a number of factors: pedagogical capacity, preparation time, appropriate materials, institutional backing, and confidence in the proposed methods. Several, if not all, of these conditions can be found in Japanese schools. A well-established system of professional development, for example, could help instructors refine their skills in inquiry-based learning. Most of the items on the items on the above list were on display in the schools I visited. Yet the absence of one or two elements—or a cadre of skeptical individuals—was enough to stall pedagogical reform. As a result, even in schools that demonstrated a strong commitment to improving instruction, most educators continued to teach the way they did prior to adoption of the relaxed-education policies.

Teacher Orientation and Accountability

One might have predicted that teachers would obediently follow government directives for relaxed education, given previous research that emphasizes the verticality of the Japanese education system and the far-reaching influence of MEXT (Horio 1988; Schoppa 1991a; Thurston 1973). My interviews with educators and observations of school activities, however, suggest that teachers have more autonomy than is commonly acknowledged. The evidence I collected reveals that the combination of central support and strong teacher capacity does not necessarily ensure smooth implementation of educational reform. Considerations rooted in the local community exerted a more direct and powerful influence over Japanese educators as they responded to policy directives than did concerns about central government expectations. Teachers made decisions with careful attention to the factors that determined their students' immediate educational prospects, their classroom experience, and the wishes of local communities, rather than MEXT priorities. The institutional cultures in which they operated had been developed—and solidified—over long periods of time.

As Hatch (2013) notes, established conventions of schooling can "sustain high-performing systems at the same time that they undermine further improvement efforts" (37). That statement, written with the United States education system as a reference point, accurately describes conditions in the schools I visited in Japan. Japanese teachers had more freedom to resist ministry authority than one might have expected. Aware that MEXT did not carefully scrutinize instructional practice in schools, instructors did not hesitate to ignore policy directives they considered impractical or inadvisable. As long as the reports submitted to MEXT pronounced that the Course of Study was being implemented according to plan, schools were free to revise the curriculum to fit their own priorities.

Teachers may have had more freedom to resist central authority than one might have expected, but they did not enjoy total independence. They were highly sensitive to the scrutiny of parents. As instructors made decisions about how to implement relaxed-education policies, they carefully considered how modifications in curriculum and pedagogy would affect their students—and how parents would react to those changes. Because parents rarely expressed their opinions directly to schools, teachers frequently made decisions based on assumptions that may or may not have had any foundation. Many complained to me about the stress that "monster parents" (*monsuta parento*)[1] created for them.[2] Educators avoided taking actions that might provoke criticism from such parents.

At the time I was conducting fieldwork, schools were concomitantly responding to changes in curriculum, students, families, and surrounding communities. This created multiple layers of uncertainty for educators who had entered the profession with expectations of workplace stability and consistency. Operating on a precarious foundation, teachers began to question the demands associated with implementation of the relaxed-education policies, as well as the rationale for *yutori kyoiku* provided by MEXT. Individuals who sensed that the local community did not agree with the goals of relaxed education often hesitated to commit to the curricular and pedagogical changes the ministry was promoting. Even those who initially agreed with the guiding principles of *yutori kyoiku* gradually developed into skeptics. Lacking assurance that the communities they served embraced the relaxed-education curriculum, Japanese instructors opted for the imperfect but familiar over the contentious promise of change. Convinced that parents would ultimately judge the success or failure of the school system based on the scores their children earned on those tests, even the most independent-minded educators focused their energies on preparing students to succeed on high-stakes tests.

The relaxed-education policies had been introduced only a few years before I conducted the fieldwork for this study and their shelf life had yet to be determined. Teachers were not sure of the long-term effects the new curriculum would have on students or the depth of MEXT's commitment to the changes that had been introduced. Given such uncertainty, resisting pressure to change constituted a logical response to the multiple pressures experienced by school-based actors. Fully committing to the plans endorsed by MEXT was risky. If *yutori kyoiku* eventually proved untenable, the reputations of its most ardent supporters could suffer. Aware of this reality, most teachers clung to the familiar.

Enduring Priorities

The relaxed-education initiatives pressed educators to move in one direction, but the foundation on which they operated remained stationary. Education officials maintained that children needed more "room to grow," but the Japanese education system is organized around a single focal point: the entrance examination. That unity of purpose provided a clear sense of order to everyone attached to the schools I visited. Even those who were highly critical of tests had difficulty resisting their influence. Sensitive to the critical role that entrance examination performance plays in determining future opportunities, education stakeholders organized their behavior to fit the demands of those tests. Students tended to focus on subjects included on entrance exams and to invest less energy on other topics. Parents went to great lengths to augment their children's chances of gaining acceptance to desirable high schools. And teachers often felt compelled to use pedagogical approaches that allowed them to transmit large bodies of information efficiently.

One might argue that the undesirable aspects of entrance examinations are outweighed by the positive outcomes. According to this line of thought, the tight coupling of entrance examination scores and future educational opportunities creates a critical incentive for students to invest in their studies. This produces widespread commitment to education and high scores on international achievement tests. In other words, the ends justify the means. I am not persuaded by this argument for a number of reasons. Japanese students as a whole may earn high marks on tests such as TIMSS and PISA, compared with their peers in other countries. However, mean test scores mask variability in performance. In all the Japanese middle schools I visited, gaps between high- and low-achieving students were glaring.

At elementary schools that served the same families, I did not observe similar contrasts in behavior or academic performance. Overall levels of student participation were consistently high. In the first- through sixth-grade classrooms I visited, rarely did an elementary school student appear withdrawn or uninterested in learning activities. That high level of engagement translated into consistent mastery of content by all pupils. Teachers worked hard to ensure that all their students could succeed. But in middle schools, as examinations became more salient and performance was increasingly measured quantitatively, the percentage of pupils who lost interest in school increased noticeably.

It is important to recognize that not all Japanese middle school students were subject to intense test-related pressures. First-year middle school classrooms (the equivalent of seventh grade in the United States) resembled upper elementary classroom in many respects. Teachers did lecture more frequently than was common in elementary schools, but they also oversaw group discussions and collaborative learning exercises. A middle school Japanese teacher reflected that with first-year students, it was still possible to encourage her pupils "to talk, discuss, interact, and think seriously about ideas introduced in language classes. The thinking process is more important than the answers." Most students responded positively to this kind of instruction and continued to display enthusiasm for learning. Rarely did I witness signs of competition among students at this level.

A critical shift occurred during the second year of middle school. At that point, studying became serious business. Interviewees acknowledged to me that the middle year of middle school served as a pivotal transition point in the education of adolescents. It was at this point of their educational careers that the demands associated with the high school entrance system began to exert a strong influence on their educational futures. During homeroom meetings, instructors shared information about how to prepare for entrance examinations. On many occasions, I observed instructors advise their students to take note of certain information that was likely to appear on an entrance test; not once did that occur in a first-year classroom I visited. Lessons became more teacher centered and the pace of learning increased. The Japanese teacher quoted in the paragraph above told me that with second- and third-year students, she couldn't often facilitate discussion-based lessons because "there are so many things we have to do. We have to cover a great deal of material in a short period of time."

A large portion of middle school students responded positively to the increased pressure placed on them; they took their studies more seriously, completed optional review exercises, and began to focus on entrance examination preparation. Many of their classmates, though, had difficulty adjusting to the new practices and expectations. Test scores cogently communicated to such individuals that their academic opportunities were limited. Branded as losers in this academic competition, they disengaged from school and channeled their energy into other activities. As a result, by the eighth grade, a sizeable subset of the population appeared to have given up on school. Test results pushed doors open for some students and slammed them shut in the faces of their less fortunate classmates.

The gap that emerged between high- and low-achieving students was exacerbated by the resources families invested in education. Some parents went to great lengths to ensure that their sons and daughters were prepared to succeed academically, both in and outside of school. This included monitoring their homework, attending special school events, and communicating with teachers. Not content that such tactics would ensure that their children gained entry to a desirable high school, parents also signed their sons and daughters up for additional tutoring sessions. Thirty-two percent of the students I surveyed indicated that they enrolled in private learning centers (*juku*) after school and/or on weekends.

My observations of *juku* operating in the area where I conducted my fieldwork suggested that the primary objective of many such operations was to give their customers a leg up on entrance examinations. Instructors employed by those businesses introduced their pupils to concepts likely to be covered on the examinations at a much faster pace than public school teachers. They also administered mock exams on a regular basis and informed students about their areas of strength and weakness. As other researchers have noted (Dawson 2010; Dierkes 2010; Tsuneyoshi 2013), supplemental instruction increases the chances that *juku* students will be accepted by reputable high schools. Having already studied much of the material before it was introduced in regular school also gives *juku* attendees greater self-confidence to participate in public school classes, which sometimes function as review sessions for them.

Recent efforts to reform schools in other Asian nations confirm that Japan's experiences with high-stakes testing are not unique. As I detail in chapter 9, several other governments in the region have enacted reform initiatives that resemble *yutori kyoiku*. Responding to criticism that the heavy emphasis on testing undermines children's intellectual and social development, education planners in China, South Korea, Singapore adopted policies designed to mitigate the influence of examinations. Confronted with evidence that students who earn high scores on standardized tests may lack the skills necessary to succeed after graduation, reform proponents encourage teachers to expand their efforts to develop pupils' critical thinking skills, creativity, and ability to communicate their ideas to others. Yet in all those settings, educators have struggled to implement the policies according to plan. The power of high-stakes tests is proving remarkably difficult to conquer, in multiple locations.

This evidence should interest and concern education stakeholders in the United States. One critical impediment to educational reform in Asia has been entrenched practices and values connected with entrance examinations. Ranking individuals and institutions based on test scores is less taxing than evaluating student learning based on more qualitative data, but it also appears to lead to more instrumental decision making by students, parents, and teachers. And once those actors organize their behavior to fit the realities of an examination-centered system, it becomes difficult to alter their orientation.

Data-driven decision making in US schools is a fairly recent phenomenon. Teachers are still in the process of determining how to prepare their students to succeed on high-stakes assessments. Many believe that the situation is bound to change soon—that public outcry about the current obsession with testing will force policy makers to lessen the impact of examinations. That window, however, appears to be closing. With each year that standardized tests continue to determine the opportunities provided to students and teachers, the more difficult it becomes to retreat from policies like NCLB and RTT. Education stakeholders would be wise to think carefully about the recent trajectory of reform in the United States. If, after examining the effects of the accountability driven approaches to education, they determine that students are better off than their peers in the pre-NCLB era, it would make sense to throw their support behind efforts to institutionalize rigorous testing at every level of the system. If, on the other hand, evidence of the damaging consequences of high-stakes tests outweighs the benefits, then it is imperative that they communicate their concerns publicly—to other parents, school board members, and government officials. For, as this study makes clear, once an education system becomes tethered to standardized tests, it is remarkably difficult to cut those strings.

Remaining Focused on the Positive

Adoption of the relaxed-education reforms did not impel extensive changes in the delivery of curricula or the context for learning in Japanese middle schools. While this evidence of resistance to change is discouraging, it is important to recognize contrasts between different levels of the system. Although middle schools continue to breed anxiety, elementary schools do an impressive job supporting the goals of *yutori kyoiku*. In all the elementary schools I studied, teachers engaged and challenged students on a daily basis. They accomplished this without relying on competition or the threat of low grades to compel children to work hard. This evidence challenges the idea that anxiety and pressure are unpleasant but necessary by-products of academic excellence. It is possible to motivate students and teachers without threatening them with negative consequences if they do not meet certain performance targets. Japanese elementary school teachers do so with remarkable consistency. They display a sense of responsibility to improve their craft, and the impetus for their dedication is rooted in the communities they serve—not a test-based accountability system.

In the elementary schools I visited, teachers set high standards for themselves and their pupils. They accomplished this feat despite the absence of high-stakes examinations. Children regularly took tests and quizzes, but the stakes were low. Pupils approached learning as members of a team rather than competitors, which fostered a strong sense of classroom community. Instructors regularly implored their charges to exert effort in tasks out of a sense of responsibility to themselves and to their classmates.

As I describe in chapter 5, instructors sometimes complained to me that the new Course of Study was not as challenging as previous versions. That may have been true. Nevertheless, the lessons I observed introduced students to concepts that were more challenging than is common in the elementary classrooms I observe in the United States. Japanese children developed a solid foundation in the three Rs, as well as other subjects that are sometimes given minimal attention in American schools. As researchers such as Cave (2007), Ma (1999), and Stigler and Hiebert (1999) have noted, teachers in Asia are expected to introduce their students to fewer concepts but to explore those ideas thoroughly. My observations in Japanese elementary classrooms support that finding. Teachers went to great lengths to design learning experiences that pushed children to understand the logic behind the knowledge they acquired. Rather than simply memorize formulas for solving mathematical problems, children were required to come up with their own problem-solving strategies, using objects, graphs, and illustrations. Furthermore, they were regularly encouraged to explain those strategies to their classmates. The focus was on depth rather than breadth—the opposite of what tends to occur in American schools subject to accountability mandates in the United States (USGAO 2009). As one sixth-grade teacher told me, "Presenting students with difficult problems often motivates them to work harder."

Clearly, elementary schools in Japan are organized to fit a set of goals and influences distinct from those that organize life in the middle schools. The absence of high-stakes tests provides teachers with the freedom to make decisions based on their analysis of the social, emotional, and intellectual needs of their pupils. I believe that sense of obligation to students is more effective than an accountability system driven by high-stakes tests. International achievement test data establish that Japanese elementary school students develop solid academic skills relative to their peers in other countries, and also maintain enthusiasm for learning.

The Roots of Academic Excellence

Observers often assume that Japanese children excel on international achievement assessments due to heavy doses of test preparation in school. At first glance, there does appear to be some logic behind this conjecture. As I have emphasized throughout this book, secondary schools in Japan are often intense settings for learning. Students as well as teachers find it difficult to shield themselves from the influence of high-stakes tests. This information might lead one to conclude that test-driven accountability provides Japanese pupils with the motivation and practical experience necessary to excel on standardized achievement tests, such as TIMSS and PISA.

Drawing from the evidence presented in this study, I offer another explanation for Japanese students' consistently high position on international league tables. To fully understand the factors that encourage children to invest in their studies, master curricular content, and acquire the skills measured on achievement tests, it is necessary to look across levels of the system. Taking such a broad view reveals the critical role that elementary education plays in preparing children for future success. I believe that the key to Japanese citizens' intellectual development is the strong foundation they develop during their early years as students. I am convinced that the absence of test-generated pressures makes it possible for teachers to create such inspiring contexts for learning. By the time most children complete the sixth grade, they develop a strong academic foundation.

International achievement test scores support this assertion. TIMSS tests are administered to fourth- and eighth-grade students. If the heavy emphasis on testing were responsible for Japanese students' academic success, we would expect to see a jump in performance between the fourth and eighth grades. Test-score data, however, do not reveal such a shift in performance. On each version of TIMSS, Japanese fourth-grade test takers have scored near the top of all participating countries both the mathematics and science sections of the test. This suggests that Japanese children begin to excel academically at the elementary level—before testing assumes a central position in the life of the school. As table 11.1 shows, middle school students do not earn higher marks than their elementary counterparts; they continue to perform at the same—or nearly the same—level as fourth graders. In other words, the external accountability introduced at the sec-

Table 11.1. Japan's average TIMSS performance over time (1995–2011)

	Fourth grade			
	Math score	International rank	Science score	International rank
1995	597	3rd	574	2nd
2003	565	3rd	543	3rd
2007	568	4th	548	4th
2011	585	5th	559	4th
	Eighth grade			
	Math score	International rank	Science score	International rank
1995	605	3rd	571	3rd
1999	579	5th	550	4th
2003	570	5th	552	6th
2007	570	5th	554	3rd
2011	570	5th	558	4th

Note: TIMSS did not test fourth graders in 1999.

ondary level is not more powerful than the internal accountability used to generate motivation in elementary school pupils. In grades one through six, children acquire knowledge and skills that equip them to succeed as they proceed through the system. Greater emphasis on testing, sorting, and ranking students at the middle school level does not improve their academic performance. Attention to high school entrance examinations may lead some adolescents to spend more time studying, but it also undercuts the motivation of many other students.

Entrance examinations also shape the behavior of teachers. Cognizant that scores on those tests will determine the academic futures of their pupils, instructors are forced to make compromises. They deliver dense lectures that allow them to introduce large bodies of information as efficiently as possible. The observation data I collected indicate that elementary school students in my sample engaged in student-centered activities and/or group work in their academic classes more than twice as often as their middle school counterparts (55% compared with 27%), and that middle school instructors lectured 73% of the time (see table 6.1). The teachers I interviewed acknowledged this reality but felt that the situation was beyond their control. A similar pattern has emerged in schools in the United States since the No Child Left Behind Act was adopted. Teachers have been pressured to make bargains—to focus on test preparation even when that approach conflicts with their core beliefs about education and their experiences working with children. Threatened with sanctions triggered by low standardized test scores, they engage in practices that undermine student engagement in learning.

Although Japanese teachers operate within social and institutional frames distinct from those that encircle American educators, the influence of examinations on decision making in Japanese schools offers some important lessons relevant to schools located in any setting. The Japanese education system provides glimpses of both the enormous potential of public schools and the extent to which high-stakes tests undermine that promise. In elementary schools, attention to the development of the whole child—rather than their performance on tests—yields impressive results. Within what appears to be a highly centralized bureaucracy, instructors enjoy a great deal of autonomy. Respected as professionals in child development and curriculum design, they collect "data" about their students on a daily basis and use that information to enhance the quality of instruction. Those data, however, do not come in the form of standardized test scores. Instead, they include a variety of measures of student behavior and performance: focused observations of children's actions in the classroom, discussions with colleagues, formative assessments that may or may not take the form of tests, input from parents, and frequent review of student work. I would argue that this amalgamation of information provides teachers with a much deeper understanding of their students' intellectual development than a standardized test can.

Great Potential, Limited Change

Japan's ambitious attempt to reshape its schools provoked passionate debates about the state of the education system, but limited changes to curriculum and instructional practice. The evidence I collected for this study demonstrates that what was billed as the nation's "Third Major Education Initiative" didn't come close to fulfilling its potential. Despite receiving unprecedented authority to tailor an initiative promulgated by the Ministry of Education to fit the needs of their students and surrounding communities, the vast majority of Japanese teachers working in the schools in and around Nishiyama eventually reverted to practices common prior to introduction of *yutori kyoiku*. Even teachers who agreed with the goals of relaxed education were hesitant to adhere to reform plans. The familiar and dependable were preferred over recommendations with unproven outcomes. Individuals may have complained about troubling aspects of that system, but they also knew what to expect from it. As a result, rhetorical support for a more-relaxed education system hovered above a system marked by tradition and stability.

Responses to the relaxed-education policies underscore the difficulties of translating ideals about the potential of public schools into concrete reform plans that are feasible and palatable to multiple constituencies. The pervasive influence of neoliberal thought in the 1990s and 2000s heightened concerns about competitiveness, productivity, and accountability that often created tensions in schools—in Japan and elsewhere. Education planners are challenged to devise reform initiatives that satisfy stakeholders concerned about academic competitiveness as well as those more focused on the affective dimensions of learning. They must weigh the relative advantages of several different possible pedagogical approaches: transmission-oriented curriculum and more student-centered approaches, teacher-directed learning and independent student investigations, enrichment activities and lessons that focus on basic academic skills. When teachers are not sure which strategies will produce the most tangible benefits, more conservative approaches tend to hold sway and the authority of quantitative measures of performance increases. Narrowing the curriculum and systematically assessing learning based on test scores may be politically palatable, but, as the Japanese case indicates, that approach to reform may have long-lasting negative consequences for children. Education-policy makers working in locations where high-stakes testing is regarded as a means of raising academic achievement should consider this evidence seriously before endorsing such measures.

EPILOGUE

Is it too early to draw conclusions about the effects of *yutori kyoiku*? Could it be that more time is necessary for the relaxed-education policies to take root? After all, Japanese government tends to institute changes, in a variety of sectors, quite methodically. Azuma has criticized researchers who rush to judgment about the effects of reform efforts, asserting that, "in education, where the results of reform are embedded in the development of young minds and may not be revealed for a decade or more, caution has its advantages" (Azuma 2002, 12–13). Was discomfort with MEXT's reform plans an unavoidable stage of the initial phase of implementation? With more time to digest and experiment with the new curriculum, will teachers gradually become more enthusiastic supporters of *yutori kyoiku*? Will parents' initial concerns about recent reforms abate after they observe the effects of those changes on their own children?

I agree with Azuma's observation that the effects of attempts to modify curriculum and instruction may not be immediately apparent. Teachers need time to carefully study a new idea before they are prepared to implement it in their classrooms. I have written elsewhere about the benefits of Japan's measured approach to reform, especially compared to the often frenetic pace of reform adoption and rejection in the United States (Bjork 2000a). But in the schools that I studied, as education stakeholders became more familiar with the concrete repercussions of MEXT's plans for change, their criticism and resistance to relaxed education become more formidable. Japan's performance on the 2003 TIMSS study heightened anxiety about recent modifications to the curriculum. Teachers found it increasingly difficult to continue supporting relaxed education amidst the vociferous claims of crisis swirling around them. I did not meet a single secondary teacher whose enthusiasm for relaxed education increased over time. During my last visit to Nishiyama, many of the changes introduced to the middle schools in the name of relaxed education had already been retracted or decimated.

In the years since I completed the primary fieldwork for this study, MEXT reconsidered its commitment to reducing academic intensity. Although the ministry did resist pressure to reinstitute a six-day school week, post-2002 revisions to the Course of Study undercut many of the changes aimed at reducing academic intensity in the schools.

As tables E.1 and E.2 document, post-*yutori* versions of the national Course of Study increased the number hours allocated to mathematics, Japanese, and foreign language. To make room for the additional time allocated to core subject matter, the hours set aside for Integrated Studies were trimmed and elective courses were eliminated from the middle school cur-

Table E.1. Changes in the elementary school curriculum

	Number of Instructional Hours—2002			
	Grade 3	Grade 4	Grade 5	Grade 6
Japanese language	280	280	210	210
Social studies	105	105	105	105
Mathematics	150	150	150	150
Science	105	105	105	105
Integrated Studies	105	105	110	110
Foreign language	—	—	—	—
	Number of Instructional Hours—2008			
	Grade 3	Grade 4	Grade 5	Grade 6
Japanese language	235	235	180	175
Social studies	70	85	90	100
Mathematics	150	150	150	150
Science	70	90	95	95
Integrated Studies	105	105	110	110
Foreign language	—	—	—	—
	Number of Instructional Hours—2012			
	Grade 3	Grade 4	Grade 5	Grade 6
Japanese language	245	245	175	175
Social studies	70	90	100	105
Mathematics	175	175	175	175
Science	90	105	105	105
Integrated Studies	70	70	70	70
Foreign language	—	—	35	35

Table E.2. Changes in the middle school curriculum

	Number of Instructional Hours—2002		
	Grade 1	Grade 2	Grade 3
Japanese language	175	140	140
Social studies	140	140	70-105
Mathematics	105	140	140
Science	105	105	105–140
Integrated Studies	35–70	35–70	35–70
Foreign language	—	—	—
Elective subjects	105–140	105–210	105–280
	Number of Instructional Hours—2008		
	Grade 1	Grade 2	Grade 3
Japanese language	140	105	105
Social studies	105	105	85
Mathematics	105	105	105
Science	105	105	105
Integrated Studies	70–100	70–105	70–130
Foreign language	105	105	105
Elective subjects	0–30	50–85	105–165
	Number of Instructional Hours—2012		
	Grade 1	Grade 2	Grade 3
Japanese language	140	140	105
Social studies	105	105	140
Mathematics	140	105	140
Science	105	140	140
Integrated Studies	50	70	70
Foreign language	140	140	140
Elective subjects	—	—	—

riculum. Do these changes portend the gradual abandonment of the goals of relaxed education, or will the reforms continue to exist in a slimmer form?

I expect that the hands-on, student-centered, stimulating learning that relaxed education was designed to promote will continue to infuse instruction in the elementary schools. I make this prediction with confidence because these practices were a regular component of primary school life in Japan long before MEXT began promoting the "new" educational framework. The instructional program for elementary schools was altered slightly, with hours set aside for most subjects reduced to make room for Integrated Studies and the five-day school week. Although teachers shared concerns about *yutori kyoiku*, most maintained a positive attitude and introduced the new curriculum according to plan. MEXT will most likely continue tinkering with the number of hours allocated to the various subjects, but Integrated Studies should remain a component of the weekly schedule. Children will continue to work on projects that require them to explore topics related to their local communities and to present their findings to their classmates. Elementary schools will augment their students' intellectual curiosity, critical thinking abilities, and "zest for life," even though debates about the mission of the schools will continue.

At the secondary level, in contrast, relaxed education will most likely die a slow death. As was common at the middle schools in my sample, teachers will find ways to circumvent official MEXT policies that do support their most immediate priorities. The goals of making learning less stressful and more personally relevant for students do not top that list. Current discourse about the state of education suggests that the public is more concerned about academic competitiveness than children's affective orientations toward school. Cognizant of this reality, middle school instructors will continue to make decisions about curriculum and instruction based on the demands associated with entrance examinations, regardless of the recommendations included in MEXT reports. Teachers may have initially been persuaded by—or at least receptive to—the ministry's claims about the need for reform, but that period of openness has passed. When initial attempts to follow reform guidelines produced additional stress and ambiguous results, middle school instructors quickly reverted to the tried and true. Public opinion, personal experience, and new MEXT policy decisions all pushed them backward. That tendency is likely to continue now that the momentum behind *yutori kyoiku* has stalled. Integrated Studies may remain in the curriculum, but in diluted form. No longer a priority in the middle schools, the subject will be treated as an unwanted encumbrance, or will exist in form only. Relaxed education will constitute little more than a catchphrase that teachers refer to in the past tense. Its influence over student learning will be negligible.

It would be erroneous to assume, however, that reducing the time allocated to relaxed-education subject matter will quickly elevate Japan's ranking on international achievement tests. Education pundits often argue that relaxed-education policies represent a threat to traditional approaches to teaching and learning. According to Takayama (2007), critics tend to frame *yutori kyoiku* as a threat to "true Japanese education" and stoke debates about educational crisis in attempt to "legitimize their own neoconservative return to the idealized past" (439). It is doubtful, though, that reducing the hours allocated to *yutori* subject matter will have such an effect. The diverse assortment of troubles the reforms were designed to address—from student apathy to weak critical thinking skills to social afflictions—are far too extensive to be remedied by minor revisions to the curriculum. Adding an hour of mathematics or eliminating a period of Integrated Studies will not induce major changes in students' attitudes toward school or their academic capabilities. Critics of *yutori kyoiku* who expect a move away from the policies enacted in 2002 to vault the nation's youths back to the top of international league tables are bound to be disappointed.

Entreaties to reinstate previous curricular frameworks frequently maintain that increasing the number of hours devoted to math and language instruction is the key to restoring Japan's academic competitiveness. Such claims may appeal to citizens with positive recollections of the nation's previous economic and educational success. Distilling the challenges associated with educating children to a simple and easy reproducible formula can be comforting. But expecting approaches used in the past to produce the same results in contemporary society is misguided. Relaxed education did not produce the maladies experienced by youths—nor will the expansion of instructional time devoted to core academic subjects solve those problems. Reinstituting a curriculum that was popular in the past will not induce pupils to adopt the same attitudes toward their studies as their peers from previous generations.

Changes in the behavior and academic performance of Japanese students that have attracted widespread outcry from education critics are rooted beyond the boundaries of school campuses. As I have emphasized, the lives of Japanese children have become extremely complex and unpredictable over the past twenty years. Changes in family structure, economic conditions, information technology, and conceptions of authority have produced children guided by priorities distinct from those common in other eras. Though required to attend school every day, many communicate through their behavior and academic performance that education is not a priority for them. Faced with uninspiring instruction or evidence of their intellectual shortcomings, they withdraw or rebel.

Reforming a national education system is an immense undertaking. It requires unified commitment across sectors of government, geographical regions, and segments of society. That sense of a clear collective purpose is notably absent from contemporary Japanese society. The education system—like many social institutions in the country—continues to search for an appropriate path forward. When that path becomes obscured visible, its members take a series of detours, but retreat when those routes do not deliver them to their desired destinations. In this context, aversion to change makes sense. Sticking to the familiar and dependable reduces risk.

The concept of *yutori kyoiku* appeals to education stakeholders when considered abstractly, but their enthusiasm dims when the idea is translated into instructional practice. Parents support proposals to make schools more stimulating institutions, but only if the costs of making that shift can be contained. Twenty-first-century skills sound appealing, but not at the expense of traditional academic subjects. Taking their cues from the communities they serve, instructors resist pressure to modify the curriculum. That pattern is likely to continue unless they become convinced that altering their behavior will provide tangible benefits to their students in the current educational marketplace. Even in what appears to be a highly centralized bureaucracy, local actors play a critical role in the educational reform process. Until teachers determine that a proposed change initiative is a clear improvement over the status quo, that reform is bound to stall, regardless of decisions made by education officials in Tokyo.

ACKNOWLEDGMENTS

This project took several years to complete. Throughout my period of research I depended on a long list of friends, colleagues, students, and scholars for support. As I designed the study and selected field sites, I reached out to friends as well as strangers to help me find teachers who would share their experiences with me, and schools willing to let a foreign researcher become a temporary member of their community. Manabu Sato, Akio Nigorikawa, Seiji Waida, Satoshi Kamada, Keiko Igarashi, Naomi Otomo, Ayako Casey, Shigeki Kubo, Shoko Hamano, and Kiyoshi Yamauchi facilitated those connections for me.

I feel fortunate to be part of a community of scholars that is so open and supportive of one another. None of the experts in Asian education I reached out to ever turned down a request for a meeting or for feedback on a piece of writing. As I shaped and reshaped the manuscript for this book, I asked a number of colleagues for input. Thank you to Gary DeCoker, Tom Rohlen, Kaori Okano, Jeremy Rappleye, David Willis, Heidi Ross, Yimin Wang, participants in workshops on Japanese education held in Montreal and Honolulu, and several anonymous reviewers for your constructive criticism. I also learned a great deal about *yutori kyoiku* through discussions I had with Hidenori Fujita, Takehiko Kariya, Akira Sakai, June Gordon, Rebecca Fukuzawa, Victor Kobayashi, Jim Shields, Takao Mimura, Stephen Murphy-Shigematsu, Penny Kinnear, Mark Langager, Walter Dawson, and Eriko Miyake.

The cross-national study of teaching reported on in chapter 10 was coordinated by the University of Tokyo Graduate School of Education. Thank you to Ryoko Tsuneyoshi, Kiyomi Akita, Christine Lee, and Catherine Lewis for inviting me to participate in that project.

During my extended period of fieldwork in Japan, a number of people helped my family adjust to our new surroundings. I am especially appreciative of the assistance provided by Carolyn Kaltenbach, Alexi Castillo, Reiko Ohdake, Midori Fujita, and the families in Nishiyama that made us feel so welcome. In addition, April Racana and Phillip Matz were outstanding hosts on my frequent trips to Tokyo.

I would also like to thank the Japan Society for the Promotion of Science and the Fulbright Association for providing the funding that allowed me to conduct my research. Everyone in the Japan-US Educational Commission in Tokyo helped me out at one point, and David Sattewhite and Mizuho Iwata were especially supportive.

While working in the United States, I depended on a crew of Vassar research assistants to locate materials, construct tables, format documents, and proofread my writing. I don't know how I would have finished the project without the assistance of those students: Nina Seligson, Becca Shubert, Katie Carpenter, Robert Woodword, Nick Pauley, and Sino Estheppan. Educators Micah Brown, David Bloom, and Michael Yarmosky all helped me find teachers willing to participate in the focus group discussions referred to in chapter 10.

I feel fortunate to have worked with such a wonderful editor. Elizabeth Branch Dyson at the University of Chicago Press responded promptly to my e-mails and phone calls, and has a real talent for expressing constructive criticism in an inspiring way.

I would also like to thank my family members for their encouragement and flexibility. My parents have always shown a great interest in my work, and served as an ongoing source of encouragement. My wife and kids have settled and resettled in a number of different places as I pursued different research projects. Having them with me kept me grounded.

Finally, I would like to recognize the educators—in Japan, the United States, and elsewhere—who shared their stories with me. As the descriptions in this book illustrate, the life of a teacher has become more complicated and stressful in recent years. I have great respect for those who remain committed to their work and their students, despite the challenges they face.

NOTES

CHAPTER ONE

1. The years attached to the various Courses of Study sometimes cause confusion. This is because some reports refer to the year the curriculum was adopted and others refer to the year it was implemented. Typically, MEXT spends several years developing a new Course of Study. After disseminating a new curriculum, the ministry pilots it in a number of schools around the country and seeks feedback from education stakeholders. After receiving that input, MEXT usually revises the curriculum, then directs all public schools to implement the modified versions of the Course of Study. In this book, I will refer to the years the Courses of Study were implemented. To make sure this information is clear, here is a summary that identifies when recent versions of the Course of Study were adopted and introduced in elementary and middle school classrooms:

   adopted 1977; implemented 1978
   adopted 1989; implemented 1992
   adopted 1998; implemented 2002

2. MEXT officially required all schools to have Integrated Studies in place by 2002, but most institutions began conducting research on the topic and phasing in IS classes prior to that deadline.
3. This is another phrase that is challenging to translate into English. Although MEXT repeatedly employs the words "zest for living" as a substitute for *ikiru chikara,* this oversimplifies the connotations of the phrase. *Ikiru chikara* encompasses a wide array of attributes seen as necessary to live comfortably and productively in contemporary society—including social, emotional, as well as cognitive qualities.

CHAPTER TWO

1. This approach has been referred to elsewhere as a "loose-tight" management strategy (Nitta 2008; Peters and Waterman 1982). It developed based on analysis of America's most successfully managed companies. According to the "loose-tight" principal, work teams are given the freedom to set their own short-term priorities but are held accountable for meeting carefully delineated goals. Teams that reach those goals receive rewards, and those that do not are sanctioned.
2. Historian Diane Ravitch writes: "At least until 1965, when the Elementary and Secondary Education Act was passed, the federal government's role had been to subsi-

dize the education of the neediest students, enforce civil rights, conduct research, gather information, and subsidize college costs. That was a significant role, but it did not involve telling local public schools what they must do to be successful or what would happen if they were not successful. All this changed with No Child Left Behind" (2010, 246–7).

3. A Department of Education was formed in 1867 but was reclassified as an office the following year. It continued to function as a bureau with limited powers until 1953, when it became part of the Department of Health, Education, and Welfare.
4. Ironically, Weiler coined the term "compensatory legitimization" to describe the decisions made by highly centralized government to delegate authority to subnational offices. With NCLB, the reverse is occurring, though many of the factors referred to by Weiler are influencing decision making at the state level.
5. This brief summary of the legislative process oversimplifies the process of negotiation that preceded passage of NCLB. A more complete and nuanced discussion of that process is provided by Manna (2006).

CHAPTER THREE

1. During the time of my research, the population of Nishiyama City was just over 200,000.
2. Before beginning my primary data collection, I also conducted a pilot study at two elementary schools located in a small city approximately an hour away. I visited each school for three weeks, observing classes and interviewing educators to gain a better understanding of their experiences implementing the relaxed-education curriculum, and trying out different surveys and observation protocols. Although that preliminary work did add to my knowledge of how schools were responding to MEXT plans for change, the data I collected at those sites are not included in the descriptions or analysis offered in this book.
3. It is important to recognize that some of the information I considered in selecting schools was anecdotal. I did research demographic information related to neighborhoods and communities, but Japanese schools are extremely protective of aspects of students' home lives considered to be confidential. I did not have access to such data when I was planning my study.
4. This includes a principal, a vice principal, a nurse, five full-time teachers (including a head teacher), and four part-time instructors.
5. There were exceptions to this pattern. On certain days of the year (such as the block of end-of-semester tests), students remained in their uniforms throughout the day.
6. Again, this figure is an unscientific estimation, but represents a sharp decrease from the figure of 30 percent supplied by instructors at the nearby elementary school.
7. This exercise is part of the procedure used to check attendance in all classrooms, in all the elementary schools I visited. The extent of such student reporting did, however, vary slightly from class to class. At the beginning of every morning meeting, for instance, a fifth-grade teacher at OES asked students three questions: Did you eat a good breakfast? Did you poop before you came to school? Did you get enough sleep?
8. At each school I asked one homeroom class per grade level to complete a student survey. According to this data, the percentage of students at CMS who attended *juku* was 23%, compared with 31% at Oka JHS and 42% at Hama JHS.
9. Because this is not a longitudinal study, I did not actually monitor individual pupils over a number of years. Instead, I compared students in different grade levels who were studying at HMS during my year of fieldwork. It is possible that the adoles-

cents in those classes were atypical and the contrasts I observed between first- and third-grade students might not have been as striking in other years. None of the interview data I collected, however, suggest this was the case.

10. Walford and Massey (1998) specify seven key elements that distinguish ethnography from other types of qualitative research: (1) the focus on the study of culture, (2) the use of multiple methods and thus the construction of diverse forms of data, (3) the direct involvement and long-term engagement, (4) the recognition that the researcher is the main research instrument, (5) the high status given to the accounts of participants and their understandings, (6) the engagement in a cycle of hypothesis and theory building, and (7) the focus on a particular case rather than on any attempts to generalize.
11. Of the 79 teachers interviewed, 30 were elementary educators and 50 taught at the middle schools. These figures do not include several teachers I spoke with who were employed at institutions not included in my sample of six schools.
12. Teacher surveys were distributed to all instructors at the six schools. At schools with two or fewer homerooms per grade level, surveys were distributed to all students; at schools with more than two homerooms per grade level, two classes at each grade level were randomly selected to take the survey.

CHAPTER FOUR

1. Individuals employed at smaller schools tended to have a longer list of responsibilities, due to the limited number of adults available to carry out that work.
2. In Japan, teachers do officially receive breaks during extended holidays (such as winter and summer vacations). However, they are usually expected to come to school and work during those times. At one elementary school faculty meeting I observed, the principal instructed teachers to bring their cell phones with them if they went out of town on any days that school was not in session so that administrators and parents could contact them if necessary.
3. Recently, most local boards of education have redesigned their teacher assessment procedures in attempt to augment professional accountability (Katsuno 2010). At the time I was conducting fieldwork, however, the schools I studied had not implemented revised teacher-evaluation procedures.

CHAPTER FIVE

1. The one curricular area that was not generally approached with such an emphasis on critical thinking and personal expression was Japanese language. In contrast with most other learning activities, teachers tended to devote a significant portion of *kokugo* lessons to drill and memorization of Japanese ideographs (*kanji*). When discussing stories included in the readers, the questions they posed almost always checked students' recall of events (rather than their opinions about the stories) and were framed to elicit a single correct response. In some instances, instructors did not facilitate any discussion of the stories at all, choosing instead to concentrate on new *kanji* included in the text.
2. This does not include the informal time I spent passing through classrooms, the pilot study I conducted in two primary schools prior to beginning my primary data collection, or single day visits I paid to schools around the country prior to 2006.
3. These observations do not apply to children who spent most of the school day in special education classrooms, which have become ubiquitous in Japan. The number of children designated for special education has steadily increased over the last de-

cade. In addition, according to a presentation given by a special education teacher at one of my schools, 6.3% of all children in Japan had ADHD at the time I was conducting my fieldwork.

CHAPTER SIX

1. I also flipped the order observations each week. For example, if I attended the elementary school in Neighborhood A one week, I attended morning classes at the middle school in Neighborhood A the next.
2. This change did not affect elementary school teachers or students.
3. These statistics are based on the instructional methods used in academic subject areas only. I did not include data from lesson observations in art, music, physical education, home economics, or special activities (such as homeroom meetings) so as to highlight the approaches used by educators to introduce curricula that was content driven. Adding data collected in subjects not considered part of the core academic subjects, I believe, would skew patterns in methodological approaches—teachers responsible for those subjects tend to employ pedagogies specific to those subjects, such as independent art projects or cooking in small groups.
4. Although several of the lessons filmed in Japanese middle schools that were analyzed in the TIMSS study captured student-centered learning activities, the teachers who facilitated those lessons were notified in advance when they would be videotaped, and that the interactions captured on tape would be studied by researchers. For this reason, I think the TIMSS videos should be treated as representations of the ideal rather than evidence of common practices in the schools.

CHAPTER SEVEN

1. Examples of the "new academic abilities" supported by MEXT included student initiative, independence, critical thinking, creativity, and the ability to investigate topics of interest to the student.
2. The word *buraku*, or "hamlet people," is used to describe a group of people who have been treated as outcasts in Japan for centuries. Historically, they lived on the edges of towns and held occupations, such as butcher or leatherworker, which others were unwilling to do. They are also sometimes referred to as *eta*.
3. For example, structural reforms endorsed by Prime Ministers Junichiro Koizumi and Shinzo Abe resulted in increased privatization of public services, an increase in the proportion of part-time and temporary employment, and widespread deregulation (Itoh 2000).
4. In 2006, *kakusa shakai* appeared on a list of the ten trendiest expressions in Japan (Caryl & Kashiwagi, 2007).
5. The tests that provoked the greatest furor were the 2003 TIMSS and the 2003 and 2006 PISA tests.
6. In most of the English elective classes I observed, an assistant language teacher (ALT) assisted the primary instructor. The presence of two adults made the task of student supervision more manageable. Teachers in other subjects did not have this luxury.
7. This helps to explain why, in the rankings of students' favorite subjects, IS trailed only physical education, music, art, and science.
8. This follows a national trend: Tsuneyoshi (2004b) found that attendance at cram schools has increased substantially since the MEXT adopted the flexible education policies.

CHAPTER EIGHT

1. The term "student guidance" (*seikatsu shido*) encompasses more diverse activities than is the case in American schools. The Japanese term involves a range of responsibilities entrusted to teachers as they mentor students. These include managing classes, mentoring individual pupils, establishing norms related to student comportment and dress, and providing advice about academic and personal plans.
2. Exclusive attention to this group model oversimplifies the nature of Japanese society. Some institutions display more egalitarianism than is implied in the brief summary above (Moeran 1986). In addition, narrowly focusing on the stability that comes with a group orientation can obscure the conflict that does occur in Japanese institutions (Krauss, Rohlen, and Steinhoff 1984).
3. I thank Mark Langager for pointing out the significance of this directive and sharing with us his experiences of its impact on middle school guidance while he was working in schools in the Tokyo area at this time.

CHAPTER NINE

1. Comparing the results of TIMSS and PISA tests is challenging because the two tests are designed to measure slightly different skills and are completed by different populations of students. The objective of PISA is "to determine the extent to which young people have acquired the wider knowledge in reading literacy, mathematical literacy and scientific literacy that they will need in adult life" (OECD 2004, p. 4). PISA tests are administered to fifteen-year-olds. TIMSS instruments assess math and science literacy among fourth and eighth graders. Most of the items included on TIMSS are multiple-choice exercises, while constructed-response questions make up the bulk of PISA instruments. In addition, as tables 9.1 and 9.2 illustrate, not all of the same countries administer both tests. Students from Finland and Mainland China did not take part in either 2003 or 2007 TIMSS. It is also difficult to compare the performance of students in China to those in other nations because separate scores are reported for Shanghai and Hong Kong. No scores for students located in other parts of China are available. Given these complications, the data included in tables 9.1 and 9.2 should be interpreted with caution.
2. For example, statistics published by the OECD indicate that Finland spends $37,293 GDP per capita on education, compared with $47,495 in the United States. (OECD 2010).
3. These highly publicized gains were later called in to question when careful analysis of test results revealed that: "the tests had become too easy and that score inflation was rampant" (Medina 2010). State officials had ignored warnings from outside experts who noted flaws in the content and administration of New York's achievement tests.
4. Oklahoma's waiver was repealed after the state chose not to follow the Common Core learning standards and failed to write a new set of standards to use in place of the CC. Washington was the first state to lose its NCLB waiver after it did not allocate what the USDOE viewed as sufficient federal funds to support private tutoring and school choice.

CHAPTER TEN

1. Groups of parents were also interviewed. Given the focus of this book, I will present only the findings of the focus group discussions with parents here.
2. Although activities filmed in Singapore, China, and the United States provoked

many interesting comments, assessments of the instruction provided in Japanese classrooms are particularly relevant to the issues that anchor this book.

CHAPTER ELEVEN

1. This phrase has become a buzzword in Japanese society, further integrated into the daily vernacular when a television drama with the title *Monster Parent*, which aired on Fuji Television, became popular in 2008.
2. Reports from researchers and teachers working in multiple locations suggest that the escalating prevalence of parental defiance was not unique to my research sites (Okano and Tsuchiya 1999; Tsuneyoshi 2008). According to Sato, "the parent-teacher relationship has changed from one of cooperation between partners sharing in the responsibility for children's upbringing and education between one of a service (the teachers) and the consumers (parents and the taxpayers. In the context of this sort of relationship, the consumers build up their lists of complaints regarding the service providers" (Sato 2005, 33). In a survey that Gordon distributed to public school teachers, only 14% of respondents responded that they felt respected by parents (Gordon 2005, p. 464).

REFERENCES

Abelmann, N., J. Choi, and S. J. Park, eds.2012. *No Alternative? Experiments in South Korean Education*. Berkeley, CA: University of California Press.

Abrams, S. E. 2011. "The Children Must Play: What the US Could Learn from Finland about Education Reform." *New Republic*, January 28. http://www.newrepublic.com/article/politics/82329/education-reform-Finland-US.

Akimoto, Makoto. 1983. *Warui nowa dareda? Gakunai boryoku* (Who is to blame? School violence). Tokyo: Tainmikku Serazu.

Altbach, Philip G. 2009. "Peripheries and Centers: Research Universities in Developing Countries." *Asia Pacific Review* 10 (1):15–27.

Amano, Ikuo. 1990. *Education and Examination in Modern Japan*. Tokyo: University of Tokyo. Press,

An, Xuehui, S. E. Hannum, and T. Sargent. 2008. "Teaching Quality and Student Outcomes: Academic Achievement and Educational Engagement in Rural Northwest China." *China: An International Journal* 5 (2):309–34.

Apple, Michael. 1982. *Education and Power*. New York: Routledge.

Arense, A. L., and L. Lundahl. 2006. "Still Social and Democratic: Inclusive Education Policies in Nordic Welfare States." *Scandinavian Journal of Educational Research* 50 (3):285–300.

Arnove, Robert. 1999. *Comparative Education: The Dialectic of the Global and the Local*. Lanham, MD: Rowman & Littlefield Publishers.

Aspinall, Robert. 2001. *Teachers' Unions and the Politics of Education in Japan*. Albany, NY: SUNY Press.

Ayers, William, ed. 1995. *To Become a Teacher: Making a Difference in Children's Lives*. New York: Teachers College Press.

Azuma, Hiroshi. 2002. "The Development of the Course of Study and the Structure of Educational Reform in Japan." In *National Standards and School Reform in Japan and in the United States*, edited by Gary DeCoker, 5–18. New York: Teachers College Press.

Azuma, Hiroshi, Kenji Hakuta, and Harold Stevenson. 1986. *Child Development and Education in Japan*. New York: Freeman.

Baker, E. L., et al. 2010. *Problems with the Use of Student Test Scores to Evaluate Teachers. EPI Briefing Paper #278*. Washington, DC: Education Policy Institute.

Baker, David, and Gerald LeTendre. 2005. *National Differences, Global Similarities: World Culture and the Future of Schooling*. Stanford: Stanford University Press.

Bambrick-Santoyo, Paul. 2010. *Driven by Data: A Practical Guide to Improve Instruction*. San Francisco: Jossey-Bass.

Barret, Brian D. 2009. "No Child Left Behind and the Assault on Teachers' Professional Practices and Identities." *Teaching and Teacher Education* 25 (8):1018–1025.

Barron, Brigid J., Daniel L. Schwartz, Nancy J. Vye, Allison Moore, Anthony Petrosino, Linda Zech, and John D. Bransford. 1998. "Doing with Understanding: Lessons from Research on Problem- and Project-Based Learning." *Journal of the Learning Sciences* 7 (3):271–311.

Beauchamp, Edward R., ed. 1991. *Windows on Japanese Education: Contributions to the Study of Education*. New York: Greenwood Press.

Beauchamp, Edward R. 1994. *Japanese Education since 1945: A Documentary Study*. Edited by James M. Vardaman. Armonk, NY: E. M. Sharpe.

Bell, Stephanie. 2010. "Project-Based Learning for the 21st century: Skills for the Future." *Clearing House: A Journal of Educational Strategies, Issues and Ideas* 83 (2):39–43.

Bjork, Christopher. 2000a. "Collaboration in Japanese and American Schools: The Challenge of Balancing Consistency and Change." *World Studies in Education* 1 (2):55–79.

———. 2000b. "Responsibility for Improving the Quality of Teaching in Japanese Schools: The Role of the Principal in Professional Development Efforts." *Education and Society* 18 (3):21–43.

———. 2005. *Indonesian Education: Teachers, Schools, and Central Authority*. New York: Routledge.

———. 2006. *Educational Decentralization: Education in the Asia-Pacific Region: Issues, Concerns and Prospects*. Dordrecht, Netherlands: Springer.

———. 2009. "Local Implementation of Japan's Integrated Studies Reform: A Preliminary Analysis of Efforts to Decentralise the Curriculum." *Comparative Education* 45 (1):23–44.

Bjork, Christopher, and Fukuzawa, Rebecca. 2013. "School Guidance in Japanese Middle Schools: Balancing the Old and New Amidst Social Change." In *Japanese Education in an Era of Globalization: Culture, Politics, and Equity*, edited by Gary DeCoker and Christopher Bjork, 47–66. New York: Teachers College Press.

Bjork, Christopher, and Ryoko Tsuneyoshi. 2005. "Educational Reform in Japan: Competing Visions for the Future." *Phi Delta Kappan* 86 (8):619–26.

Boon, G. C., and S. Gopinathan. 2006. *The Development of Education in Singapore since 1965*. Background paper presented to the Asia Education Study Tour for African Policy Makers. Washington, DC: The World Bank.

Borovoy, Amy. 2005. *The Too-Good Wife: Alcohol, Codependency, and the Politics of Nurturance in Postwar Japan*. Berkeley: University of California Press.

Bray, Mark. 2009. *Confronting the Shadow Education System—What Government Policies for What Private Tutoring?* Paris: International Institute for Education Planning/UNESCO.

Caryl, C., and A. Kashiwagi. 2007. "The Gap Society." *Newsweek*.

Cave, Peter. 2001. "Educational Reform in Japan in the 1990s: 'Individuality' and Other Uncertainties." *Comparative Education* 37 (2):173–91.

———. 2007. *Primary School in Japan: Self, Individuality, and Learning in Elementary Education*. London: Routledge.

Central Council of Education. 1996. *The Model for Japanese Education in the 21st Century*. Tokyo: Ministry of Education.

Clayton, Thomas. 1998. "Beyond Mystification: Reconnecting World-Systems Theory to Comparative Education." *Comparative Education Review* 42 (4):479–96.

Coburn, Cynthia E. 2004. "Beyond Decoupling: Rethinking the Relationship between the Institutional Environment and the Classroom." *Sociology of Education* 77 (3):211–44.

Cohen, David K., and James P. Spillane. 1993. "Policy and Practice: The Relations between Governance and Instruction." In *Designing Coherent Education Policy*, edited by S. Fuhrman, 35–95. San Francisco: Jossey-Bass.

Colvin, Richard Lee. 1997. "Why Tiny Singapore Is at the Top of the Class." *Los Angeles Times*, February 23, 1997. http://articles.latimes.com/1997-02-23/news/mn-31772_1_tiny-singapore.

Cuban, Larry. 1990. "Reforming Again, Again, and Again." *Educational Researcher* 19 (1): 3–13.

———. 1992. "What Happens to Reforms That Last? The Case of the Junior High School." *American Educational Research Journal* 29 (2):227–51.

Cummings, William. 1980. *Education and Equality in Japan*. Princeton, NJ: Princeton University Press.

———. 1982. "The Egalitarian Transformation of Postwar Japanese Education." *Comparative Education Review* 26 (1):16–35.

Cummings, William, and Atsushi Naoi. 1974. "Social Background, Education, and Personal Advancement in a Dualistic Employment System." *The Developing Economies* 12 (3):245–73.

Dall, Anna. 2011. *A Cross-National Comparative Study of Cultural Factors Underpinning 15-Year Old Students' Performance in Reading Literacy in Finland, Sweden and Indonesia*. Unpublished doctoral dissertation. University of the Sunshine Coast.

Dawson, Walter. 2010. "Private Tutoring and Mass Schooling in East Asia: Reflections of Inequality in Japan, South Korea, and Cambodia." *Asia Pacific Education Review* 11 (1):14–24.

Day, Christopher. 2002. "School Reform and Transitions in Teacher Professionalism and Identity." *International Journal of Educational Research* 37 (8):677–92.

DeCoker, Gary. 2013. "Enduring Issues, New Contexts." In *Japanese Education in an Era of Globalization: Culture, Politics, and Equity*, edited by Gary DeCoker and Christopher Bjork, 3–17. New York: Teachers College Press.

DeCoker, Gary, ed. 2002. *National Standards and School Reform in Japan and the United States*. New York: Teachers College Press.

Dello-Iacovo, Belinda. 2009. "Curriculum Reform and 'Quality Education' in China: An Overview." *International Journal of Educational Development*, 29 (3): 241–249.

Deng, Zhong, and Donald Treiman. 2007. "The Impact of the Cultural Revolution on Trends in Educational Attainment in the People's Republic of China." *American Journal of Sociology* 103 (2):391–428.

Derthick, Martha, and Joshua Dunn. 2009. "False Promises: The Accountability in Education." *Harvard Journal of Law and Public Policy* 32 (3):1015–1034.

Desimone, Laura. 2002. "How Can Comprehensive School Reform Models Be Successfully Implemented?" *Review of Educational Research* 72 (3):433–79.

Dewey, John. 1900. *The School and Society*. Chicago: University of Chicago Press.

Diamond, John B. 2007. "Where the Rubber Meets the Road: Rethinking the Connection between High-Stakes Testing Policy and Classroom Instruction." *Sociology of Education* 80 (4):285–313.

Dierkes, Julian. 2010. "Teaching in the Shadow: Operators of Small Shadow Education Institutions in Japan." *Asia Pacific Education Review* 11 (1):25–35.

Doi, Takeo. 1971. *The Anatomy of Dependence*. Tokyo: Kodansha International.

Donnelly, Kevin. 1998. "East Beats West in Classroom." *Australian Financial Review*, January 5, 1998.

Dore, Ronald, ed. 1967. *Aspects of Social Change in Modern Japan*. Princeton, NJ: Princeton University Press.

Duke, Benjamin. 1973. *Japan's Militant Teachers*. Honolulu: University Press of Hawaii.

———. 1975. "Statistical Trends in Postwar Japanese Education." *Comparative Education Review* 19 (2):252–66.

———. 1986. "The Liberalisation of Japanese Education." *Comparative Education* 22 (1): 37–45.

Dyck, Brenda A. 2006. "People Get Ready . . . A Call for Data Driven Instruction." *National Middle School Association* 9 (3):39–40.

Economic Policy Institute (EPI). 2010. *Problems with the Use of Student Test Scores to Evaluate Teachers*. EPI Briefing Paper #278. Washington, DC: Economic Policy Institute.

Elementary and Secondary Education Bureau of MEXT. 2002. *Heisei 12 nen-do no seito no shomondai no genjou ni suite* (Current problems in instructing students in 2001). Tokyo: MEXT.

Ellen, R. F. 1984. *Ethnographic Research: A Guide to General Conduct*. London: Academic Press.

Elmore, Richard F. 2004. *School Reform from the Inside Out: Policy, Practice, and Performance*. Cambridge, MA: Harvard Education Press.

Evers, Will J. G., André Brouwers, and Welko Tomic. 2002. "Burnout and Self-efficacy: A Study on Teachers' Beliefs When Implementing an Innovative Educational System in the Netherlands." *British Journal of Educational Psychology* 72 (2):227–43.

Finnish National Board of Education (FNBE). 2004. *National Core Curriculum for Basic Education 2004*. Helsinki, Finland: FNBE.

Fausset, Richard. 2014. "Trial Open in Atlanta School Cheating Scandal." *New York Times*, September 30, A17.

Fernandez, C. 2002. "Learning from Japanese Approaches to Professional Development: The Case of Lesson Study." *Journal of Teacher Education* 53 (5):393–405.

Finch, Janet. 1988. "Ethnography and Public Policy." In *Education, Training and the New Vocationalism: Experience and Policy*, edited by Andrew Pollard, June Purvis, and Geoffrey Walford, 185–201. Buckingham: Open University Press.

Fujita, Hidenori. 2010. "Whither Japanese Schooling? Educational Reforms and Their Impact on Ability Formation and Educational Opportunity." In *Challenges to Japanese Education: Economics, Reform and Human Rights*, edited by June A. Gordon, Hidenori Fujita, Takehiko Kariya, and Gerald LeTendre, 17–53. New York: Teachers College Press.

Fujiwara, Masahio, and Yoshiko Sakurai. 2006. *The Sorry State of Japanese Education*. Tokyo: Chuo Koron.

Fukuzawa, Rebecca. 1994. "The Path to Adulthood According to Japanese Middle Schools." *Journal of Japanese Studies* 20 (1):61–86.

Fukuzawa, Rebecca, and Gerald LeTendre. 2001. *Intense Years: How Japanese Adolescents Balance School, Family, and Friends*. New York: RoutledgeFalmer.

Fullan, Michael. 1995. "The Schooling as a Learning Organization: Distant Dreams." *Theory into Practice* 34 (4):230–35.

———. 2000. "Three Stories of Educational Change." *Phi Delta Kappan* 81 (8):581–84.

Fullan, Michael G., and Matthew B. Miles. 1992. "Getting Reform Right: What Works and What Doesn't." *Phi Delta Kappan* 73 (10): 745–52.

Fuller, B., K. Gesicki, E. Kang, and J. Wright. 2006. *Is the No Child Left Behind Act Work-*

ing? The Reliability of How States Track Achievement. Working paper 06–1. Berkeley, CA: Policy Analysis for California Education.

Furlong, Andy. 2008. "The Japanese *Hikikomori* Phenomenon: Acute Social Withdrawal among Young People." *The Sociological Review* 56(2):309–25.

Garelick, Barry. 2006. "Miracle Math: A Successful Program from Singapore Tests the Limits of School Reform in the Suburbs." *Education Next*, 6 (4): 38.

Geertz, Clifford. 1960. *The Religion of Java*. London: The Free Press.

Gehrke, Natalie J. 1979. "Rituals in the Classroom." In *Children in Time and Space*, edited by K. Yamamoto, 103–27. New York: Teachers College Press.

Glazer, Nathan. 1976. "Social and Cultural Factors in Japanese Economic Growth." In *Asia's New Giant: How the Japanese Economy Works*, edited by H. Patrick and H. Rosovosky, 813–816. Washington, DC: Brookings.

Global Agricultural Information Network. 2011. *Prefecture Report 2011*. Washington, DC: US Department of Agriculture.

Goetz, Judith P., and Margaret D. LeCompte. 1984. *Ethnography and Qualitative Design in Educational Research*. San Diego: Academic Press.

Goldenberg, Claude, and Ronald Gallimore. 1991. "Local Knowledge, Research Knowledge, and Educational Change: A Case Study of Early Spanish Reading Improvement." *Educational Researcher* 20 (8):2–14.

Goodman, Roger, David Phillips, eds. 2003. *Can the Japanese Change Their Education System?* Wallingford: Symposium Books.

———. 2005. "The Crumbling Pedestal: Changing Images of Japanese Teachers." *Journal of Teacher Education* 56 (5):459–70.

Gordon, June. 2008. *Japan's Outcaste Youth: Education for Liberation*. Boulder, CO: Paradigm Publishers.

Gordon, J., H. Fujita, T. Kariya, and G. LeTendre. 2009. *Challenges to Japanese Education: Economics, Reform, and Human Rights*. New York: Teachers College Press.

Gowen, Annie. 2001. "East Meets West in Math Classes: Four Schools Import Curriculum from Singapore." *The Washington Post*, October 18.

Groen, Mark. 2012. "NCLB—The Educational Accountability Paradigm in Historical Perspective." *American Educational History Journal* 39 (1):1–14.

Hannum, Emily. 1999. "Political Change and the Urban-Rural Gap in Basic Education in China, 1949–1990." *Comparative Education Review* 43 (2):193–211.

Hanson, E. Mark. 1998. "Strategies of Educational Decentralization: Key Questions and Core Issues." *Journal of Educational Administration* 36 (2):111–28.

Harris, D., and C. Herrington. 2004. "Accountability, Standards, and the Growing Achievement Gap: Lessons from the Past Half-Century." Paper presented at the American Education Finance Association Meeting, Salt Lake City, Utah.

Hatch, Thomas. 2013. "Innovation at the Core." *Phi Delta Kappan* 95 (3):34–38.

Hernandez, J. and R. Gebeloff. 2013. "Test Scores Sink as New York Adopts Tougher Benchmarks." *New York Times*, August 7. http://www.nytimes.com/2013/08/08/nyregion/under-new-standards-students-see-sharp-decline-in-test-scores.html.

Hersh, David. 2007. "Assessing No Child Left Behind and the Rise of Neoliberal Education Policies." *American Educational Research Journal* 44 (44):493–518.

Hess, Robert D., and Hiroshi Azuma. 1991. "Cultural Support for Schooling: Contrasts between Japan and the United States." *Educational Researcher* 20 (9):2–8.

Hill, Benjamin. 1996. "Breaking the Rules in Japanese Schools: Kosoku Ihan, Academic Competition, and Moral Education." *Anthropology & Education Quarterly* 271 (1):90–110.

Holloway, Susan D. 2010. *Women and Family in Contemporary Japan*. Cambridge: Cambridge University Press.

Hood, Christopher. 2001. *Japanese Education Reform: Nakasone's Legacy*. New York and London: Routledge.

———. 2003. "The Third Great Reform of the Japanese Education System: Success in the 1980s Onwards." In *Can the Japanese Change Their Education System?*, edited by R. Goodman and D. Phillips, 73–85. Oxford: Symposium Books.

Horio, Teruhisa. 1988. *Educational Thought and Ideology in Modern Japan*. Tokyo: University of Tokyo Press.

Hurst, G. Cameron. 1984. "Japanese Education: Trouble in Paradise." *UFSI Reports* 40.: 1–11.

Illich, Ivan. 1971. *Deschooling Society*. New York: Harper & Row.

Ishii, Yuri. 2003. *Development Education in Japan*. New York: RoutledgeFalmer.

Ishii, Yuri, and Mari Shiobara. 2009. "Teachers' Role in the Transition and Transmission of Culture." In *Asian Perspectives on Teacher Education*, edited by Suzuki, Shin'ichi, and Edward R. Howe, 11–25. New York: Routledge.

Itoh, Mayumi. 2000. *Globalization of Japan: Japanese Sakoku Mentality and US Efforts to Open Japan*. New York: St. Martin's Press.

Japan External Trade Organization (JETRO). n.d. "Investing in Japan: Regional Information." Tokyo: Japan External Trade Organization. Accessed March 26, 2012. http://www.jetro.go.jp/en/invest/.

Johnson, Chalmers A. 1982. *MITI and the Japanese Miracle: The Growth of Industrial Policy, 1925–1975*. Stanford, CA: Stanford University Press.

Kang, Mi Ok. 2012. "Why Not National Standardized Testing? A Policy Ecologies Analysis Regarding National Testing in South Korea and Its Impacts on Democratic Education." In *International Struggles for Critical Democratic Education*, edited by M. Knoester, 89–110. New York: Peter Lang.

Kariya, Takehiko. 1985. "The Mechanism of Educational Selection through the Hierarchical Structure of High School: A Study of the Cooling-Out Process of the Educational Aspiration." *Koutou Kyouiku Kenkyuu Kiyou* 4:11–28.

———. 2000. "Confused Thinking about Equality and Education." *Japan Echo* 27 (6):8–13.

———. 2002. *Kyoiku kaikaku no genso* (The illusion of educational reform). Tokyo: Chikuma Shobo.

Kariya, Takehiko, and Jeremy Rappleye. 2010. "The Twisted, Unintended Impacts of Globalization on Japanese Education." *Research in Sociology of Education* 17:17–64.

Kariya, Takehiko, Kokichi Shimizu, Mutsumi Shimizu, and Yuko Morota. 2002. "The Truth about Declining Scholastic Achievement." *Japan Echo* 4 (4): 12–17.

Kato, K., and K. Takaura, eds. 2001. *Gakuryokuteikaron hihan* (Criticizing the advocates of the achievement crisis). Tokyo: Reimei Shobo.

Katsuno, Masaaki. 2010. "Teacher Evaluation in Japanese Schools: An Examination from a Micro-Political or Relational Viewpoint." *Journal of Education Policy* 25 (3):293–307.

Kendall, Nancy. 2004. *Global Policy in Practice: The "Successful Failure" of Free Primary Education in Malawi*. Unpublished doctoral dissertation, Stanford University.

Kida, Hiroshi. 1986. "Educational Administration in Japan." *Comparative Education* 22 (1):7–12.

Kim, J. W. 2004. "Education Reform Policies and Classroom Teaching in South Korea." *International Studies in Sociology of Education* 14 (2):125–44.

Kipnis, Andrew. 2001. "The Disturbing Educational Discipline of Peasants." *The China Journal* 46:1–24.

———. 2006. "Suzhi: A Keyword Approach." *The China Quarterly* 186:295–313.

Klein, Alyson. 2012. "Obama Uses Funding, Executive Muscle to Make Often-Divisive Agenda a Reality." *Education Week* 31 (35):1–28.

Kobayashi, S., K. Yoshida, H. Noguchi, T. Tsuchiya, and J. Ito. 2003. "'Shakaiteki hikikomori' o kakeru kazoku ni kan suru jittai chousa" (Research for parents of children with 'social withdrawal'). *Seishin Igaku* (*Clinical psychiatry*) 45 (7):749–56.

Kobayashi, Tetsuya. 1976. *Society, Schools, and Progress in Japan*. Oxford: Pergamon Press.

Koh, Thiam Seng, and Lee, Sai Choo. 2008. *Information Technology in Education: Singapore's ICT Masterplans 1997–2008*. Singapore: World Scientific Publishing Company.

Kojima, Hideo. 1986. "Child Rearing Concepts as a Belief-Value System of the Society and the Individual." In *Child Development and Education in Japan*, edited by H. S. Stevenson, H. Azuma, and K. Hakuta, 39–54. New York: Freeman.

Kondo, Dorinne K. 1990. *Crafting Selves: Power, Gender, and Discourses of Identity in a Japanese Workplace*. Chicago: University of Chicago Press.

Kongshem, Lars. 2002. "Failure Is Not an Option: An Interview with US Secretary of Education Rod Paige." *Scholastic Administrator*, Back to School edition:16–18.

Korean Educational Development Institute (KEDI). 2001. *The Development of Education*. Seoul: KEDI.

Kotler, Philip. 1982 . "The World's Champion Marketers: The Japanese." *Journal of Business Strategy* 3 (1):3–13.

Kotloff, Lauren. 1996. "And Tomoko Wrote This Song for Us." In *Teaching and Learning in Japan*, edited by Rohlen, Thomas and Gerald LeTendre, 98–118. Cambridge: Cambridge University Press.

Krauss, Ellis S., Thomas P. Rohlen, and Patricia G. Steinhoff, eds. 1984. *Conflict in Japan*. Honolulu: University of Hawaii Press.

Laskey, Sue. 2005. "A Sociocultural Approach to Understanding Teacher Identity, Agency and professional Vulnerability in a Context of Secondary School Reform." *Teaching and Teacher Education* 21 (8):899–916.

Lauen, D. L., and S. M. Gaddis. 2012. "Shining Light or Fumbling in the Dark? The Effects of NCLB's Subgroup-Specific Accountability on Student Achievement." *Education Evaluation and Policy Analysis* 34 (2):185–208.

Lebra, Takie. 1984. "Nonconfrontational Strategies for Management of Interpersonal Conflicts." In *Conflict in Japan*, edited by Krauss, Ellis, Thomas Rohlen, and Patricia Steinhoff. Honolulu: University of Hawaii Press.

Lee, Jaekyung. 2001. "School Reform Initiatives as Balancing Acts: Policy Variation and Educational Convergence among Japan, Korea, England and the United States." *Education Policy Analysis Archives* 9 (13):1–11.

Leithwood, Kenneth, and Teresa Menzies. 1998. "A Review of Research Concerning the Implementation of Site-Based Management." *School Effectiveness and School Improvement* 9 (3):233–85.

LeTendre, Gerald. 1995. "Disruption and Reconnection: Counseling Young Adolescents in Japanese Schools." *Educational Policy* 9 (2):169–84.

LeTendre, Gerald K. 1996. "Shido: The Concept of Guidance." In *Teaching and Learning in Japan*, edited by Thomas Rohlen and Gerald LeTendre, 275–94. New York: Cambridge Press.

———. 1998. "The Evolution of Research on Educational Attainment and Social Status in

Japan." In *Education and Training in Japan*, volume 1, edited by Thomas Rohlen and Christopher Bjork, 135–67. New York: Routledge.

———. 2000. *Learning to Be Adolescent: Growing up in US and Japanese Middle Schools*. New Haven: Yale University Press.

———. 2002. "Setting National Standards: Educational Reform, Social Change, and Political Conflict." In *National Standards and School Reform in Japan and in the United States*, edited by Gary DeCoker, 19–32. New York: Teachers College Press.

Lewis, Catherine. 1984. "Cooperation and Control in Japanese Nursery Schools." *Comparative. Educational Review* 28:69–84.

———. 1995. *Educating Hearts and Minds: Reflections on Japanese Preschool and Elementary School Education*. New York: Cambridge University Press.

Lewis, Catherine, and Ineko Tsuchida. 1998. "A Lesson Is Like a Swiftly Flowing River: How Research Lessons Improve Japanese Education." *American Educator* 22 (4): 12–52.

Lipsky, Michael. 1983. *Street-Level Bureaucracy*. New York: Russell Sage Foundation Publications.

Little, Judith W. 1993. "Teachers' Professional Development in a Climate of Educational Reform." *Educational Evaluation and Policy Analysis* 15 (1):129–51.

Lortie, Dan C. 1975. *Schoolteacher: A Sociological Study*. Chicago: University of Chicago Press.

Ma, Liping. 1999. *Knowing and Teaching Elementary Mathematics: Teachers' Understanding of Fundamental Mathematics in China and the United States*. New York and London: Routledge.

Mandinach, Ellen B., and Sharnell S. Jackson. 2012. *Transforming Teaching and Learning through Data-Driven Decision Making*. Thousand Oaks, CA: Corwin.

Manna, Paul. 2006. "Leaving No Child Behind." In *Political Education: National Policy Comes of Age*, edited by Christopher Cross, 126–81. New York: Teachers College Press.

Marton, Andrew M. 2006. "The Cultural Politics of Curricular Reform in China." *Journal of Contemporary China* 15 (47):244–45.

Marx, Ronald W., Phyllis C. Blumenfeld, Joseph S. Krajcik, and Elliot Soloway. 1997. "Enacting Project-Based Science: Challenges for Practice and Policy." *Elementary School Journal* 97:341–58.

MacDonald, Laurence. 2006. *Curriculum Reform as a Reflection of Tradition and Change: Japanese Teachers' Approaches to Dimensions of Difference via the Integrated Curriculum*. Unpublished doctoral dissertation. College Park, MD: University of Maryland.

McCann, Claire. 2012. "Waiver States with Race to the Top Grants Slow to Reform." Washington, DC: New America Foundation, May 31. http://edmoney.newamerica.net/blogposts/2012/waiver_states_with_race_to_the_top_grants_slow_to_reform-68046.

McGinn, Noel, and Susan Street. 1986. "Educational Decentralization: Weak State or Strong State?" *Comparative Education Review* 30 (4):471–99.

McLaren, Peter. 1985. "The Ritual Dimensions of Resistance: Clowning and Symbolic Inversion." *Journal of Education* 167 (2):84–97.

McLaughlin, Milbrey W. 1987. "Learning from Experience: Lessons from Policy Implementation." *Education Evaluation and Policy Analysis* 9 (2):171–78.

McLaughlin, Milbrey W., and Talbert, Joan E. 2001. *Professional Communities and the Work of High School Teaching*. Chicago, IL: University of Chicago Press.

McMurrer, Jennifer. 2007. *Choices, Changes, and Challenges: Curriculum and Instruction in the NCLB Era*. Washington, DC: Center on Educational Policy.

Mathis, William J. 2006. *The Accuracy and Effectiveness of Adequate Yearly Progress, NCLB's School Evaluation System*. East Lansing, MI: Great Lakes Center for Education Practice and Research.

Mausethagen, Solvi. 2013. "A Research Review of the Impact of Accountability Policies on Teachers' Workplace Relations." *Educational Research Review* 9 (June):16–33.

Medina, Jennifer. 2010. "On New York School Tests, Warning Signs Ignored." *New York Times*, October 10. http://www.nytimes.com/2010/10/11/education/11scores.html.

Miller, Aaron. 2010. "Taibatsu: 'Corporal Punishment' in Japanese Socio-Cultural Context." *Japan Forum* 21 (2):233–54.

Mimizuka, H., M. Kaneko, and Y. Morota. 2002. "Seneika suru gakuryoku no nikyoku bunka (The increasing polarization of achievement)." *Ronza* 11:212–27.

Ministry of Education, Culture, Sports, Science and Technology (MEXT). 2000. *Toward a Culturally Oriented Nation: Japanese Government Policies in Education, Science, Sports, and Culture*. White paper. Tokyo: MEXT.

———. 2002. *Creating the Dreams for Japan's Tomorrow: The Role of the Ministry of Education, Culture, Sports, Science and Technology*. Tokyo: MEXT.

———. 2003. *School in the New Era: Elementary and Secondary Education Reform in Progress*. Tokyo: MEXT.

———. 2004. *Government Policies in Education, Science, Sports, and Culture*. White paper. Tokyo: MEXT.

———. 2006. *Urgent Recommendations on Ijime Prevention*. Tokyo: MEXT.

Ministry of Education, Science, and Technology (MEXT). 1994. "About the 'Convention on the Rights of the Child' (Notice)," May 20. Accessed May 1, 2011. http://www.mext.go.jp/a_menu/kokusai/jidou/main4_a9.htm.

———. 1997a. *The Model for Japanese Education in the Perspective of the 21st Century: The 2nd Report by the Central Council for Education*. Tokyo: MEXT.

———. 1997b. *Program for Educational Reform*. Tokyo: MEXT.

Ministry of Education and Culture (MOEC). 1992. *Japanese Government Policies in Education, Science and Culture*. Tokyo: MOEC.

———. 1994. *Japanese Government Policies in Education, Science and Culture*. Tokyo: MOEC.

Ministry of Health, Labor & Welfare (MOHLW). 2001. *Guidelines for Intervention in Local Mental Health Activities for Hikikomori*. Tokyo: MOHLW.

———. 2003. *Community Mental Health Intervention Guidelines Aimed at Socially Withdrawn Teenagers and Young Adults*. Tokyo: MOHLW.

Moeran, Brian. 1984. "Individual, Group and *Seishin*: Japan's Internal Cultural Debate." *Man* 19 (2):252–66.

———. 1986. "Individual, Group and Seishin: Japan's Internal Cultural Debate." In *Japanese Culture and Behavior: Selected Readings*, edited by Takie Lebra and William Lebra, 62–79. Honolulu: University of Hawaii Press.

Moore, Karen, Nicola Jones, and Emma Broadbent. 2008. *School Violence in OECD Countries*. Surrey, Australia: Plan International.

Mori, R. 2002. "'Shin no manabi' no sozo 'gakuryoku teika ron' e no cyosen." (Creation of 'real learning:' Challenging the 'achievement crisis debate')." In *Gakuryoku Teikaron e no Chosen* (A challenge to the "dropping achievement theories"), edited by T. Muto, 16–27. Tokyo: Gyosei.

Motani, Yoko. 2005. "Hopes and Challenges for Progressive Educators in Japan: Assessment of the 'Progressive Turn' in the 2002 Educational Reform." *Comparative Education* 41 (3):309–27.

Mullis, Ina V. S., and Michael O. Martin. 2008. *TIMSS in Perspective: Lessons Learned from IEA's Four Decades of International Mathematics Assessment*. Boston: TIMSS & PIRLS Study Center.

Murakami, Yasusuke. 1981. "The Age of New Middle Class Politics: The Case of Japan." *Journal of Japanese Studies* 8 (1):29–72.

Muta, Hiromitsu. 2006. "Trends and Issues in Deregulation and Decentralization of Educational Administration in Japan." *Educational Decentralization: Asian Experiences and Conceptual Contributions*, edited by Christopher Bjork, 97–114. Dordrecht, Netherlands: Springer.

Nabeshima, Yoshiro. 2010. "Invisible Racism in Japan." *Challenges to Japanese Education: Economics, Reform, and Human Rights*, edited by June A. Gordon, Hidenori Fujita, Takehiko Kariya, and Gerald LeTendre, 109–30. New York: Teachers College Press.

Nakane, Chie. 1986. "Criteria of Group Formation." In *Japanese Culture and Behavior: Selected Readings*, edited by Takie Lebra and William Lebra, 171–87. Honolulu: University of Hawaii Press.

National Center for Educational Statistics (NCES). 1996. *Pursuing Excellence: Initial Findings from the Third International Math and Science Study*. Washington, DC: The US Department of Education.

———. 2004. *Highlights from the Trends in International Mathematics and Science Study (TIMSS) 2003*. Washington, DC: The US Department of Education.

National Commission on Excellence and Education (NCEE). 1983. *A Nation at Risk: The Imperative of Educational Reform*. Washington, DC: NCEE.

National Institute of Educational Policy Research (NIER). 2001. *Research and Study on Learning Motivation*. Tokyo: National Institute of Educational Policy Research.

Ng, Jennifer C. 2006. "Understanding the Impact of Accountability on Preservice Teachers' Decisions about Where to Teach." *Urban Review* 38 (5):353–72.

Ng, Pak Tee. 2008. "Educational Reform in Singapore: From Quantity to Quality." *Educational Research for Policy and Practice* 7 (1):5–15.

Nichols, Sharon L., Gene V. Glass, and David C. Berliner. 2005. *High-Stakes Testing and Student Achievement: Problems for the No Child Left Behind Act*. Unpublished policy brief. Tempe, AZ: Education Studies Laboratory. http://nepc.colorado.edu/files/EPSL-0509-105-EPRU.pdf.

———. 2007. *Collateral Damage: How High-Stakes Testing Corrupts America's Schools*. Cambridge, MA: Harvard Education Press.

Nishimura, Kazuo, ed. 2001. *Gakuryoku teika ga kuni wo horobosu* (Declining Academic Achievement Is Destroying Our Nation). Tokyo: Nihon Keizai Shinbun.

Nishimura, Kazuo, N. Tose, and T. Okabe. 1999. *Bunsu ga dekinai daigakusei* (College Students Who Cannot Solve Problems with Fractions). Tokyo: Keizai Shinposha.

Nitta, Keith. 2008. *The Politics of Structural Education Reform*. New York: Routledge.

No Child Left Behind Act of 2001 (NCLB). 2001.

Noah, Harold. 1984. "The Use and Abuse of Comparative Education." *Comparative Education Review*, 28 (4): 550–562.

Nomi, Tomoaki. 2006. "Inequality and Japanese Education: Urgent Choices." *Japan Focus* 13, (February):

———. 2013. "Government Spending, Socioeconomic Backgrounds and Academic Achievements in Tokyo." In *Japanese Education in an Era of Globalization: Culture, Politics, and Equity*, edited by Gary DeCoker and Christopher Bjork, 147–163. New York: Teachers College Press.

Ohmori, Fujio. 2000. "The Flawed Consensus on Reform." *Japan Echo* 27 (December):14–17.

Okano, Kaori. 1993. *School to Work Transition in Japan: An ethnographic study*. Clevedon, Avon, and Philadelphia, PA: Multilingual Matters.

Okano, Kaori, and Motonori Tsuchiya. 1999. *Education in Contemporary Japan: Inequality and Diversity*. Cambridge: Cambridge University Press.

Organization for Economic Cooperation and Development (OECD). 1971. *Reviews of National Policies for Education: Japan*. Paris: OECD.

———. 2004. *Measuring Student Knowledge and Skills*. Paris: OECD.

———. 2010. *Strong Performers and Successful Reforms in Education: Lessons from PISA for the United States*. Paris, OECD.

Ota, Haruo. 1993. "Political Teacher Unionism in Japan." In *Japanese Schooling: Patterns of Socialization, Equality, and Political Control*, edited by James Shields, 243–259. University Park, PA: Pennsylvania State University Press.

Paige, Rod. 2006. "No Child Left Behind: The Ongoing Movement for Public Education Reform." *Harvard Educational Review* 76 (4):461–73.

Park, Hyunjoon. 2008. "Growing Inequality of Academic Achievement among Japanese Students." Paper presented at the annual meeting of the Comparative and International Education Society, New York City, 17–21.

———. 2013. "Growing Educational Inequality in Japan during the 2000s." In *Japanese Education in an Era of Globalization: Culture, Politics, and Equity*, edited by Gary DeCoker and Christopher Bjork, 131–146. New York: Teachers College Press.

Park, S. J., 2011. "Mothers and the Private After-School Market." In *No Alternative? Experiments in South Korean Education*, edited by N. Abelmann, J. Choi, and S. J. Park, 115–31. Berkeley, CA: University of California Press.

Park, Yung H. 1975. "The Central Council for Education, Organized Business, and the Politics of Educational Policy-Making in Japan." *Comparative Education Review* 19 (2):196–311.

Passin, Herbert. 1965. *Society and Education in Japan*. New York: Teachers College–Columbia University.

Peak, Lois. 1986. *Learning to Go to School in Japan: The Transition from Home to Preschool Life*. Berkeley, CA: University of California Press.

Pennington, Matthew. 1999. "Asia Takes a Crash Course in Educational Reform." *UNESCO Courier* July–August, 17–22.

Pepper, Suzanne. 1996. *Radicalism and Education Reform in 20th Century China*. Cambridge: Cambridge University Press.

Peters, Tom, and Robert Waterman. 1982. *In Search of Excellence: Lessons from America's Best-run Companies*. New York: HarperCollins.

Popham, W. J. 2010. *Everything School Leaders Need to Know about Assessment*. Thousand Oaks, CA: Corwin.

Prime Minister's Commission on Japan's Goals in the 21st Century. 2000. *The Frontier Within: Individual Empowerment and Better Governance in the New Millennium*. Tokyo: Japan's Goals in the 21st Century, January. http://www.kantei.go.jp/jp/21century/report/htmls.

Rappleye, Jeremy. 2009. *Decline of the Tokyo Technocrats in Educational Policy Formation? Exploring the Loss of Ministry Autonomy and Recent Policy Trends with Reference to "Globalisation" and Educational Transfer*. Shiga, Japan: Afrasian Centre for Peace and Development Studies.

Ravitch, Diane. 2010. *The Death and Life of the Great American School System: How Testing and Choice Are Undermining Education*. New York: Basic Books.

Rhoten, Diana. 2000. "Education Decentralization in Argentina: A 'Global-Local Conditions of Possibility' Approach to State, Market, and Society Change." *Journal of Education Policy* 15 (6):593–601.

Ritter, G. W. et al. 2004. "Keeping Score: What Do We Know About the Impact of Statewide Accountability Programs on Student Achievement?" Paper presented at the annual meeting of the Association for Public Policy Analysis and Management, Atlanta, GA.

Rohlen, Thomas P. 1980. "The Juku Phenomenon: An Exploratory Essay." *Journal of Japanese Studies* 6 (2):207–42.

———. 1983. *Japan's High Schools*. Berkeley, CA: University of California Press.

———. 1989. "Order in Japanese Society: Attachment, Authority and Routine." *Journal of Japanese Studies* 15 (1):5–40.

Rohlen, Thomas P., and Christopher Bjork. 1998. *Education and Training in Japan*. New York: Routledge.

Rosegaard, Marie H. 1998. *Moving Mountains: Japanese Education Reform*. Aarhus: Aarhus University Press.

Rosenbaum, James E., and Takehiko Kariya. 1989. "From High School to Work: Market and Institutional Mechanisms in Japan." *The American Journal of Sociology* 94 (6):34–65.

———. 1991. "Do School Achievements Affect the Early Jobs of High School Graduates in the United States and Japan?" *Sociology of Education* 64:78–95.

Ross, E. Wayne, and Rich Gibson, eds. 2007. *Neoliberalism and Education Reform*. Cresskill, NJ: Hampton Press.

Rowan, Brian. 1990. "Commitment and Control: Alternative Strategies for the Organizational Design of Schools." *Review of Research in Education* 16:353–89.

Ruzzi, Betsy B. 2005. *Finland Education Report*. Washington, DC: National Center on Education and the Economy.

Sahlberg, Pasi. 2007. "Education Policies for Raising Student Learning: The Finnish Approach." *Journal of Education Policy* 22 (2):147–71.

———. 2009. *A Short History of Educational Reform in Finland*. Unpublished paper. http://www.oxydiane.net/IMG/pdf/Finland-Sahlberg.pdf.

———. 2011. *Finnish Lessons: What Can the World Learn from Educational Change in Finland*. New York: Teachers College Press.

Sakikabara, Eisuke. 2001. "First Reform the Educational Bureaucracy." *Japan Focus*, June, 23–26.

Sarason, Seymour B. 1993. *The Case for Change: Rethinking the Preparation of Educators*. San Francisco, CA: Jossey-Bass.

Sato, Manabu. 2005. "Kaikaku ni yotte kakudai suru kiki (Expanding crises resulting from reform." *Ronza*, February, 30–37.

Sato, Nancy. 1991. *Ethnography of Japanese Elementary Schools: Quest for Equality*. Unpublished doctoral dissertation. Stanford, CA: Stanford University School of Education.

———. 2003. *Inside Japanese Classrooms: The Heart of Education*. New York: Routledge-Falmer.

Sato, Nancy, and Milbrey McLaughlin. 1992. "Context Matters: Teaching in Japan and in the United States." *Phi Delta Kappan* 75 (5):359–66.

Savada, A. M., and W. Shaw. 1990. *South Korea: A Country Study*. Washington, DC: GPO for the Library of Congress.

Schemo, Diana Jean. 2000. "Worldwide Survey Finds U.S. Students Are Not Keeping Up." *The New York Times*, December 6. http://www.nytimes.com/2000/12/06/us/worldwide-survey-finds-us-students-are-not-keeping-up.html.

Schoppa, Leonard. 1991a. *Education Reform in Japan: A Case of Immobilist Politics*. New York: Routledge.

———. 1991b. "Zoku Power and LDP Power: A Case Study of the Zoku Role in Education Policy." *Journal of Japanese Studies* 17 (1):79–106.

———. 2006. *Race for the Exits: The Unraveling of Japan's System of Social Protection*. Ithaca, NY: Cornell University Press.

Schriewer, Jürgen. 2003. "Globalisation in Education: Process and Discourse." *Policy Futures in Education* 1 (2):271–83.

Schwartz, Robert B., and Jal D. Mehta. 2011. "Finland: Superb Teachers—How to Get Them, How to Use Them." In *Surpassing Shanghai*, edited by M. Tucker, 51–77. Cambridge, MA: Harvard Education Press.

Scott, James C. 1990. *Domination and the Arts of Resistance: Hidden Transcripts*. New Haven: Yale University Press.

Seth, Michael. 2012. "South Korea's Educational Exceptionalism." In *No Alternative? Experiments in South Korean Education*, edited by N. Abelmann, J. Choi, and S. J. Park, 17–27. Berkeley, CA: University of California Press.

Shimahara, Nobuo K. 1986. "Japanese Education Reforms in the 1980s." *Issues in Education* 4 (2):85–100.

———. 1998. *Politics of Classroom Life: Classroom Management in International Perspective*. New York: Routledge.

———. 2002. *Teaching in Japan: A Cultural Perspective*. New York: RoutledgeFalmer.

Shimahara Nobuo K., and Akira Sakai. 1992. "Teacher Internship and the Culture of Teaching in Japan." *British Journal of Sociology of Education* 13:147–62.

———. 1995. *Learning to Teach in Two Cultures: Japan and the United States*. New York: Garland.

Shirley, Dennis, and Andy Hargreaves. 2006. "Data-Driven to Distraction." *Education Week* 26 (6):32–33.

Simon, Roger I. 1992. *Teaching against the Grain: Texts for a Pedagogy of Possibility*. Westport, CT: Bergin & Garvey.

Singapore Ministry of Education. n.d. "About Us." Accessed August 20, 2014. http://www.moe.gov.sg/about/.

Slavin, Richard. 2002. "Evidence-Based Policies: Transforming Educational Practice and Research." *Educational Researcher* 3 (7):15–21.

Sorenson, Clark W. 1994. "Success and Education in South Korea." *Comparative Education Review* 38 (1):19–35.

Spillane, James P., Brian J. Reiser, and Todd Reimer. 2002. "Policy Implementation and Cognition: Reframing and Refocusing Implementation Research." *Review of Educational Research* 72 (3):387–431.

Stassen Berger, Kathleen. 2007. "Update on Bullying in School: Science Forgotten?" *Developmental Review* 27 (1):90–126.

Steiner-Khamsi, Gita. 2004. *The Global Politics of Educational Borrowing and Lending*. New York: Teachers College Press.

———. 2012. "Understanding Policy Borrowing and Lending: Building Comparative Studies." In *World Yearbook of Education*, edited by G. Steiner-Khamsi and F. Waldow, 3–13. New York: Routledge.

Stevenson, David L., and David P. Baker. 1992. "Shadow Education and Allocation in

Formal Schooling: Transition to University in Japan." *American Journal of Sociology* 97 (6):1639–1657.

Stevenson, H., S. Lee, and J. Stigler. 1986. "Mathematics Achievement of Chinese, Japanese, and American Children." *Science* 231 (4739):693–99.

Stevenson, Harold W. 1991a. "The Development of Prosocial Behavior in Large-Scale Collective Societies: China & Japan." *Cooperation and Prosocial Behavior*, edited by Robert Hinde and Jo Groebel, 89–105. Cambridge: Cambridge University Press.

———. 1991b. "Japanese Elementary School Education." *The Elementary School Journal* 92 (1):109–20.

Stewart, Vivian. 2011. "Singapore: A Journey to the Top, Step by Step." In *Surpassing Shanghai*, edited by Marc Tucker, 113–37. Cambridge, MA: Harvard Education Press.

Stigler, James, and James Hiebert. 1999. *The Teaching Gap: Best Ideas from the World's Teachers for Improving Education in the Classroom*. New York: The Free Press.

Stigler, James, and Harold Stevenson. 1991. "How Asian Teachers Polish Each Lesson to Perfection." *American Educator* 15 (1):43–47.

Stinson, Roddy. 2006. "More Test-Cheating Proof Found (but Nobody Cares)." *San Antonio Express-News*, May 28. http://www.schoolsmatter.info/2006/05/more-test-cheating-proof-found-but.html.

Strauss, Valerie. 2013. "China's New Education Reform: Reducing Importance of Test Scores." *Washington Post*, June 25. http://www.washingtonpost.com/blogs/answer-sheet/wp/2013/06/25/chinas-new-education-reform-reducing-importance-of-test-scores/.

Stritikus, Tom T., and Ann-Marie Wiese. 2006. "Reassessing the Role of Ethnographic Methods in Education Policy Research: Implementing Bilingual Education Policy Research at Local Levels." *Teachers College Record* 108 (6):1106–131.

Sunderman, G. L, C. A. Tracey, J. Kim, and G. Orfield. 2004. *Listening to Teachers: Classroom Realities and No Child Left Behind*. Cambridge, MA: The Civil Rights Project, Harvard University.

Sutton, Margaret, and Bradley Levinson, eds. 2001. *Policy as Practice: Toward a Comparative Sociocultural Analysis of Educational Policy*. Stamford, CT: Ablex Publishing.

Tachibanaki, Toshiaki. 2005. "Jakusha no hinkonka ga kakusa o jocho shite iru (Dark age of gray-haired freeters)." *Ronza*, June, 102–7.

Takayama, Keita. 2007. "A Nation at Risk Crosses the Pacific: Transnational Borrowing of the US Crisis Discourse in the Debate on Educational Reform in Japan." *Comparative Education Review* 51 (4):423–46.

———. 2011. "Reconceptualizing the Politics of Japanese Education, Reimagining Comparative Studies of Japanese Education." In *Reimagining Japanese Education: Borders, Transfers, Circulations, and the Comparative*, edited by David Willis and Jeremy Rappleye, 247–80. Oxford: Symposium Books.

Tan, Jason, and S. Gopinathan. 2000. "Education Reform in Singapore: Towards Greater Creativity and Innovation." *NIRA Review*, Summer, 5–10.

Tan, Sophia H. 2010. "Singapore's Educational Reforms: The Case for Un-Standardizing Curriculum and Reducing Testing." *AASA Journal of Scholarship and Practice* 6 (4):50–58.

Thomas, John W. 2000. *A Review of Research on Project-Based Learning*. San Rafael, CA: Autodesk Foundation.

Thurston, Donald. 1973. *Teachers and Politics in Japan*. New York: Columbia University Press.

Tobin, J., H. Yeh, and M. Karasaw. 2009. *Preschool in Three Cultures Revisited: China, Japan, and the United States*. Chicago and London: University of Chicago Press.

Tobin, J., D. Wu, and D. Davidson. 1991. *Preschool in Three Cultures: Japan, China, and the United States*. New Haven, CT: Yale University Press.

Tokutake, Yasushi. 2000. "Educational Reform." *Japan Echo*, December, 6–7.

Tominaga, Ken'ichi. 1969. "Trend Analysis of Social Stratification and Social Mobility in Contemporary Japan." *The Developing Economies* 7:471–98.

Treiman, Donald J., and Kazuo Yamaguchi. 1993. "Trends in Educational Attainment in Japan." In *Persistent Inequality: Changing Educational Attainment in Thirteen Countries*, edited by Yossi Shavit and Hans-Peter Blossfeld, 229–50. Boulder, CO: Westview Press.

Tsuchimochi, Gary. 1993. *Education Reform in Japan: The 1946 US Education Mission*. Tokyo: University of Tokyo Press.

Tsuneyoshi, Ryoko. 2001. *The Japanese Model of Schooling: Comparisons with the United States*. New York: RoutledgeFalmer.

———. 2004a. "A Japanese Vision of 21st Century Abilities: The Integrated Period, Basics, and the New Reforms." In *Reconsidering Japanese Education: 21st Century Abilities in the Japanese Context*, edited by Tsuneyoshi, Ryoko. Tokyo: University of Tokyo Graduate School of Education.

———. 2004b. "The New Japanese Educational Reforms and the Achievement 'Crisis' Debate." *Educational Policy* 18 (2):361–94.

———. 2013. "Junior High School Entrance Examinations in Metropolitan Tokyo: The Advantages and Costs of Privileges." In *Japanese Education in an Era of Globalization*, edited by Gary DeCoker and Christopher Bjork, 164–82. New York: Teachers College Press.

Tsuneyoshi, Ryoko, Kaori H. Okano, and Sarane Boocock, eds. 2011. *Minorities and Education in Multicultural Japan: An Interactive Perspective*. New York: Routledge.

Tucker, Marc S., ed. 2011. *Surpassing Shanghai: An Agenda for American Education Built on the World's Leading Systems*. Cambridge, MA: Harvard Education Press.

Tucker, Marc S., and Betsy Brown Ruzzi. 2011. "Japan: Perennial League Leaders." In *Surpassing Shanghai: An Agenda for American Education Built on the World's Leading Systems*, edited by Marc S. Tucker, 79–109. Cambridge. MA: Harvard Education Press.

Tyack, David, and Larry Cuban. 1995. *Tinkering toward Utopia*. Cambridge, MA: Harvard University Press.

UNICEF. 1996. *The Progress of Nations*. New York: UNICEF.

United States Department of Education (USDOE). 2001. *No Child Left Behind Act of 2001*. Washington, DC: USDOE.

———. 2004. *A Guide to Education and No Child Left Behind*. Washington, DC: USDOE.

———. 2007. *Mobilizing for Evidence-Based Character Education*. Washington, DC: USDOE.

———. 2012. "Overview: The Federal Role in Education." Last modified February 13. http://www2.ed.gov/about/overview/fed/role.html.

———. 2013. "Waivers Granted under No Child Left Behind." Last modified December 12. http://www2.ed.gov/nclb/freedom/local/flexibility/waiverletters/index.html.

———. 2014. "Race to the Top Fund." Last modified March 25. http://www2.ed.gov/programs/racetothetop/index.html.

United States Government Accountability Office (USGAO). 2009. *Access to Arts Education*. Washington, DC: USGAO.

———. 2013. *K–12 Education: States' Test Security Policies and Procedures Varied*. Washington, DC: USGAO.

Valli, L., and D. Buese. 2007. "The Changing Roles of Teachers in an Era of High-Stakes Accountability." *American Educational Research Journal* 44 (3):519–58.

Vogel, Ezra. 1979. *Japan as Number One: Lessons for America*. Cambridge, MA: Harvard University Press.

Wada, Hiroshi. 2002. *Kyoritsu sho chu ko kara Todai ni hairu hon* (Getting into the University of Tokyo from a Public Elementary or Junior High School). Tokyo: Gentosha. 2002.

Waida, Seiji, Lin Minghuang, Zhikui Niu, and Myung Woo Shin. 2006. "Differences and Similarities in Curricular Reform and Integral Learning in Some East Asian Countries." *Joetsu University of Education Bulletin* 24 (2):575–610.

Walford, Geoffrey. 2002. *Debates and Developments in Ethnographic Methodology*. Amsterdam: JAI Press.

Walford, Geoffrey, ed. 2001. *Ethnography and Education Policy*. Oxford: Emerald Publishing.

Walford, Geoffrey, and Alexander Massey, eds. 1998. *Children Learning in Context: Studies in Educational Ethnography*, volume 1. London/Stamford: JAI Press.

Weiler, Hans. 1984. "The Political Dilemmas of Foreign Study." *Comparative Education Review* 28 (2):168–79.

———. 1989. "Education and Power: The Politics of Educational Decentralization in Comparative Perspective." *Educational Policy* 3 (1):31–43.

White, Merry. 1987. *The Japanese Educational Challenge: A Commitment to Children*. New York: The Free Press.

———. 1993. *The Material Child: Coming of Age in Japan and America*. New York: The Free Press.

Wiggins, Grant, and Jan McTighe. 1998. *Understanding by Design*. Alexandria: Association for Supervision and Curriculum Development.

Winerip, Michael. 2003. "Houston's 'Zero Dropout.'" *Rethinking Schools Online*, Fall 2003. http://www.rethinkingschools.org/special_reports/bushplan/drop181.shtml.

Wu, Xiaogang. 2007. *Economic Transition, School Expansion, and Educational Inequality in China, 1990–2000*. Ann Arbor, MI: University of Michigan, Institute for Social Research.

Yamamura, Yoshiaki. 1986. "The Child in Japanese Society." In *Child Development and Education in Japan*, edited by Harold S. Stevenson, Hiroshi Azuma, and Kenji Hakuta, 28–38. New York: Freeman.

Yoneyama, Shoko. 2007. *The Japanese High School: Silence and Resistance*. London & New York: Routledge.

Zakaria, Fareed. 2006. "Across Globe, We Have a Lot to Learn." *Charleston (West Virginia) Gazette*, January 4, 2006.

INDEX

Abe, Shinzo, 224n3 (chap. 7)
Abelman, Nancy, 169–70
ability grouping, 49
Abrams, S. E., 175
absenteeism, 59
academic achievement: achievement gap in Japan, 97–98, 120–23, 131–40, 159, 204–5; achievement gap in United States, 1, 177–79, 182; comparison of Japan and United States, 1, 3–5, 9, 25, 96; and the construction of "crisis," 15, 18, 30; crisis rhetoric in Japan, 13, 27–29, 82, 134, 198, 213–16; crisis rhetoric in other Asian locations, 170; crisis rhetoric in United States, 34; emphasis on, 51, 119–24, 165–68; and family background, 120–40; measurement of, 94–97, 142; and NCLB, 19–24, 177–83, 186–87; pressure related to, 2–3, 8, 51–52, 198–99
academic intensity, 1–5, 11–12, 18, 26, 34, 161, 172, 196–99, 214
accountability: arguments for, 97; evidence of impact, 4, 9, 117, 202–10; in Finnish schools, 164, 176–77; for Japanese teachers, 34, 73–76, 79; and NCLB, 29–32, 93–94, 164, 176–86; questions about, 17, 142, 177; reform trends, 1; and school guidance, 161; teacher opinions about, 195–97; and testing, 13–14, 20–24
adequate yearly progress (AYP), 21, 31
Ad Hoc Council on Education (AHCE, or *Rinkyoshin*), 3
Ainu, 37, 121
amae. *See* indulgence
Amano, Ikuo, 2
American Schools Act, 20
An, Xuehui, 169
Arense, A. L., 176
Arnove, Robert, 3
Aspinall, Robert, 73
Ayers, William, 23
Azuma, Hiroshi, 79, 100, 213

Baker, David, 120, 137
Bambrick-Santoyo, Paul, 1
Barrett, Brian, 181
Barron et al., 130
Bell, Stephanie, 130
Berliner, David, 23, 25, 178
birthrate, declining, 38
Bloomberg, Michael, 177
Boocock, Sarane, 9, 37, 121
bowing exercises, 146–49
Bray, Mark, 137
Brouwers, André, 201
Buese, Daria, 181
bullying, 26, 43, 145
Burakumin, 121, 224n2 (chap. 7)
Bush, George W., 20–21, 24, 30, 179

career education, 103, 129
Caryl, C., 224n4 (chap. 7)

Cave, Peter, 2, 3, 65, 208
Center on Education Policy (CEP), 180
ceremonies: graduation, 60, 116, 135; tea, 42
charter schools, 26
cheating, evidence of, 179–80
childhood: Japanese beliefs about, 48, 144, 151; relation to adolescence, 151
China: achievement test results, 163–67; cultural revolution, 165; Education for Quality (*Suzhi Jiaoyu*), 169–72; participation in video study, 183–85, 196; reform outcomes, 172–73, 182–83; residents in Japan, 121; response to criticism of schools, 168–69, 206; student happiness, 27; visitors to Kita, 54
Choi, 169–70
classroom collapse (*gakkyu hokai*), 43
class system and discrimination, 121
Clinton, Bill, 20, 24, 168
clubs. *See* extracurricular activities
Coburn, Cynthia, 36
Cohen, David, 106
College Board, 19
Colvin, Richard, 168
Committee of Ten Report, 180
Common Core learning standards, 178, 225n4
community: connections to schools, 12, 41, 135; impact on school decision-making, 17, 69, 73–76, 203; role in relaxed education, 27, 63, 93, 186, 189–205; service, 25
competition: among students, 46, 154, 186; attempts to reduce, 118, 168–69; related to entrance exams, 26, 170, 205–6
Council for Education Rebuilding (CER), 28
counseling, 141
Course of Study (*Gakushu Shido Yoryu*): attention to emotional development, 32; challenges associated with, 76–80, 99–101, 105–6, 113, 124; and electives, 8; initial responses to, 110; instructional methods associated with, 92; and Integrated Studies, 98–99; level of rigor, 97, 207–8; local input into, 28, 66, 119, 199; and national goals, 79; parent responses to, 63; questions related to, 85, 95–96; recent versions of, 214–15; reconfiguration of, 110–11; reductions in instructional hours, 72, 114, 214–15; as a resource, 105; revisions to, 2, 6, 29, 199; teacher comments about, 67, 72–74, 82–83, 94–95, 207–8; and teacher responsibilities, 2, 119; 2002 version, 9, 13, 29, 68; years adopted and implemented, 221n1 (chap. 1)
cram schools for high school entrance. See *juku*
Creating Dreams for Japan's Tomorrow, 27
creativity, 2–3, 9, 17, 26, 30–32, 168–71, 188, 193–96, 201, 206, 224n1 (chap. 7)
critical thinking: in Asian schools, 2, 168–71, 206; evaluation of, 201; and "new" abilities, 185; parent support for, 137; questions about, 168; and relaxed education, 89, 196, 216–17, 224n1 (chap. 7); teacher comments about, 190–92; in US schools, 17
Cuban, Larry, 4, 99, 114, 115, 201
cultural festivals (*bunkasai*), 44
culture: and community, 89, 103; behavior influenced by, 112, 115; of schools, 11, 16, 40, 61–62, 116, 123, 158, 161, 184; of systems, 114, 152, 202; teaching, 107; trust-based, 174
Cummings, William, 120
curriculum: in Asian countries, 168–73, 196–97; authority over in United States, 31; control over, 194–95; differences across countries, 193–95; effects of testing on, 3, 116–17, 195–97; effects on communities, 141; in Finland, 175–76; frameworks, 1; in Japan, 179–81, 197. *See* Course of Study; No Child Left Behind Act (NCLB)

Dall, Anna, 176
data-driven instruction, 1, 21–22, 31, 93, 97, 206
Davidson, Dana, 185, 189
Dawson, Walter, 137, 206
Day, Christopher, 181
decentralizing education, 15, 24, 26, 30–31, 64–65
DeCoker, Gary, 64, 79, 80, 100
Dello-Iacovo, Belinda, 162, 169, 173
Deng, Zhong, 165

Derthick, Martha, 20
Desimone, Laura, 201
Dewey, John, 86
Diamond, John, 35
Dierkes, Julian, 206
discipline. *See* school guidance
discrimination and class system, 121–22
Donnelly, Kevin, 168
Dore, Ronald, 120
dress code, 46–48, 58, 149
drop-out rates, 178
Duncan, Arnie, 188
Dunn, Joshua, 20
Dyck, Brenda, 1

economic development, 121, 141, 164–65
Economic Policy Institute (EPI), 178–79, 181
educational opportunity, 16, 119–40
education policy/reform: analysis of, 10, 35–36, 213; challenges associated with, 186–87, 195–97; comparison of Japanese and American, 1, 9, 18–19, 25–35, 184; conditions for success, 114–15; debates about, 3, 34, 69, 198–99, 216–17; fundamental vs. incremental, 4, 114–15; impact on teachers, 13–14, 35–37, 63, 66–79, 110–12; implementation, 13–14, 35–36, 63–64, 78–82, 114–15; institutionalization of, 78; and local control of education, 28–30, 64–65; obstacles to, 172–74, 195–96; for social integration, 164–68; and teacher beliefs, 13–14, 66–69, 78–79, 81–82, 102–15; tensions associated with, 186, 211; ties to business, 10, 20, 26–30; trends across Asia, 163–83
elective subjects (*sentaku no jugyo*): assessment of student learning in, 108–9; expansion of, 7–8, 28, 66, 103–4; lesson descriptions, 104–9, 120, 125–27; resistance to, 110–15; student attitudes toward, 107–9, 132–33; teacher attitudes towards, 109–15
elementary and secondary education, contrasts between, 39–40, 81–82, 101–6, 114–18
elementary schools: absence of test pressure in, 16, 96, 204–5, 210; academic rigor of, 94–98, 204, 207–11; attention to the whole child, 210; comparisons of Japanese and US schools, 188–97; descriptions of campuses, 41–44, 47–50, 54–56, 187–88; implementation of relaxed education policies, 94–101, 207–8; learning environments, 31, 42, 81–101, 184–88, 207; lesson descriptions, 86–93; lesson design, 13, 85–87, 112–13; with limited enrollment, 38; pilot schools, 36, 222n2 (chap. 3); promotion of independent thinking, 87–89; teacher attitudes, 82–85; test-related pressure in, 194–97; trends in instructional time, 6–7, 210–14; video study conducted in, 185–86
elite education, 172
Ellen, R. F., 60
emotional development, 32, 136, 181
ethnic diversity, 9, 20–21, 25, 121, 180
ethnopedagogy, 75
Evers, Will, 201
examinations: arguments in favor of, 14, 20–24, 204; attitudes toward, 13–14, 136–37; in China, 169–70; comparison of Japanese and US, 18–19, 93–94, 117–18; cultural foundation for, 115; debates about, 168, 186, 198–99; and education reform, 4, 117–18, 161; and elective courses, 10, 125–27; examination hell, 2; in Finland, 164, 174–77; historical use of in Japan, 2, 9, 113, 203–4; impact on curriculum, 14, 73, 194–96; impact on instruction in Japan, 13–14, 116–25, 144, 200–207, 216; impact on instruction in United States, 194–96; impact on student attitudes, 26, 87–94, 124–54, 161–62, 210; impact on student-teacher relationships, 181; parent views about, 74–75, 136–37; position in Asian systems, 1–2, 172–74, 182–83, 205; preparation for, 14, 111; and school improvement, 4, 14, 93–94, 177–83; in Singapore, 170–71; and social status/sorting, 117–18; in South Korea, 169–70; stability created by, 154, 203–4; stress created by, 26, 30, 169–70
experiential learning, 8
extracurricular activities, 47, 57, 60–61, 68, 112, 161

faculty meetings, 56, 223n2 (chap. 4)
family: background and educational achievement, 119–23, 134–39; changes in, 53, 157–59, 202–3, 217; connections to schools, 53, 75; responsibilities, 138–40, 153–59, 204–7; role in relaxed education, 12, 27, 134–39
Fausset, Richard, 179
Fernandez, Clea, 106
field trips, 67, 189
Finch, Janet, 82
Finland: achievement test results, 163–67, 175–76, 183; development of education system, 174–76; financial outlays, 175; national matriculation examination, 176; skills emphasized, 175; tests, attention to, 174, 183
Finnish National Board of Education (FNBE), 175
frontier schools, 112, 141
Fujita, Hidenori, 3, 28
Fukuzawa, Rebecca, 11, 39, 112, 113, 117, 141, 143, 144, 159
Fullan, Michael, 114–15
Fuller, Bruce, 4

Gaddis, S. M., 177
Gallimore, Ronald, 201
gap society (*kakusa shakai*), 121
Garelick, Barry, 168
Gebeloff, R., 178
Geertz, Clifford, 153
gender, 43, 146, 150, 153–55
Gesecki, K., 4
Glass, Gene, 23, 25, 178
Global Agricultural Information Network, 38
Goals 2000: Educate America Act, 20, 24
Goetz, Judith, 65
Goldenberg, Claude, 201
Goodman, Roger, 75
Gopinathan, S., 171
Gordon, June, 9, 37, 121, 226n2
Gowen, Annie, 168
Groen, Mark, 117, 180
group harmony (*wa*), 143, 150, 154
guidance practices. *See* school guidance

Han, 147
Hannum, Emily, 169
Harris, D., 178
Harvard Civil Rights Project, 180
Hatch, Thomas, 202
Hernandez, J., 178
Herrington, C., 178
Hess, Robert, 100
Hiebert, James, 16, 65, 106, 115, 208
Hill, Benjamin, 144
homerooms: descriptions of, 45–46, 57; responsibilities for, 49, 59, 67–68; student behavior in, 55, 112; topics covered in, 115
homework, 117, 131, 169, 205
Hood, Christopher, 28, 75, 137
Horio, Teruhisa, 64, 202

immigrants, 37, 176
implicit cultural logic, 79
indulgence (*amae*), 145, 159
instruction: changes in, 2, 8–10, 53, 99, 169, 202; classroom discussions in, 158, 181, 191–92, 204–5; for community building, 42, 65, 188, 190, 207; comparisons between Japanese and US, 117; constructivist, 77–78, 100, 192, 200; data-driven, 15, 31, 93; discovery-oriented, 79, 106, 112, 191–92, 208; experimentation with, 97, 99, 113; goals for, 66–67, 77–78, 93, 126; impediments to innovation, 103, 107, 183, 193–95; innovation, 8–10, 111–15, 183, 192–93, 199–200; lecture style, 8, 53, 105, 111–12, 116, 169, 200–201, 210–11; project-based, 71, 78, 88–89, 130–32; shifting expectations related to, 69–71; small group lessons, 49; standards, 73; student-centered, 66–67, 70, 79, 86–87, 102, 113, 210–11, 215; teacher beliefs about, 99, 109–14, 184–97; test-driven, 3, 14, 110, 118, 144; traditional approaches, 8, 32, 69–71, 111–12; transmission-oriented, 105, 116, 172
Integrated Studies (*sogotekina gakushu*): American teacher responses to, 189–91; assessment of impact, 28, 84–85; assessment of student performance, 84–87, 104, 131–34; community connections, 92; contrasts to traditional curricula, 93, 105; development of, 7, 66; future

of, 216–17; goals for, 6–7, 92; impact on other subjects, 72–73, 103–4, 214–17; lesson descriptions, 89–91, 120, 189–91; parent attitudes toward, 73–76, 134–39; place in the curriculum, 6–7, 28, 103, 214–17; student attitudes toward, 84–85, 91–92, 106–7, 132–33; student research projects, 84, 105, 128–34; teacher attitudes toward, 66–71, 83–85, 94–109; themes of, 66, 89, 103, 128
international achievement tests, 1–5, 19, 140, 163–83, 208–11, 216
Itoh, Mayumi, 121, 224n3 (chap. 7)

Jackson, Sharnell, 1
Japanese Business Federation (*Keidanren*), 26
Japan External Trade Organization (JETRO), 38
juku, 51, 75, 137–38, 205–6

Kang, E., 4
Kang, Mi Ok, 170
Karasawa, Mayumi, 79
Kariya, Takehiko, 120, 121, 122–23, 140
Kashiwagi, A., 224n4 (chap. 7)
Katsuno, Masaaki, 223n3 (chap. 4)
Kendall, Nancy, 61
Kida, Hiroshi, 12, 64
Kim, J. W., 170
Kipnis, Andrew, 169
Klein, Alyson, 182
Koizumi, Junichiro, 224n3 (chap. 7)
Korea. *See* South Korea
Krauss, Ellis, 150, 198, 225n2 (chap. 8)

Laskey, Sue, 181
Lauen, D. L., 177
Lebra, Takie, 150–51, 159–60
LeCompte, Margaret, 65
Lee, Jaekyung, 170
lesson study/research lessons, 61, 65, 100, 106
LeTendre, Gerald, 39, 46, 115–16, 120, 121, 137, 141, 143, 144, 148, 149
Levinson, Bradley, 60
Lewis, Catherine, 65, 71, 100, 106, 200
Lipskey, Michael, 35
Lortie, Dan, 23
Lundahl, L., 176

Ma, Liping, 187, 208
MacDonald, Laurence, 8
Mandinach, Ellen, 1
Manna, Paul, 24, 222n5 (chap. 2)
Marx et al., 130
Massey, Alexander, 61, 223n10
Mausethagen, Solvi, 181
McGinn, Noel, 74
McLaren, Peter, 154
McLaughlin, Milbrey, 35, 61, 65, 78
McMurrer, Jennifer, 117, 180
McTighe, Jay, 87
media influence, 26, 40–43, 83, 136, 165–66
Medina, Jennifer, 177, 225n3 (chap. 9)
Mehta, 174
Meiji reformation, 2
middle schools: comparisons of US and Japanese, 115–16, 195–96; connections to elementary schools, 103, 115–18, 208; curriculum, 7, 94, 102–18, 124–28, 215; discipline and class management, 141–62; and education reform, 102–18, 213–18; extracurricular activities, 47, 57, 60–61, 68, 112, 161; goals of, 142–44, 204–5, 208; instructional approaches in, 102, 105–15, 139–40, 200–203; learning environment in, 115–18, 128–34, 142, 204–6; role of teachers, 102–18, 199–207; socialization, 141–62; special activities, 112, 151
Miles, Matthew, 114–15
Miller, Aaron, 8, 144, 150
Ministry of Education, Culture, Sports, Science, and Technology (MEXT): authority, 12, 28, 78–80, 113–15, 202–3; concerns about emotional development, 32; concerns about low achieving students, 119; concerns about student stress, 15, 68, 73, 92; and curriculum development, 10, 103, 221n1 (chap. 1); goals for Integrated Studies, 91–93; goals for relaxed education, 25, 29, 85; influence on teacher behavior, 64–69, 74–78, 100–106, 130–31, 202–3, 218; reform priorities, 6–9, 27–28, 214–18;

Ministry of Education (*continued*)
role in education reform, 2–6, 63–74, 114, 214–18; and school guidance, 142–46, 162; support for decentralization, 26, 31–32, 199–200; support for elective courses, 124; support for five-day school week, 138; support for "new abilities," 89, 224n1 (chap. 7); support for pedagogical innovation, 8, 10, 107, 200–201
minority students and groups, 21, 25, 31, 120–21, 176–77
Moeran, Brian, 112, 225n2 (chap. 8)
moral development/education, 22, 48, 141–42
Mori, Arinori, 2
Murray, David, 2

Nabeshima, Yoshiro, 121
Nakane, Chie, 112, 143, 144
Naoi, Atsushi, 120
National Assessment of Educational Progress (NAEP), 178–79
National Commission on Excellence and Education (NCEE), 19–20
National Council on Education Reform (NCER), 19–20
National Education Association, 24
Nation at Risk, A, 19–20
neoconservatism, 101, 216
neoliberalism, 26, 121, 140, 211
new academic abilities, 8, 85, 100, 119–24, 133, 185
new public management, 26
New York State Regents' Examinations, 179
Ng, Jennifer, 181
Ng, Pak Tee, 171
Nichols, Sharon, 23, 25, 178
Nitta, Keith, 24, 26, 28, 29, 221n1 (chap. 2)
Noah, Harold, 4–5
No Child Left Behind Act (NCLB): Adequate Yearly Progress (AYP), 177; adoption of, 18–24; and distribution of authority, 30–31; financial incentives and, 23–24, 181–82; goals for, 1, 4, 14, 18, 20–25, 188; highly qualified teachers, 189; impact on curricula, 180–81; impact on instruction, 195–97, 210; impact on teachers, 23, 93, 186; impact on student achievement, 11–14, 177–81; impact on student-teacher relationships, 181; opinions of teachers about, 193–97; reporting categories, 20–21, 31; requirements, 20–24, 31
Nomi, Tomoaki, 122, 140

Obama, Barack, 24, 181
Okano, Kaori, 9, 37, 120, 121, 135, 226n2
Okinawans, 121
orderliness, socialization for, 141–42
Organization for Economic Cooperation and Development (OECD), 5, 166–67, 174–75, 225n1 (chap. 8), 225n2 (chap. 8)

Paige, Rod, 14, 20–24, 179, 188, 195
parents: attitudes toward education reform, 9, 12, 73–76, 134–39, 218; changes in, 38, 53–54, 82–83, 153–59, 202–3; concern for the education of their children, 14–15, 21, 71, 75, 134–36, 205–7; economic resources, 120–24, 205–6; education level, 120–24, 138–39; opinions about relaxed education, 13, 73–76, 134–39; participation in school activities, 82–83, 155–56; relationships with children, 138–40, 149–53; responsibilities, 53–54, 82–83, 153
Park, Hyunjoon, 122, 140, 169
Park, S. J., 169–70
Pepper, Suzanne, 169
Peters, Tom, 221n1 (chap. 2)
Phillips, David, 75
physical punishment in schools, 8–9, 145–46
Politics of Structural Reform, The, 26
Popham, W. J., 1
Preschool in Three Cultures, 185, 189
principals/school administration: obligations to students, 53, 152; opinions about relaxed education, 71, 83; oversight of teachers, 51, 59, 73, 223n2 (chap. 4); reflections on parenting, 155, 158; responsibilities, 47–49, 64, 66
Programme for International Student Assessment (PISA): anxiety generated by, 213–14; limitations of, 204, 225n1

(chap. 9); media attention to, 165–68; motivation generated by, 208; rankings/results, 3, 5, 121, 166, 174–76; use of, 165, 168, 204, 225n1; video study, 224n4
PTA, 135

Race to the Top: accountability system, 14, 180; effects on curriculum, 4; emphasis on testing, 1, 4, 182, 206–7; funding, 182; goals for, 1, 4; implications of, 75, 181–83, 205–6; waivers, 182
Rappleye, Jeremy, 123
Ravitch, Diane, 178, 221n2 (chap. 2)
recommendation letters (*suisen*), 154
reform. *See* education policy/reform
Reimer, Todd, 35
Reiser, Brian, 35
relaxed education (*yutori kyoiku*): assessment of impact, 19, 24–29, 91–98, 162, 213; assumptions about, 11, 78; awareness of, 2, 12–13, 23, 34; community involvement in, 84–85, 89–92; components of, 2, 5–9, 103–4; contrasts with traditional programs, 93, 216–17; criticism of, 92, 196, 213–18; debates about, 3, 136, 198–201, 216–18; goals for, 2, 10–12, 16, 88, 93; justification for, 2, 6, 9–12, 18–19, 26, 81–85; links to academic achievement, 82, 119, 122–28; policy development, 1–3, 5–10, 18, 25–28; resistance to, 110–13, 200–202, 207–12, 216; role of families in, 134–39, 155–59; role of teachers in, 63–69, 98–99, 103, 119; and school guidance, 141–62; student opinions about, 132–34; tensions associated with, 43–44, 66–78, 94–98, 102–8, 124–26, 201
research methodology, 11, 36–41, 60–62, 65, 81–82, 185
Rhoten, Diana, 35
Rinkyoishin (Ad Hoc Council on Education), 3
Ritter et al., 178
Rohlen, Thomas, 8, 39, 121, 137, 143, 150, 198
Rosegaard, Marie, 79
Rosenbaum, James, 120
routines, use of in schools, 46, 60, 143–45, 148
Rowan, Brian, 36
rules and rule enforcement, 43–46, 52, 59, 142–45, 156–59

Sahlberg, Pasi, 175–76
Sakai, Akira, 11, 76, 100, 141, 200
Sarason, Seymour, 23
Sargent, Tanja, 169
Sato, Manabu, 226n2
Sato, Nancy, 65, 71, 106
Schemo, Diana, 168
Scholastic Aptitude Tests (SATs), 19
school choice, 26
school cleaning (*soji*), 145
school guidance: anticipatory management, 150–51; comparisons of Japanese and US, 143; cooperation and self-governance, 125, 144, 148; at different levels, 115–16, 144; historical foundations, 142–45; policies, 8–9, 145–46; and relaxed education, 8–9, 16–17, 145–46, 151–52; shifting practices and student behavior, 8–9, 125, 141–62; and social change, 142; student responses to, 153–55; teacher roles and responsibilities, 8–9, 154–55, 160–62, 252
School in the New Era, 31
school nurse, 38, 59, 129, 222n4
school refusal syndrome (*hikikomori*), 53
school research sites, descriptions of, 41–60
school uniforms. *See* uniforms
school violence (*konai boryoiku*), 26, 59, 145
school week, length of, 6, 12, 74–75, 134–39
Schoppa, Leonard, 12, 64, 202
Schwarz, Robert, 174, 175
senior-junior (*Sempai-kohai*) relationships, 50, 53, 58, 60, 144–45
Seth, Michael, 165, 181
Shimahara, Nobuo, 11, 64–67, 76, 79, 100, 200
Simon, Roger, 112
Singapore: achievement test results, 163–68, 170–71; influence of testing, 173; Master Plan for Information Technology, 171; Ministry of Education, 171; reform efforts, 165; Singapore Math, 168;

Singapore (*continued*)
Teach Less, Learn More, 171; Thinking Schools, Learning Nation, 171–73
Slavin, Richard, 4
social class, 119–24
social-emotional development of children, 32, 86, 93, 161, 189, 208
social hierarchy, 161
social integration, 11, 164–65
South Korea: achievement test results, 163–67; criticism of schools, 169–70; influence of examinations, 1, 170, 206; Presidential Committee on Education Reform, 170; reform efforts, 169–71; residents of Japan, 121; teachers' union, 170
special education, 49–50
Spillane, James, 35, 106
sports, 51, 58, 150–51
sports festivals, 61, 135
Sputnik, 19
Steiner-Khamsi, Gita, 19
Steinhoff, Patricia, 150, 198, 225n2 (chap. 8)
Stevenson, David, 120
Stevenson, Harold, 67, 71, 100, 106
Stewart, Vivian, 165, 171
Stigler, James, 16, 65, 106, 115, 208
Stinson, Roddy, 179
Strauss, Valerie, 169
Street, Susan, 64
Stritikus, Tom, 60
structural reforms, 26, 31, 224n3
student guidance approaches. *See* school guidance
students: academic abilities, 19–25, 43, 94–98, 121–26; attitudes toward education, 6–14, 48, 52–56, 81–85, 216–17; autonomy, 87–89, 128–32, 143, 153–55; behavior in school, 46–48, 55–59, 87, 145–62; enthusiasm for learning, 10, 85–86, 115, 128, 190–92; motivation, 2–8, 10–19, 59–60, 81–87, 117, 145–62; motivation, comparisons between countries, 83, 96, 165–71; opinions about relaxed education, 91–94, 132–34; performance on tests, 4–5, 95–96, 177–82, 210; relationships with teachers, 70–72, 76–78, 141–62, 181, 201; resistance, 52, 58–60, 148–50, 153–55, 159–60; social issues, 25–29, 50–60, 82–83
suicide, 159
Sunderman et al., 117, 180
supplementary education. See *juku*
Sutton, Margaret, 60

Takayama, Keita, 18, 121, 216
Talbert, Joan, 36, 61
Tan, Jason, 171
Tan, Sophia, 170, 171, 173
teachers: accountability, 4, 13, 32–33, 79–80, 195–96, 202–8; authority, 66, 86, 152; autonomy, 1, 23, 28–30, 63–66, 71, 79–80, 93–94, 97, 110–11, 139–40, 195, 199–202, 208; cheating, evidence of, 179–80; collaboration, 49, 65, 106; education and training, 25–27, 70; evaluation of, 73, 182; extracurricular responsibilities, 47, 52–53, 56, 67–68; feelings of frustration, 59, 106–7, 153; instructional responsibilities, 7–11, 43–44, 64–68; isolation, 106; opinions about relaxed education, 63–80, 83–85, 94–101, 104–15, 200–201; relationships with students, 70–72, 76–78, 141–62, 181, 201; roles in implementing reform policies, 28–33, 64–69, 78–80, 211–12; supervision of students, 8–9, 52–60, 97, 151–53; work-related stress, 43–44, 56–59, 128, 155
teaching. *See* instruction
tests. *See* examinations
Texas Education Agency (TEA), 178
textbooks, 28, 60, 67, 70–71, 105, 124–27, 168, 192, 201
Third International Math and Science Study (TIMSS): anxiety generated by, 213–14; limitations of, 204, 225n1 (chap. 9); media attention to, 165–68; motivation generated by, 208; performance of Asian students, 3; rankings, 3, 167; use of results, 165, 168, 204, 225n1; video study, 224n4
Third Major Education Initiative, 3, 199, 211
Thomas, John, 130
Thurston, Donald, 202

Title I funding, 24
Tobin, Joseph, 79, 85, 189
Tomic, Welke, 201
Tominaga, Ken'ichi, 120
Total Quality Management (TQM), 22
Treiman, Donald, 120, 165
Tsuchida, Ineko, 65
Tsuchiya, Motonori, 37, 121, 135, 226n2
Tsuneyoshi, Ryoko, 2, 9, 10, 29, 32, 35, 37, 119, 121, 124, 137, 206, 224n8, 226n2
Tucker, Marc, 4–5, 176
twenty-first century abilities, 12, 30, 73, 218
Tyack, David, 4

UN Convention on the Rights of the Child, 145, 170
uniforms, 46, 48, 58, 116, 157
universal primary education, 163
University of Tokyo Graduate School of Education, 185
US Department of Education (USDOE), 4, 23, 30–31, 93, 167, 177, 182, 187–89
US Government Accountability Office (USGAO), 117, 179–80, 208

Valli, Linda, 181

Walford, Geoffrey, 60–61, 65, 82, 223n10
Walt Disney, 187
Waterman, Robert, 221n2 (chap. 2)
Weiler, Hans, 24, 222n4 (chap. 2)
White, Merry, 11, 86, 100, 120, 143, 153, 200
Wiese, Ann-Marie, 60
Wiggins, Grant, 87
Winerip, Michael, 179
worksheets, 90–92, 111, 126–27, 128–29, 140
Wright, J., 4
Wu, David, 185, 189
Wu, Xiaogant, 165

Yamaguchi, Kazuo, 120
Yamamura, Yoshiaki, 142
Yeh, Hsueh, 79
youth culture, 9–10, 25–27, 58, 81–82, 145, 217
yutori kyoiku. *See* relaxed education

Zakaria, Fareed, 168
zest for living (*ikiru chikara*), 8, 85–87, 93, 127, 201, 216